12
LADDERS
TO WORLD CLASS
PERFORMANCE

D1488105

12

LADDERS
TO WORLD CLASS
PERFORMANCE

how your organization can compete with the best in the world

INSTITUTE OF DIRECTORS

DAVID DRENNAN
STEUART PENNINGTON

KOGAN
PAGE

First published 1999

Apart from any fair dealing for the purposes of research or private study, or criticism or review, as permitted under the Copyright, Designs and Patents Act 1988, this publication may only be reproduced, stored or transmitted, in any form or by any means, with the prior permission in writing of the publishers, or in the case of reprographic reproduction in accordance with the terms and licences issued by the CLA. Enquiries concerning reproduction outside these terms should be sent to the publishers at the undermentioned addresses:

Kogan Page Limited
120 Pentonville Road
London
N1 9JN
UK

Kogan Page Limited
163 Central Avenue, Suite 4
Dover
NH 03820
USA

© David Drennan and Steuart Pennington, 1999

The right of David Drennan and Steuart Pennington to be identified as the authors of this work has been asserted by them in accordance with the Copyright, Designs and Patents Act 1988.

British Library Cataloguing in Publication Data

A CIP record for this book is available from the British Library.

ISBN 0 7494 3000 1

Typeset by Saxon Graphics Ltd, Derby
Printed and bound in Great Britain by Biddles Ltd, Guildford and King's Lynn

Contents

Preface

This is a practical book. It is meant for managers and companies who want to know what 'world class' actually means in practical terms, and to find out just what you have to do to get there . . . and stay there.

The book does not debunk everything you've been doing hitherto, and urge you to adopt some wonderful new concept that by itself will completely revolutionize your business. On the contrary, it looks at companies who are already world class in their field, and examines what practical things they did to get there. And the point is: if they did it, so can YOU.

That doesn't say it's easy. It isn't. It takes know-how, hard work and dedication. The know-how is here. You just need to supply the hard work and dedication.

Looking at the lifeskills of world class companies, the book will help you understand not only where your business is now, but the steps you need to take on the journey to becoming world class.

Note on gender use

We have generally used the term 'he' throughout the publication for ease of reading. However, this does not reflect a gender specific reference, but should be read as referring to people of both sexes.

Introduction

Becoming *world class* is on everyone's mind. As the world becomes a global market, the standards applied to 'World Class Performance' are becoming increasingly expected by customers and buyers everywhere. Global competitiveness then becomes an international search exercise as firms scan the world for best practices that will keep them ahead of the pack. And as organizations begin to focus on thinking globally while acting locally, finding new ways to stay competitive, to meet and beat ever-rising customer expectations, to compete with the best, is the talk of our time.

World class is as widely written about as any subject in management today. But by the time you have absorbed the works of Drucker, Peters, Kanter, Porter, Handy and the rest, the subject becomes confusing and clichéd to managers and workers alike.

The organizational graveyard is filled with failed attempts at culture change, total quality management, re-engineering and all the rest. Managers have become increasingly cynical about the next 'flavour of the month' fad. Experience has shown that real competitive edge is in going back to basics, and single-mindedly re-establishing focus.

This requires systematic analysis and agreement amongst the firms' stakeholders on areas where improvement is to be focused, and how such improvements are to be measured. And while the language of world class is becoming increasingly common across borders and across cultures, we believe it is critically important to make choices, ie to focus on those specific areas that will make your company truly a world class performer.

When one mentions the words 'world class' in product or business terms, people often think of the Japanese. We often ask members of our audiences: who has *not* got a Japanese product at home? Generally no hands are raised at all. When we ask why they buy Japanese products in preference to anything else, they say they are: 'good quality', 'reliable', 'value for money', and so on. In fact, in the mind of the public Japanese products have become synonymous with quality – so much so that one large UK retailer deliberately labels many of its British-made products with the Japanese-sounding brand name 'Matsui', so its customers will be automatically convinced of their quality.

But it wasn't always so. In David Drennan's boyhood days, his mother taught him to avoid Japanese products, because they were tinny, unreliable, cheap imitations of better-made Western products. These days are changed. Look what has happened. Japanese products have gone from:

tinny	to	well-made
cheap	to	good value
unreliable	to	reliable
imitation	to	innovative.

They have completely changed their image . . . but it took them nearly 40 years to get there.

ATTAINING WORLD CLASS STATUS TAKES TIME

That's the first point to realize. There is no great tablet you can swallow that will make you world class within six months. There is no revolutionary concept that will throw out all the common-sense things you have been doing over the years, and turn you into a world class performer within the year. It takes time. It takes effort. It takes teamwork. It takes commitment. In short, it is not a technique. It is an attitude of mind. It is a way of life.

This is not a one-off event, it's a journey. But a journey where you will enjoy the stops along the way, where you will enjoy the pleasure of repeatedly breaking your own records, in which you will enjoy getting to places where you've never been before. And when you can genuinely compete with the best in the world, it brings a pride and enthusiasm among your people that is quite unique. It is hard work, but it's thrilling too.

WHAT IS 'WORLD CLASS'?

World class means 'being able to compete with the best in the world at what you do'. It doesn't mean winning the gold medal every time. No company manages to do that. It just means being able to compete credibly with the best anywhere. Let's look at some of those companies that we could put in the world class category. Many appear in the *Fortune* magazine Global 500 list. These companies no doubt became big by satisfying a lot of customers, and they certainly qualify as players on a world scale.

The companies in the *Fortune* Global 500 are classified on the basis of size and financial performance. Let's look at a selection from *Fortune's* 1998 list (see Table 0.1).

With few exceptions most of these companies would be categorized as world class in their field. Microsoft, Intel, Disney and Merck all appear in the top 10 of 'most admired companies' in America in 1998. More people travel in Boeing planes round the world than any other type, while British Airways have won the 'Best Airline' title 10 years in a row. Marks and Spencer, despite temporary troubles, is a legend with its customers in the United Kingdom, while Wal-Mart has taken serving customers so seriously, it has well

Table 0.1 Size and financial performance of selected *Fortune* Global 500 companies

	Sales per employee ($)	Profits per employee ($)	Profit % on sales	Return on assets (%)
Intel	391,719	108.516	27.7	24.0
Microsoft	510,885	155,361	30.4	24.0
Motorola	198,627	7,867	3.9	4.3
Boeing	191,632	(744)	(0.4)	–
British Airways	233,519	12,423	5.3	3.9
Merck	439,330	85,762	19.5	17.9
Dupont	419,773	24,442	5.8	5.6
Glaxo Welecome	248,985	57,713	23.2	21.8
Disney	208,083	18,204	8.7	5.2
Sony	318,110	10,457	3.4	3.7
General Electric	329,130	29,721	9.0	2.7
GEC (UK)	143,045	15,452	10.8	11.4
Matsushita (Panasonic)	232,934	2,765	1.2	1.2
Wal-Mart	144,605	4,274	3.0	7.7
Tesco	216,941	6,660	3.1	6.8
Marks & Spencer	280,829	28,237	10.1	10.6
Federal Express	106,828	3,348	3.1	4.7
British Post Office	52,192	2,959	5.7	6.4
Proctor & Gamble	337,396	32,217	9.5	12.4
Unilever	169,899	19,034	11.2	17.2

surpassed long-time No. 1 US retailer Sears Roebuck to become the biggest retailer in the world by far.

But these companies are not all world class performers in financial terms. The companies are not all directly comparable, of course, but they have been grouped into related fields. Yet look at the variability in performance of these companies. Intel and Microsoft are the exceptions – despite their 1998 stock market sufferings they win the gold medal on financial performance whichever measure you use. But would the customers of Wal-Mart class the company as ordinary because they make only a third of the profit of Marks and Spencer, or they achieve only half the sales per employee of M&S? Of course not. Would we reject Boeing because they made a loss in 1997? The users and buyers of their aircraft wouldn't say so. Would we condemn Matsushita, makers of Panasonic products, because they made only a measly 1.2 per cent profit on sales? We don't think so. In fact, the vast majority of people who buy these companies' products or use their services have no idea about their sales volume or profitability. And they don't much care either. They only know that their products and service are the best around.

WHAT CUSTOMERS SEE AS TRULY WORLD CLASS

So if it's not just financial performance that makes companies world class, what is it? Well, it doesn't mean perfection. World class is a comparative measure. It implies: is this good enough to be compared to the best in the world? And the ultimate judges on these matters are customers themselves. What makes companies world class *in the customers' eyes*? Just this.

- *The quality of the product or service*. Does the product fulfil all the requirements it promised? Does it work first time out of the box? Is it simple enough that I don't need an 80-page instruction book to work it? Is this the best service I can get for my purpose compared to what I could get elsewhere?

  In making their choices, customers are forever evaluating their alternatives. Is this the best I can get? Companies who cannot regularly meet their customers' expectations first time with their products or service have little chance of becoming world class.
- *Value for money*. Is the value I perceive in getting this product or service greater than the money I have to part with? How does that compare with the price-value I could get elsewhere? This is where perception plays a key part in the customer's decision. If the item concerned is a branded product with identical features, then price becomes the main consideration. More often than not, however, there's always 'added value' that companies can add to their product that customers will perceive as worth paying for, and will distinguish them from the competition. That's something world class companies excel at.
- *Service*. Is it a pleasure to deal with this company? Are they easy to do business with? Are they as concerned to help after the sale as before? Do they put themselves out to resolve your problems? Do they respond speedily to your problems? Are they concerned about *you*? Do they really put customers first?

  Or do they move you from pillar to post and let you fight your way through their system to get your problem attended to? Are you greeted by a mechanical voice on the telephone that forces you through a number-punching sequence before you get to talk to a real person? Are you compelled to listen to the eternal canned music as you hang on?

  In an age when companies catch up on each other's technology in relatively short order, quality of service may well be the key factor that distinguishes one company from another. That is something of which world class companies are acutely aware.
- *Reliability*. Here, the kind of questions customers ask themselves are: will the company actually deliver when they say they will? Will the product actually prove to be reliable in practice? Is the quality of their product or service consistent? Do they phone you back when they say they will? Do

they keep their promises? Can you trust them? In that respect, are they better than all the rest?

This is an area where the Japanese are the all-time champions. They taught the rest of the world what real quality and reliability looked like. Cars are complicated products, and for a long time we all accepted that things would inevitably go wrong from time to time. Today you can buy a Japanese car that might have 10,000 parts in it, all requiring design, manufacture and assembly – and nothing goes wrong. Nothing. That's remarkable. But you can't get there without having spent years working on quality and having every employee paying attention to the detail every minute of the day. That's what it takes to reach world class standard.

- *Innovation.* What won the gold medal at the last Olympics may well not be good enough to win next time. Standards – in business as well as in sport – improve all the time. So to stay at world class standard means constant change and innovation, always trying to produce something that beats the customer's expectations. And that's quite exciting – for employees as well as customers.

One company that makes constant innovation into a cherished principle is US company Rubbermaid. They make plastic and rubber products. They work to ensure that 25 per cent of their sales in any year come from products introduced in the previous five years. In 1993, they introduced some 365 new products. That was the year they won the title of 'Most Admired Company' in America. That's world class.

WORLD CLASS COMPANIES ARE NOT MARVELLOUS AT EVERYTHING

When sportsmen aspire to Olympic standards, no one expects to win medals at the 400 metres and at weightlifting too. They know they can't be world standard at everything. They have to choose. So they concentrate on their strengths and work on them until they can compete with the best in the world. It's just the same with companies. You have to choose what you want to be best at.

Do you know what you want to be best at? What do you want to concentrate on? Market share? Operating efficiency? Customer service? How well you manage and use your employees? Below is a list of performance measures used by real companies around the world. They are divided into five categories. Have a good look through the list and choose what you think should be the priorities for your company.

Customers

- order to delivery time/waiting time;
- right first time: service and product;
- on time in full (OTIF) delivery;
- customer complaints;

- speed of problem resolution;
- phone response time;
- letter response time;
- customer survey scores.

Employees

- sales per employee;
- profit per employee;
- standard hours vs attended hours;
- absence;
- staff turnover;
- employee survey scores.

Financial performance

- return on capital/assets;
- profit percentage on sales;
- investor returns;
- share price;
- unit costs.

Market performance

- market share;
- product innovation;
- sales growth.

Internal efficiency

- sales per square foot;
- profit per square foot;
- added value time vs process cycle time;
- standard hours vs attended hours;
- stock turns;
- overall machine efficiency;
- costs of quality;
- inspection costs and delays:
  - re-work;
  - scrap;
  - customer returns;
  - costs;
  - penalty costs;
- time to market.

So, what measures would be most important to your organization? What would have the biggest impact on your performance? What would be most appreciated by your customers? Whatever you decide, remember, don't choose too many. Concentration is the key to excellence.

YOU MAY ACHIEVE RESULTS YOU NEVER THOUGHT POSSIBLE

When you do start down the road to world class, it looks like a daunting journey. But over time companies can reach levels of performance they never dreamt were possible. Here is one example. Back in 1979, Motorola senior management held a three-day conference together in Chicago. Near the end, one of the sales managers stood up and said: 'Our customers think our quality stinks.' The audience was dumbfounded. Their measured defect rate was already good and it was something they were working on constantly. However, the company was so stung by the criticism that it decided to make quality its prime goal. And look what happened.

We'll assume their defect rate was already a pretty good 0.5 per cent to start with. But that still means:

5 parts were wrong	in 1,000, or
50	in 10,000
500	in 100,000, and as many as
5,000	in 1,000,000

That's a lot of faulty bits getting out to customers. Over the following years the company kept 'raising the bar', setting new targets. By 1992, they were into their Six Sigma quality programme. That year the target they set was 'no more than 3.4 defects in a million parts produced'. Only 0.5 per cent scrap sounds pretty good to most people, but the company's 1992 performance standard is not just 10 times better or even 100 times better. It's *1,400 times better*. Now that's world class!

That kind of achievement takes time, effort, determination and teamwork. But it has a threefold benefit. Customers soon notice and start trusting you with more of their business. Employees feel a great sense of pride and accomplishment. And the bottom line improves markedly.

WORLD CLASS COMPANIES ARE ALL AROUND US

Wherever you live and work there are large international companies in operation. With their resources of management talent and global reach, these companies tend to seek out good practices wherever they can find them, and put them into operation across their organizations. And these are the companies that set the standards that everyone else has to follow.

Take McDonald's, the fast food chain, as a case in point. Wherever they go in the world, McDonald's know exactly what they want. They know the kind of locations they need for their restaurants and just how they should be laid out, decorated and furnished. They know exactly what kind of meat and vegetables they need, and so do their local suppliers, in minute detail. Their restaurant staff may be young, but there's a thick tome laying down in excruciating detail how the food should be prepared, exactly how long it should be cooked and at what temperature, when it should be thrown away if not used, how customers should be greeted, how orders should be taken, etc. They don't just hope. They rely on thorough planning, preparation and training.

The indigenous population soon gets used to the new standards set by such companies. Their expectations rise. They get impatient with local companies who get stuck in their old ways. They begin to give them less of their business. The fact is, for any business who wants to thrive and survive, there is no alternative but to actively seek out these best practices and make them your own.

YOU DON'T HAVE TO RE-INVENT THE WHEEL

The good news is: you don't have to start from scratch. You can get a leg up by learning from the experience of others who have gone before. You can avoid some of the mistakes they made, and adopt or adapt the techniques and processes that took other companies to world class levels of performance. Of course, you won't become world class overnight. As we know, it takes time and it takes practice. But you can enjoy all your steps of achievement along the way.

And, surprising as it may seem, those companies who are world leaders in their field are not uniquely filled with exceptional people. But they do have focus, they know what they want to be good at, they seek to serve their customers better than anybody, and they involve and enthuse every one of their employees in doing it.

THE 12 LADDERS TO WORLD CLASS PERFORMANCE

To make the whole issue of progress to world class more accessible and practical, we have distilled what is a complex subject into 12 key factors, each of which we know can make significant differences to the performance of any organization. They have been composed from directly observing a great variety of world class companies, and studying what practical things they did to take themselves to that level of achievement. This is workable know-how you can put into operation in your own organization, and which fills the rest of this book.

Each of the factors has been subdivided into five levels, representing progress from ordinary performance right up to world class standard. There are good reasons for this:

- It helps you see just where you are now.
- It shows you what practical things you have to do to get to the next level.
- It recognizes that getting to world class is a step-by-step process. It is a journey, not an event.

Here are the 12 Ladders:

1. Aligning Management Objectives
2. Customer Focus
3. Organizing the Workplace
4. Visible Measurement Systems
5. Managing for Quality
6. Eliminating Waste
7. Best Operating Practices and Continuous Improvement
8. Teamwork
9. Staff Empowerment and Involvement
10. Rewards and Recognition
11. Purposeful Communication
12. Continuous Learning.

Now look into the book. It is a treasure chest of ideas and well-tested processes. They have the capacity to take your organization to levels of performance you have never reached before.

 O N E

Aligning Management Objectives

LEVELS	MEASURES
Level 1	Managers give orders; workers only do as much as they have to. Some people don't know who their boss is. Objectives are not written; the goalposts seem to keep moving. Managers say: 'We don't need objectives, we know what to do.'
Level 2	Each person's responsibilities are clearly defined. There is a well-defined organization chart. Top management have defined their goals but junior management are not sure what they can do about them. Objectives are written, but not seriously followed up.
Level 3	Top management decide on their annual objectives as a team. These are turned into more specific team objectives at each lower level of management. Regular follow-up reviews measure progress to date. At least 80% of objectives are achieved by year end.
Level 4	The company's goals are clear and actionable by all. Employees all understand exactly how they can contribute. Management co-ordinate their efforts across departments. At least 90% of objectives have been achieved by year end.
Level 5	Measurable objectives are agreed annually in every department. Teamwork and co-operation are expected at every level. People work to achieve the goals even under changing conditions. 100% of objectives are achieved, or exceeded, by year end.

LEVEL 1

'Managers give orders; workers only do as much as they have to'

Surprisingly enough, many managers prefer simply to issue orders and have staff do just what they're told. Why? Because the power flatters their ego, it takes less time, and they feel they're in control. Some staff prefer it too – they don't have to think, they don't have to accept any responsibility, and if you're only doing what the boss told you, then you keep yourself safe and out of trouble.

The problem with that is that staff act powerless when the boss is not there, and they don't take initiatives to solve problems or to do it right for the customer at the time. In fact, they don't think about customers, they just do what will keep the boss happy. They know he is there all the time, they have to live with him every day, whereas customers they may never see again, so why bother? At times also, staff will do what the boss orders even when they know it is wrong, either just to be able to say 'Ya boo!', or because they know they have the protection of saying later 'Well, that's what you told me to do!' That's a terrible waste of time and talent.

You're never going to reach world class if you treat employees like automatons who just take orders. You have to use all the developable talent they've got. Our strong advice is: don't let staff push all the responsibility on to the boss, even if he is willing to take it, and they want it that way. Determine to train your staff well, give them all the information and materials they need to do a good job, and show them clearly what a good job looks like. After that, insist that staff take responsibility for the work they do, ie its quality and its quantity. Overtly, the basic philosophy should be: 'We're not going to treat you like children. We're going to treat you like adults, but in return we expect you to act like adults. That means we expect you to work effectively by yourself without having to be supervised into it.' That act by itself will release a lot of formerly wasted managerial time. Some staff will be apprehensive at first, but later as they realize you are actually trusting them more, they will begin to appreciate being treated like a sensible adult and won't want to go back to the old ways.

'Some people don't know who their boss is'

In an organization of any size, people need to know who their boss is. It brings order into any organization; it makes for clear working relationships. When you don't know who your boss is, it makes life confusing, as you find yourself taking conflicting orders from different people etc. For example, it's quite common for front-line workers on rotating shifts to work for different bosses who themselves are not on rotating shifts. That's a mess of an idea. That kind of woolly thinking and confusion needs to be banished in organizations aspiring to be world class. Fundamentally, people need structure in their lives, so at work at least make it clear to them who their boss is.

'Objectives are not written; the goalposts seem to keep moving'

Exercise

When managers say they already know what their objectives are (without having them written), try this little test. Ask them to write down what the company's or department's top three priorities are. Give them a few minutes, then list their suggestions. We guarantee you'll get two flipcharts full of different suggestions.

It's our view that the lack of clear, commonly understood objectives among management is the most common cause of conflict in companies and subsequent mediocre performance. Of course, the goalposts in some companies seem to keep moving even when the objectives are written, but writing them down as a discipline brings distinct advantages:

- First, it demands thinking. You have to work out what should be the priorities, and to say exactly what you intend. That process is much more likely to bring clarity and constancy.
- Second, you have to be specific. When you have to state exactly what will be achieved by when, that's sobering.
- Third, if the objectives are then made public, one feels much more the onus of responsibility. And that can be really motivating.

'Managers say: "We don't need objectives, we know what to do"'

We often find this tendency in organizations where there is no bottom line, eg government departments, charity organizations, etc. In such cases, of course, performance can be much more difficult to measure, but it is never impossible, and it needs to be done. It is useful to account for how an organization's money was spent, but it's even more important to detail what was achieved for the spend. Often managers can get quite articulate defending the undesirability of having objectives that are too specific, but often the real reason is they don't want anything written down because that way they can't later be held to anything! That's a tendency that should be resisted.

LEVEL 2

'Each person's responsibilities are clearly defined'

People need to know simple things, like what they are responsible for, how they will know when they are doing a good job, and what they will be measured by. That way, life is simpler, easier, and more open for boss and subordinate alike. It's basic, simple, good management.

Part of that process can be to identify who the job-holders' customers are, ie the people who get the result of their work. These may be both internal (members of the same company) or external. Getting the job-holders to visit their customers – especially the more important ones – can be transformational in getting them to realize that the quality of their work is best judged by the real customers they serve. And the act of visiting 'internal customers' can help encourage inter-departmental co-operation, and break down the 'Chinese walls' that often develop.

'There is a well-defined organization chart'

An organization chart tells you quite a lot about a company, eg whether it is well structured with clear job titles, the number of departments and reporting layers, and how up-to-date things are (from the changes, crossings-out, gaps, etc). If a company has stopped producing organization charts because they say there are so many changes, that tells you something about its stability. A good rule-of-thumb timescale for publishing updated organization charts is every six months.

'Top management have defined their goals, but junior management are not sure what they can do about them'

Top management sometimes define their objectives or goals, but they often don't go much further than the board room. That's a problem if you want the rest of the organization to follow. Quite often when you ask top managers what their objectives are you find they can't remember them. If you find they have to scrabble about in a drawer to find them, then they are not affecting their everyday behaviour (and they should).

There can also be a tendency at times to make the goals only applicable to top management, eg 'To maintain our return on equity' or 'To be No. 1 in our market'. Often, lower echelons of staff do not know what that means, or think there is nothing they can do to help. Often too, front-line departments will decide on objectives quite oblivious of what top management's objectives are, and therefore have little connection with them. All of these problems contribute to misunderstanding and misalignment.

'Objectives are written, but not seriously followed up'

Departments may set objectives at the beginning of the year, which then languish in a document somewhere with no effective follow-up. That is largely a waste of time. Follow-up – whether in one-to-one meetings between managers and subordinates or in department meetings convened for the purpose – means you are serious, and when you follow up religiously you find several things begin to happen:

1. People start focusing on, and working on, the objectives they set in the first place.
2. People don't agree to unrealistic objectives at the outset.
3. Individuals, departments, and the company start achieving things.
4. People actually like working for companies who know where they want to go and make a habit of getting there.

LEVEL 3

'Top management decide on their annual objectives as a team'

'These are turned into more specific team objectives at each lower level of management'

It is fairly common in companies for managers to agree individual objectives with their subordinates for the coming year, but much less common for departments to agree objectives for the team as a whole. The contribution to the business of the whole team will generally supersede that of any one individual, so getting clarity on *team* priorities, and close co-operation between team members on achieving these, can often be vitally important. That's where a systematic process can be a great help. In our work with clients we use a Team Objectives Meeting (TOM) cascade process.

Normally this starts in the first year with a top management Strategy TOM, where those reporting to the MD (or equivalent) decide on their goals for the following three years, the values (behaviours) they want to encourage in the company, etc. Then those who are team members in the top team conduct TOMs with their teams in turn, with the MD appearing as 'Super-Boss' at the end to endorse their decisions. In this way it cascades down the whole organization. (The entire process is described later in this chapter.)

'Regular follow-up reviews measure progress to date'

'At least 80 per cent of objectives are achieved by year end'

No matter how well-fashioned the objectives you set, the whole process is dead in the water without serious and regular follow-up. For individuals, depending on the nature of the work, formal face-to-face meetings on progress on objectives should take place at least twice a year. For team get-togethers, we recommend every three months or so. What makes that work even better is if the team head's boss also attends. Team members then tend to put on a 'hurry-up' to get things achieved before the meeting, and take more trouble with their presentations.

LEVEL 4

'The company's goals are clear and actionable by all'

'Employees all understand exactly how they can contribute'

Companies are becoming quite sophisticated by this point. For example, they know how to produce simple, actionable goals that take the company where it wants to go, are measurable, are easily understood by the whole workforce, and are something everyone can contribute to. That sounds good, but it's not easy. Later in this section, we describe what good goals look like.

In many companies we visit, front-line staff don't have a clue what the company's goals are, and don't know how that should affect them and their work. Yet the vast majority of managers we meet are convinced people much prefer to do the best job they can. Clearly, then, if they knew the company's chosen goals their natural tendency would be to do what they could to help. That's why we encourage our clients to conduct attitude surveys that deliberately ask staff whether they understand the company's goals, and how they can personally contribute to them. That is invaluable information any company and its managers can use.

'Management co-ordinate their efforts across departments'

At this level, the company will have been conducting TOMs or their equivalent for some time. Part of their conclusions and actions will have been making agreements or 'contracts' with their customer departments. This part of the TOM system, ie identifying customers, talking with them face-to-face and making deals with them, is one of the most powerful and successful aspects of the process. And that often leads in turn to full-blown cross-departmental TOMs to agree ongoing commitments and relationships.

'At least 90 per cent of objectives have been achieved by year end'

To reach this kind of achievement on a regular basis depends essentially on writing only realistic objectives in the first place. There is both art and science to producing good objectives – it needs good rules and sensible judgement. This is our firm philosophy on the important matter of objectives:

- If you are going to create a 'success culture' in your business – and we believe that is fundamentally important – you have to set objectives that are realistic. That means objectives where the team or the individual has an 80% chance of success. Why 80%? That way there's going to be some stretch in the objective, but four out of five times they are likely to succeed. And no organization succeeds better when there is that kind of success feeling all over the business. It's infectious.
- Many managers think it is their job to set objectives for their subordinates.

That doesn't get any ownership on the part of the subordinates, and that means a lot less commitment on their part. Getting subordinates to propose their own stretch objectives first, which they then discuss and agree with their boss, is the much better option. Real commitment on the subordinates' part to the objectives they themselves proposed means a lot more determination to succeed when obstacles appear and the pressure is on.

- Another tendency – especially among sales managers – is to set objectives that they know are realistically beyond their subordinates' reach, but are set nevertheless in the hope that they will try harder, and perhaps do even better than they would have done with more realistic objectives. That is a mistake. Ambitious objectives may look good on paper at the beginning of the year, but everyone then gets to feel a failure every month as the results repeatedly fail to match the plan. That's bad for morale. Then when the manager congratulates subordinates even when they have fallen short of their objectives, he implies that failure is OK. That's dangerous.

- The acid test of a well-written objective is: 'Will the team or individual know, without having to ask their boss, when they have succeeded?' Objectives need to be clear and unambiguous, so that everyone knows just when they've passed the winning post. That avoids conflict at review or appraisal time, and creates a positive, no-surprises environment.

We should add: we make a distinction between the words 'goal' and 'objective'. Goals for us are longer-term targets that keep you stretching year by year. Objectives, on the other hand, are the specific things you plan to achieve in the next time period, normally this year. A short glossary of terms and how we use them appears at the end of this chapter.

LEVEL 5

'Measurable objectives are agreed annually in every department'

'Teamwork and co-operation are expected at every level'

At Level 5, companies have been using a TOM-type process for a number of years. People take it as commonplace that teams set objectives year by year and measure their progress. Individuals will be setting themselves personal objectives in agreement with their boss as a routine, or the process is built into an established appraisal process that extends right to front-line staff. It's even better if personal awards reinforce achievement, or there is a profit-sharing arrangement that ties company success to additional personal rewards.

At this level too, you should be able to ask staff at any level what the company goals are and hear the same story, and they should be able to tell you just what they are personally contributing to their achievement. It should be like Blackpool rock – the same message from top to bottom.

'People work to achieve the goals even under changing conditions'

This item is probably best illustrated by a real-life story. Mars, the international food and confectionery company, is well known the world over. Their biggest plant in the United Kingdom is Pedigree Petfoods. Some years back several events nearly stopped the plant: a national transport strike (no lorries moving); a national steel strike (no food cans); and a drought. The company's competitors all closed down or stopped production during these times, but Pedigree employees were confident their management would find a way to continue, even though they then produced over 4 million cans of petfood a day. And they did. In the transport shortage case, their own employees drove hired lorries, and worked unusual hours and night shifts to get essential materials in and finished goods out. Production was down only 3 per cent. Before the steel strike took place, the company bought rolls of tin-plate steel from Belgium and Japan, put them into storage, and fed their supplies to Metal Box, their can-makers, when they themselves ran out of tin-plate. They even airlifted can ends in huge Galaxy aircraft into East Midlands airport from America. It was quite an operation. During the drought that hit them, they found a private lake and transported water from there to the factory in milk tankers to prevent their production lines from stopping. That is what we mean by 'work to achieve the goals even under changing conditions'.

'100 per cent of objectives are achieved, or exceeded, by year end'

Based on the policy of objective writing elaborated earlier in this chapter, it becomes a *habit* in world class companies regularly to meet and beat their stretching objectives. That 'expectation of success' is an invaluable commodity. It can often be the key difference between the winners and those who come second.

IDEAS AND TECHNIQUES YOU CAN USE

Contents of this section:

- producing great company goals;
- aligning management behind the goals;
- what good objectives should look like;
- explanation of key terms.

Producing great company goals

The first task in aligning management objectives is to produce a set of long-term goals for the business that will be understandable to employees at all levels and to which they can all make a positive contribution. This is not easy. Being clear, simple and galvanizing all at the same time is hard. But it's crucial.

We use a set of rules for goal-setting that have been helpful to a whole variety of businesses. Here they are:

1. Make sure your goals are few and simple.
2. Make your goals actionable by everybody in the business.
3. Make your goals constant.
4. Make your goals measurable.
5. Lead by example.

Make sure your goals are few and simple

Make your goals so clear and simple, you know that everyone in the business will be able to *understand them without further explanation.* If you don't, your employees will not be able to help you make them come true. Make them few enough that everyone will be able to carry them round in their head. That way, they will affect their behaviour every day.

Take an example or two. Many years ago, Marks and Spencer directors decided they would not stock items of a quality they would not be pleased to have in their own homes. To reinforce their commitment, they were one of the first to offer a no-quibble take-it-back guarantee to anyone with faulty or unsuitable goods. Marks and Spencer's commitment to quality affects everything they do. It's so clear every director knows it, every manager, every member of staff, even every customer. Is there anything about your company that is so clear that it affects every employee's behaviour every day, and which all your customers would recognize too?

Well, it happens at Federal Express. For years their commitment to delivery of customers' parcels has been 'absolutely, positively overnight'. And everyone in the business knows just what that means: the item has to reach its destination next day before 10.30 am or the customer doesn't have to pay. It's that simple. The managers know it, the office people know it, the delivery people know it, and the customers know it. There's no confusion – everyone knows exactly what they have to do every day. That kind of clarity brings an energy and teamwork across the business that is difficult to generate any other way.

Make your goals actionable by everybody in the business

The best example we can give you here is that of the London Metropolitan police who several years ago commissioned consultants to investigate their poor image with the public. The consultants concluded: 'There is no overall consistency of view on the mission of the Met nor on how each individual contributes to the whole . . . That is why different standards of behaviour and action co-exist, and why they have been noticed by both police and public.' The then Commissioner of Police decided to draw up a Statement of Common Purpose, which he defined as:

● to uphold the law firmly and fairly;

- to maintain public peace;
- to act with honesty and integrity;
- to adopt the highest standards;
- to be compassionate and courteous to others;
- to uphold individual rights;
- to behave in a manner which is neither sexist nor racist;
- to serve the public;
- to be a cost-effective service;
- to co-operate with and consult with the community and other agencies in pursuing police purposes.

The list was well intentioned despite looking like mere 'motherhood' statements. The problem is: will they actually help the constable doing his everyday job on the beat? For example, what does 'to adopt the highest standards' actually mean in practice? Would the constable know how to change his behaviour as a result? If he's called on to sort out a family feud, which 'individual rights' should he choose to uphold? Will he get support for his decision later if he tries to follow the guidelines? When staff don't know quite what you mean, they tend to take the safest route, which is not to act at all, or to send the problem upstairs for someone else to decide.

Consider the difference, however, if the police (or the Met) had decided on just three simple actionable goals:

- to reduce crime;
- to make it safe for anyone to walk anywhere at any time in the United Kingdom;
- to treat everyone fairly.

No list is perfect, of course, but simple goals like these have several crucial advantages:

1. Every member of the force at every level would be able to understand them without further explanation. The point seems obvious, but it's crucial.
2. Everyone in the police could carry the goals around in their head and *do something about them every day*. And everyone would realize that they had a personal contribution to make that was important to the success of the whole organization.
3. Based on the goals, objectives could be agreed at every level throughout the force – at country level, region, district, section, right down to individuals – and performance measured against them. And if you can't measure it, you can't tell whether you're making progress.
4. Most importantly, working on exactly the same goals, the whole organization would at last be seen to be pulling in the same direction. And that is true teamwork!

When you first see simple, actionable goals like those above, it all looks quite easy. It isn't. It takes contemplation, effort, discussion and struggle. But it is fundamentally important if you are going to get the willing support of your people to make your goals a reality.

Make your goals constant

Don't keep moving the goalposts. When you're beginning to have trouble with the current concept, it's always very tempting to jump on the new bandwagon as an easy solution to the problem. It may be tempting, but here are the things that can happen as a result.

Staff and junior managers think that top management don't know what they're doing. Just as they're getting used to one idea, the company moves on to another. There's a tendency to give only lip service to the new concept, knowing that if they hold on long enough the new idea will fade away or be replaced by another.

Top management sometimes give the impression that the new concept or technique is bigger than their own vision for the company. No concept should be that big. It should be the servant of the company's long-term purpose, a means to an end, not the end itself. Whatever new concept or technique comes along, it should only be adopted if it takes the organization nearer to the goals it has already decided on.

If you look again at the suggested goals for the police in the last section, you'll see that they are likely to last for a very long time. You might set some specific objectives for reduction in different types of crime in year one, and further objectives in year two, but the ongoing goal 'to reduce crime' would remain unchanged, in year one, two, three and thereafter.

Make your goals measurable

Companies measure what is important to them – things like sales, costs, profitability, stock-holding, market share, etc. But the corollary is also true, namely: what gets measured *becomes important*. You can never know if you are really making progress on your goals unless you measure the difference. Goals without measures are nothing more than dreams.

Many managements are reluctant to introduce measures because they might later be held to account. 'If we ask our customers what they think, we might not like the answers we get.' So it's easier not to ask. 'If we survey the opinions of our employees, we could raise their expectations and then we'd have to do something about them.' Better not to ask. But that's managing blind. We've never met the management who could manage better blind than by having hard data, and taking action on the data to make measurable progress.

Later in the Ladders (Ladder 4) we not only promote the value of measurement, but the benefits of using visible measures. By making the chosen measures visible right at the place of work, staff and managers are made aware on a daily basis of what the company wants everybody to concentrate on. That shapes behaviour. And if employee rewards are linked to company progress (see Ladder 10), then that adds to the focus and energy put behind them by everyone.

Lead by example

Whatever goals you set yourselves as an organization, employees look on to see if you are serious in what you say. If you choose to focus on 'superior customer service', for example, staff wait to see if you will define in detail what you mean, if you will give them the necessary training to deliver something better, if you will spend money on the technology that will allow them to be more effective, etc. They wait to see if you change your old habits. They want to know if you're really serious. Only then do they jump on board.

You see, it's not the words that count. It's the *example*. Your actions are 10 times more powerful than your words. What they see you do is what they will believe in. The words are only window dressing. Equally, they look to see if the senior management team are all backing the goals with the same fervour. It is vitally important that the top team are 'as one' on the subject. If everyone's divisional or departmental head is not right behind the goals and the new ideas, the whole initiative will soon start to founder with all the disappointment, repercussions and embarrassment that that can involve. Words by themselves won't change the business. Action and genuine commitment will.

Aligning management behind the goals

Getting any management fully behind the company's goals starts at Board level. If it doesn't happen there, it doesn't go anywhere else. But with robust managers and thinkers at senior level, it is difficult to achieve that unity without a definitive process. It also helps to use an experienced independent facilitator to run the process. With previous experience in business he can ask the appropriate 'naïve' question at the right time, introduce ideas that get managers to think 'out of the box', and with no in-company career aspirations to worry about, he can raise important subjects that might otherwise be taboo.

The tested process we ourselves use starts with an executive Team Objectives Meeting or TOM, at which the goals and strategy for the business for the next three years are decided. That session is followed by a series of TOMs held by each working department. There they turn the goals decided by the top team into operational objectives. So the plans and goals of the business cascade down the whole organization. This is how the process works, first with the top team.

Preparation phase

1. *Individual interviews.* Asking directors some searching questions, and about their vision of the future of the business gets serious (and essential) thinking started.

2. *Pre-TOM seminar.* The facilitator 'opens windows' on concepts and ideas that have taken other companies into the 'world class' league, which the team might consider interesting for their own company. Without the injection of new thinking, the strategy meeting is likely to produce many of the same old ideas as before.
3. *Pre-think document.* Team members each get a booklet asking them to put down their considered views on a number of key questions affecting the company, including what goals and performance measures they feel they ought to be setting themselves for the following three years.

Team Objectives Meeting

The team spends two or three days together, considering the ideas and views from individual Pre-thinks, and coming to team agreement on their key goals for the next three years. Two rules apply:

1. Nothing becomes a decision unless it is agreed by the team 100%. (If you don't 'pay the price' by hammering out differences at this stage, the price is paid later by individuals showing little commitment back at work.)
2. Those actions which are agreed become commitments, ie the team undertakes to do whatever it takes to see them achieved.

Action phase

1. *Action document.* The flip-charted goals and decisions are transferred to an action document distributed to all team members, and which becomes the organization's blueprint for action.
2. *Formal reviews.* So many organizations start with heart-felt good intentions, but fail to follow up. That is fatal. So every quarter or so, the team meets formally to ask hard questions and do the reality check: 'Are we doing what we said we would do?' That sends the critical message that the company is serious about its goals.

Cascading management TOMs

Having agreed the company's longer-term goals, the hardest job is then to come: getting all of management fully behind the goals. The only successful way to get them on board is to make them the 'drivers of change'. And that means giving them the time to think through in their working teams what objectives they can set, or what practical actions they can take, to help make the company's goals come true in their area.

This is achieved by each of the directors from the original strategy team conducting TOMs with their own divisional teams, ie with the managers who report directly to them. Normally this is confined to a group of fewer than 10 people. The process is similar to the top team TOM, with some important differences:

Preparation phase

1. *Individual interviews.*
2. *Pre-TOM seminar.* The facilitator introduces some new ideas as before, but also explains some of the thinking behind the goals chosen by the company. It is enormously helpful here that the team boss, who himself was at the top team TOM, can explain the 'music behind the words'.
3. *Pre-think document.* Issued to each team member, this time concentrating on what objectives they think their Division can set to make their contribution to the company's new goals.

Team Objectives Meeting

Generally this is held off-site but certainly in a location where the team will be undisturbed. The 100 per cent agreement rule applies as before. There is one key difference. The team head's boss arrives at the end of day two to hear what they have decided. They present their actions and commitments to him. That's when real ownership and public commitment takes place. After all, the chief executive cannot be accused of dominating. He didn't take part in the meeting. Obviously the objectives the team set have to fit with the company goals their own boss agreed with, but the actions they have listed are all theirs, and every one of them 100 per cent agreed. That's locked-in commitment.

Action phase

1. *Action document.* Composed from the TOM, this is distributed to each team member, but can also usefully be sent to supplier and customer departments.
2. *Formal review.* Held at least twice in year one. The whole team presents their progress to a Board Meeting formally convened for the purpose. The more high-powered you make it, the more teams treat the matter seriously and indulge in 'hurry up' actions to get things done before their deadlines.

The TOM process then cascades down the organization (see Figure 1.1), with each TOM's agreed output being formally endorsed by an end-of-TOM visit by the manager one level above.

This way, the objectives throughout the organization are understood, aligned, owned and committed to. That kind of alignment is the indispensable starting-point to begin climbing the Ladders to world class performance.

What good objectives should look like

Written objectives have a habit of coming true. Writing down your intentions presses you into getting focused and specific. It leads to less ambiguity, confusion and post-event rationalization. They are an essential tool for

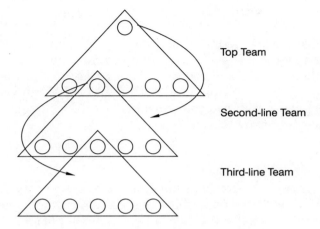

Top Team

Second-line Team

Third-line Team

Figure 1.1 TOM process cascade

performance-oriented companies. But few managers find the process easy. Often they need training, practice and some sensible rules to follow. The rules we commend to you are easy to remember and to the point. Here they are.

Make sure the objectives you decide upon are S.M.A.R.T., that is:

- Specific
- Measurable
- Agreed
- Realistic
- Time-bounded.

Specific

Write objectives about specific things to be achieved. Don't just write vague generalities about 'creating greater quality awareness' or 'reducing paper-work'. Say in what specific areas, by when and how much. Then apply the key test to each objective you propose: 'Will we all know, without having to ask the boss, when success has been achieved?'

Measurable

Make your objectives depend on measurable facts, not opinion. The best measures are those which can be answered with a 'yes' or 'no', ie 'Was the objective achieved, yes or no?' Decide what data should be used, or what data should be collected, to measure each objective.

Set priorities: Priority 1 = essential, must be done; Priority 2 = important; Priority 3 = desirable. Write no more than three or four Priority 1 objectives. Concentrate on the critical few.

Agreed

Objectives that are imposed from above tend to get much less commitment from staff than those that are agreed. Your boss may not accept everything you say without question, of course. In your discussions you may need to make changes to fit the current needs of the business. When you do agree, however, objectives become commitments. That means doing whatever it takes to make the objectives come true.

Realistic

Write objectives that are stretching but achievable, ie where you feel you and your team have an 80 per cent chance of succeeding. Don't write ambitious objectives that look good at the time but set you up for failure. Using the 80 per cent rule will give you objectives with enough stretch to keep the team learning and growing, but makes it tempting to go for success. And we want yours to be an organization where success is the norm.

Time-bounded

Make clear the timescale in which each objective is to be achieved, ie exactly what, by when. This should apply both to one-off objectives and ongoing standards, such as despatching orders, or responding to customer enquiries, etc.

Explanation of key terms

One of the stumbling-blocks for managers involved in making change is the plethora of terms that are meant to help but often serve to confuse. Is 'mission' the same as 'vision'? Are 'goals' the same as 'aims and objectives'? Is there a difference between 'values', 'principles' and 'beliefs'? If managers find it all too confusing, they often find the safe way to deal with it all is just not to get involved. Our strong advice to you is not to get over-elaborate in your terminology. Keep it simple. Choose your terms carefully and say what you mean by them. When your people understand, they are much more likely to come on board. For this reason, you may find the following glossary useful.

Company goals   These are ongoing aims that keep a company continually striving in a chosen direction. They may or may not be quantified. Their constant characteristic is that they can keep being repeated year by year. For example: 'To increase company earnings by 15 per cent year on year' (Rubbermaid). 'To be first or second in any market in which we operate' (General Electric).

Objectives   These are the key tasks for this year. Each objective will be quantified, and have time scales attached. The job-holder or team will know, without anyone telling them, when they have passed the winning post. For example: 'System to be installed to customer's satisfaction (ie sign-off) by 30 September.'

Standards   These describe the performance expected on recurrent job requirements. For example, a standard of performance on producing accounts figures might be: 'produced, error-free, by the 10th working day of each month'.

Accountability   This describes what a manager can be 'called to account for'. For example, the manager may not have done something personally, but will still be expected to 'account for' what happens in departments under his control.

Responsibility   This is what any manager is personally responsible for, ie it describes what the manager does himself, his unique contributions to the business.

Business definition   This is a succinct description that makes clear the areas of activity the company is *not* in, and keeps its managers 'sticking to the knitting'. In other words, the definition helps them stick to the areas they know best, and that give them the best chance of commercial success. For example: 'Our business is renting cars without drivers' (Avis).

Longer-term objectives   These are objectives that are set for a longer time horizon, eg for the next 3 to 10 years. For example: 'We aim to double our sales and profits over the next three years.'

Strategy   This describes how any objective set is to be achieved. For example, the objective of the Duke of Wellington at the Battle of Waterloo was to defeat Napoleon. His strategy was about how he deployed his resources – men, equipment, and timing – to achieve victory. Strategy is not the goal itself.

Policy   This describes a standard way of dealing effectively with repetitive situations. A laid-down policy avoids having to take a decision each time the event occurs, and ensures the matter is dealt with consistently. An example of a policy might be: 'It is our policy to pay checked invoices at the end of the month following receipt.'

Note: Other terms and meanings also exist, of course, but we have found the terms and descriptions laid out here to be the clearest and most useful definitions in practice.

T W O

Customer Focus

LEVELS	MEASURES
Level 1	Employees think sales and marketing look after customers. Managers believe they are 'professionals' and already know what customers want. Many managers and staff don't think they have customers.
Level 2	Everyone realizes that the paying customer is the most important person in the business. In-company, people know their customer is the next process. Customer complaints are seen as a nuisance, and something to get rid of as soon as possible. At least 80% of orders delivered to customers on time.
Level 3	The company uses real survey data to measure performance. Internal customers make contracts across departments. Written service standards established in every department. Complaints seen as an opportunity to create improvements. At least 90% of orders delivered in full and on time.
Level 4	Customer data discussed regularly at Board meetings. Service standards met and exceeded across the company. Cycle time, order to delivery, reduced by 50%. At least 95% of orders delivered in full and on time.
Level 5	Regular surveys and focus groups keep company 'in touch'. Visible service improvements made year on year. Cycle time, order to delivery, reduced by 80%. Complaints under 0.5% and at an all-time low. 100% of orders delivered in full and on time.

LEVEL 1

'Employees think sales and marketing look after customers'

It is quite amazing how many people in organizations never think of the customer. This applies as much to managers as to front-line staff. They assume they are there 'to do their job', and that their salary will automatically materialize at the end of the month. Somehow they see the company like a fruit machine that pays out as long as they pull the handle; they do not think about the need to keep putting money in the back of the machine for it to keep producing. Everyone in commercial organizations needs to realize that their current and future salaries are actually in the pockets of real customers outside the walls, and they will only keep giving the company money if they satisfy their needs as well as, or better than, the competition.

It is surprising also how many chief executives and directors do not know who their biggest customers are, what they sell them, how much they sell to them, what margins they make, etc. Even sales or marketing executives often have to look in their drawers to find the figures. Customers are the life-blood of any business. Everyone needs not only to be aware of who they are, but to realize the company's continued existence depends on serving them well.

'Managers believe they are "professionals" and already know what customers want'

In some companies, especially where the products or services are technically complex (eg specialist machinery, computer systems, financial services, etc), executives will often call themselves 'professionals', ie 'we know what we are doing', or 'we do the type of job that would be admired by other professionals in our business'. Often, however, this can mean they actually don't listen to customers (because they know better), and that is dangerous. There is no professional who cannot do a better job by first listening to customers, and then doing something about what they say.

'Many managers and staff don't think they have customers'

When first asked who their customers are, staff and their managers will often say they do not have 'customers' as such. They are wrong. Everyone has customers in that they are doing the work for use by someone. Who is that someone? That is what must be identified.

For example, when first asked the question, the R&D department managers at the Bank of England Printing Works felt they did not have customers; if they did, there was only one, ie the Chief Cashier (the man whose signature appears on the banknotes). In discussion, however, they conceded that the commercial banks were probably customers too, perhaps High Street retailers, maybe big note users like London Underground or betting shops, and eventually maybe even the man in the street. Astonishingly, customer consultation had not previously been part of the process before designing banknotes. They felt they were 'the professionals'. Today, it is different. Not only do they have long lists of customers divided into four major categories, they talk to them too. And they are forever striving to make the notes serve the needs of the customer better, eg easier to go through an ATM machine, easier to manufacture, harder to forge, easier for the public to tell a genuine note from a counterfeit, etc.

LEVEL 2

'Everyone realizes that the paying customer is the most important person in the business'

L L Bean is a US company that sells fishing and game sporting goods by mail order. They have a legendary order fulfilment and warehousing system that is regularly benchmarked by other companies seeking to reach world class standard. And it has all come out of their fundamental attitude – inculcated by the original owner – to customers. This is the statement they have posted on the wall throughout the company:

What Is A Customer?

- A Customer is the most important person in this office . . . whether in person, by mail or telephone.
- A Customer is not dependent on us . . . we are dependent on him.
- A Customer is not an interruption to our work . . . he is the purpose of it. We are not doing a favour by serving him . . . he is doing us a favour by giving us the opportunity to do so.
- A Customer is not someone to argue or match wits with. Nobody ever won an argument with a Customer.
- A Customer is a person who brings us his wants. It is our job to handle them profitably for him and for ourselves.

This is an attitude we thoroughly endorse. The points that follow are the arguments we ourselves use to reinforce the point that the paying customer is king in any commercial business:

1. The salary and benefits of every person in the business – yours and mine – come out of the pocket of the customer. That is the only place they can come from. Our job security and standard of living all come from him. That is why he is the most important person in this business.
2. The only reason the customer parts with his money is because he sees the value of what we are giving him as worth more than the money he has in his hand. No other reason. And it is not just the product or service he gets that counts. It is also the courtesy he experiences, the speed and accuracy with which we fulfil his request, the quality of the product in practice, getting things right the first time, the concern we show for resolving his problems quickly, etc.

3. Normally the customer can choose to go elsewhere, if he doesn't like the product quality, the price, the delivery, the treatment he gets, etc. So we are always in competition. That is why we have to be doing better than our competitors to keep his business. Customers have some loyalty to their suppliers of course, but eventually they will buy from those who offer the best overall value in meeting their needs. We are only as good as our last game.

4. The customer can only judge us by what he *perceives*. There may be a lot of work going on behind the scenes, but the customer only gives us credit for the things he himself sees. The customer may be a large company, of course, in which case our product and service is perceived by a number of people, each of whom only sees part of the picture.

    For example, if we are delivering products, they are first seen by the receiving warehouse, who see how the products are delivered, who note the helpfulness of the driver, etc. The products may then be inspected by quality control people, who see whether the products regularly meet the specifications laid down. The production people who use the product judge how well they are made, how reliable they are in practice, etc. The warehouse people make judgements about the paperwork that is sent. The accounts people find out whether the invoices sent tie up with the deliveries and are easy to work with. The buyers meet the company's salespeople and come to conclusions about their prices, their quality, whether they are a believable company, etc.

    That means we have to make sure that wherever there is an interface between the company and its paying customers, we give them an overall good experience every time they deal with us. That is what keeps them coming back, and keeps us all in a job.

Exercise

A good exercise to go through with managers or staff is to ask: what are all the interfaces our company has with the customer (from the reception desk to problem-solving post delivery)? What experiences do you think customers are getting in each of these? What must we or can we do to improve these?

---

5. We have to value the customer not just for the benefit we get from one sale, but for all the sales he can bring us in the future. If a housewife spends, say, £50 per week on her groceries, that is £2,500 a year, or £25,000 over a 10-year period. That is what staff should see stamped on the customer's forehead every time they serve her: £25,000! That is their future salary standing right there. If you are selling cars or other high-value items, then the numbers will be even higher.

Also, if a satisfied customer refers you to another customer, then the original customer's value could double or treble . . . Truly, the customer is the most important person in the business.

A word of caution, however. It is quite easy to identify customers when there are paying clients and their satisfaction shows through in a profit bottom line. It is much harder when there is no bottom line, eg a government department, a church, a charity, a library, a hospital, the armed forces, etc. In state-owned enterprises the 'Who cares?' syndrome often prevails, as you appear to get paid whether you do your job well or not. That is just more of a challenge. There may not be profit targets to aim for, but there are service *standards* that can be set and met. You can still identify customers (especially the most important, or the most frequent), you can ask them what improvements they would like to see, and set realistic goals.

Our definition of 'standards' is: objectives you aim to achieve repeatedly. For example: 'answer the telephone within five rings'; 'reply to letters within five days'; 'all orders received by 4 o'clock will be despatched the same day', etc. Commercial manufacturing companies have the advantage that they can see the products they make going out of the door, they can count them, and control them to that extent. Controlling service quality can be that much harder: it is less tangible, and it gets delivered in thousands of *'moments of truth'* when the customer interfaces with one of your staff.

A moment of truth refers to the fact that you often only get one chance: *you either did it right at the time or you did not.* The member of staff dealt with *is* the company to the customer at that moment, whether it is the receptionist, the telephonist, the credit controller, the salesperson, the delivery driver, or whoever. Managers in any company may see less than 1 per cent of these transactions, so it is imperative that all staff who deal with customers are both trained and motivated to do it well. Not easy!

'In-company, people know their customer is the next process'

The service delivered to the ultimate (paying) customer can never be better than the worst links in the chain of events needed to produce that service. That is why everyone in any company needs to know exactly who their internal customers are (by name preferably), and to be working to explicit standards in delivering the product or service for which they are responsible.

To help explain the concepts of 'internal customer' and 'chain of customers' we use the example of building a car. This is a complex process of course, so we have grossly simplified the procedure to bring out the essential points involved (see Figure 2.1).

The first step in making a car is to bend the sheets of metal received from the steel producer into the required shapes, eg like boot lids, bonnets, wings, etc. In the Press Shop, big 300 to 1,000-ton presses bend the metal into shape in one big thump. It is the operator's job:

1. To check the metal before he uses it for defects, imperfections, etc; that is, he becomes the company's initial quality control checker.
2. To do what it takes to do his job 'right first time'.

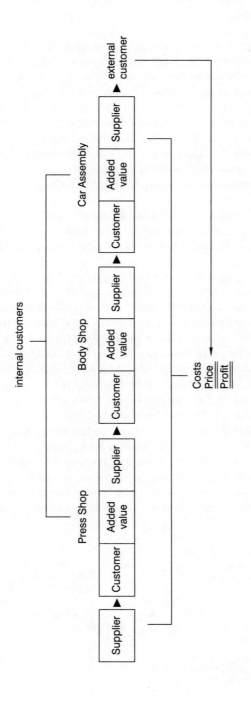

Figure 2.1 The customer chain

3. To check the part he has made before he passes it on to the next person in the line, ie the next process.

At the point when he receives the bare metal from the outside supplier, he is a *customer*, ie he acts as receiver on behalf of the company. His job then is to *add value*, ie to change the material in a way that will be of value to the customer. In this case, his customer is the next process, the next person in the line. This is what we call the 'internal customer' (as opposed to the ultimate paying customer). And when he is passing over material like this, the operator acts in the role of *supplier*. As such, the operator should only pass on to his customer that which allows him to do a *zero-defect* job. Only if we have zero-defects at each stage can we hope to give our ultimate customer (the one who pays all our salaries) the perfect product you have effectively promised and he thinks he is buying.

The same can be applied to the work done at the next stage, ie in the Body Shop (where they weld together the metal parts to make a complete car body) and then in the Assembly Shop (where they add an engine, steering wheel, seats, instruments, etc).

All the work done in building the car has so far only added costs. No one has paid the car manufacturer anything yet. And no customer is going to pay to the company anything unless he thinks that what it is offering is of more value than the price he has to pay. That is why he parts with his money – he sees the product or the service as worth more to him than the notes he has to give up to get it. Hopefully, the price he pays will also be more than the total cost, for that is the only way the company can make a profit. And making a profit is the only way the company can stay in business. Every employee's job security is tied up in getting the company's act together internally well enough to satisfy the customer and keep him coming back.

It should also be remembered that the paying customer never just looks at one company's product or service by itself. He also looks at what he can get elsewhere (see Figure 2.2). The customer will only give you his business if he thinks that overall he is getting a better deal with you than with your competitors. Like you and me, he looks for the best value for his money. So working well together as a team of internal customers is the best guarantee

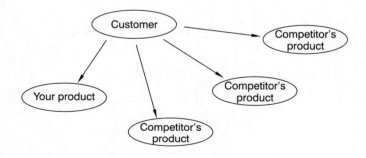

Figure 2.2 Customer comparison of products

of ensuring that your customers will keep on coming back. They have the power to decide your fate. They keep us all in a job.

In summary, the basic lessons for every employee are:

1. You can be a customer and a supplier at the same time. Ensure your supplier gives you what you need to do a good job.
2. Every person's task is to add value. Adding value means changing the material or information you work with in a way that is useful to the customer.
3. The customer is the next person in the process. That is, the person who gets the result of your work.
4. Quality means fulfilling the customer's requirements. That means giving customers what they want, when they want it, how they want it. Quality, therefore, is not what we say it is, it is what the customer says it is.
5. No commercial company can stay in business unless the customer pays you a price greater than your costs. It is therefore the job of every employee to deliver a value greater than his cost.

'Customer complaints are seen as a nuisance, and something to get rid of as soon as possible'

Many companies are today much more positive about handling customer complaints, but many more still see complaints as something to get rid of as soon as possible. For example, a few years ago it was quite a common experience for the UK manufacturer of certain sit-upon farm vehicles to have customers phoning in about problems they were experiencing with their engines, causing them both inconvenience and extra cost, and ask what the company was going to do about it; they might suggest the company should pay for the repair because, although the engine guarantee might have run out, the vehicle had 'not been used for months' and therefore it was unfair for the customer to foot the bill. The natural instinct of the company's technicians was to go on the defensive, and start asking some searching questions. Had they been treating the engine right? Did they have it serviced properly at the stated intervals by an approved dealer? Are they sure they followed instructions and didn't put unusual strain on the engine?

To some extent they felt that by interrogating the customer, questioning points, they might thereby mitigate the cost of any subsequent claims. Sometimes it would take a while to get a decision, but whereas some might hope the customer would get fed up and withdraw, generally they would not. In fact, they often got more irate, rejected first offers, or demanded to speak to the Managing Director. The MD found he could have a lot of problems on his plate, and found himself having to make concessions to placate upset customers. He was well aware that this would not do the company any good in their chosen market, if current owners were to start relating their experiences to their friends.

Today in the company the situation is quite different. Technicians realize the key objective of handling a customer complaint is to resolve it so well the customer *wants to buy from the company again*. The first thing they do is listen. They have a personal target to resolve any problem within seven days maximum. If it isn't, the whole technician team sits down together to attack the problem and resolve it. And they know the problem is only finally resolved when the customer says 'thanks'. Customer feedback tells them the customers really notice and appreciate the positive attitude. The MD doesn't hear from irate customers with technical problems any more. He knows his technicians treat these matters with urgency – they know everyone's security is tied to having banks of customers who are pleased with the product and pleased with the service.

There are a number of lessons to be drawn here:

1. It is better to pay the costs of getting the product or service right the first time inside the business. It is the cheapest cost option. If you don't, you will pay even more later putting things right.
2. While resolving 'things gone wrong', not only are your costs increasing, you are irritating the customer who expected you to get it right the first time. In other words, you find yourself paying more cost for no extra benefit whatsoever.
3. Delaying putting a fault or a complaint right not only adds further cost, it adds to the customer's irritation as well.
4. Getting into a contest with the customer is bad business. It elevates the customer's settlement threshold (it costs you more in the end), and he pays you back even after a higher settlement by bad-mouthing you in the market.
5. A complaint that reaches the MD will have several characteristics: the customer has been sandbagged and annoyed to the point where he is at the pitch of his irritation; you can be sure he wants compensation not just for his complaint, but for his frustration as well (always more expensive than early settlement).
6. Once the MD starts handling complaints, customers do not want to talk to anybody else. That seriously debilitates other staff. And people at lower levels do not try as hard. No point – we may as well leave it to the MD to decide.

Any legitimate complaint by a customer means you haven't delivered on what you originally promised. If you broke a promise to a friend you'd want to do something to make up, ie to show you are sorry and to make sure you stayed friends. It should be exactly the same with your customers. Don't delay: put it right immediately and say you are sorry.

'At least 80 per cent of orders delivered to customers on time'

There are three levels of 'on time' measurement:

1. The *company determines* when the customer will get the product.

2. The company meets the date *mutually agreed with the customer.*
3. The company meets the date *demanded by the customer.*

Most companies cannot even manage number 1. Some companies actually tell fibs via their sales people (promising delivery dates they know will not be fulfilled) to get the order. That's a thoroughly bad idea. Often it happens because sales people do not communicate with production people. They say it is bad enough getting the order without production people complaining about tight deadlines. Production people then telephone customers themselves to sort out the problems. Companies like this simply convince their customers that they do not know what they are doing. Would you want to deal with a company like this any more than you have to?

The fact is that customers cannot do any real production planning at their end unless they know what to expect in reality. As a result they build in time buffers since they know they cannot believe the supplier. This spells disaster for any company that is serious about becoming world class. Step 1 is to tell customers the truth, which may come as an initial shock to them, but they definitely prefer it. But when you do tell the truth, you have to meet your own deadlines. That is the very first stage of on-time delivery.

When you have mastered meeting your own delivery dates, ie more than 80 per cent achievement three months in a row, then you can think of 'raising the bar'. Companies may find they have to move much faster on this subject than they envisaged as they face 'heat' from the competition. Whatever the pressure, customers generally prefer reliability of supply to speed *per se.* They do not want the inconvenience of changing suppliers unless they really have to, so if a company is genuinely trying – and succeeding – they will generally stay loyal.

LEVEL 3

'The company uses real survey data to measure performance'

Many companies never ask their customers what they think. In some cases, it is because they are too internally focused and never think about it. In other cases, it is because they feel they have enough problems and do not want to hear about any more. Of course, such an attitude is short-sighted, and does not become a company intent on becoming world class. Especially since customers can provide many clues to the simple things that could be done should you want to improve your products or service.

Often customers tell you things you had not even been thinking about. Then, instead of slaving away at things they are not concerned about, it becomes obvious where efforts should be concentrated. A good case in point is Volvo Penta, the Division of Volvo that produces engines for all kinds of water craft: in 1993 the company was intent on improving the service quality delivered by their 90 agents around the United Kingdom to help counter the threat from Japanese competition. First, their senior managers got together to draw up a list of possible improvements, of which the following is a selection:

- dealer easy to find via direction signage;
- open at convenient hours;
- Volvo name at least in the telephone directory and yellow pages;
- dealer accepts credit cards, at least Visa and Access;
- premises are clean and smart;
- work is complete when promised;
- repair works first time;
- engineers leave no dirt or stains on customer's boat;
- dealer gives customer clean (not grubby) bills or paperwork.

On the face of it, this looks like a pretty good list.

Then they conducted a survey among real boat-owners at the London Boat Show who hardly mentioned any of that. This is what *they* said they wanted:

- fixed-price servicing;
- firm estimate of repair costs pre-job;
- final charge matches estimate;
- no extra work done unless authorized by the customer;
- opening hours convenient to customers, ie weekends and holidays;
- good advice given irrespective of size of purchase;
- contact with customer always friendly and helpful.

Following a national conference with their dealers, the company introduced a new Code of Practice for customers, which appears as a large poster where customers are dealt with in every dealership. This is what it says:

> We want you, our customers, to be fully satisfied both with our products and our service. That is why we have developed this Code of Practice, so that you know you can always expect a fair deal and courteous treatment from all Volvo Penta dealers.

> In striving to offer you the very best service we can, we undertake to:

> - treat your boat and equipment with care and work in a clean and tidy fashion;
> - give you a fair estimate of the work required and cost before we start;
> - name the person in the dealership who will be responsible for any work done on your equipment;
> - carry out any service work according to the laid-down company schedules using only genuine Volvo Penta parts and Volvo Penta trained personnel;
> - inform you immediately of any complications or delays, and to get your personal go-ahead for any additional work before carrying it out;
> - inform you about what has been done about any special items you have raised with us, and have available for you where requested all parts removed from your equipment;
> - have the work completed for you on time;
> - charge a final price for the work carried out in line with the estimate we gave you;

- have commonly used parts available immediately, and any part available for you normally within 72 hours.

To ensure that the company is doing what it has promised, a customer questionnaire is now attached to every service invoice handed to a customer. Each is addressed to the Managing Director himself, postage pre-paid. Both dealers and customers realize the company is genuinely serious about service.

'Internal customers make contracts across departments'

The 'customer chain' was described on the previous pages. To consolidate full understanding of this internal customer process, the following sequence is the pattern we ourselves use with client companies:

1. Staff are educated about the 'customer chain' and how each of the links has to play its part to satisfy the customer (see Figure 2.1). The customer can never receive a zero-defect product or service (ie what we have promised), unless we get zero defects at every stage of the process.
2. Work teams then name their internal customers, ie they make a list. This should include naming 'supplier departments' (like Planning or Finance who supply them with the right information to enable them to do their job), as well as the next person or department that receives the result of their work.
3. Team members then each visit, say, two named internal customers to ask them:
   (a) what they should continue doing (that they are already doing well);
   (b) what they would most like them to improve.

Normally, the 'customers' are surprised to be visited by 'suppliers', who, far from bringing complaints, have actually come to listen, and to ask how they might improve their service to them. Our experience is that the process is a powerful start to breaking down barriers and encouraging cross-department co-operation.

4. Once the work team has made a number of improvements requested by their customers, they then 'make contracts' for the future on a regular basis. We deliberately use the word 'contract' to imply obligation, ie 'our word is our bond'. Contracts should cover items such as:
   (a) what quantities of what material or information you can expect;
   (b) what (error-free) quality you can expect;
   (c) when you will get it;
   (d) in what form you will get it;
   (e) who to contact in case of trouble, and how to contact them.

'In what form' may need some further explanation. It may mean, for example, how you want the financial information you need laid out or presented, in what detail, or how often. In the case of a manufacturing shop floor, it may mean how much material should be delivered at a time, how often, in what type of container (otherwise it may be too heavy to lift or manoeuvre), where it should be put, etc. We repeat: quality is not what the producer decides it is, it is what the customer says it is.

'Written service standards established in every department'

Service standards describe the quality of service customers can expect on a regular basis. They also describe the performance staff are expected to deliver day by day. Service standards are typically written like this:

'We will answer phones within five rings.'
'All orders received by 4 o'clock will be delivered by 9 o'clock the next day.'
'Customer enquiries will be answered within 24 hours. Quotations will normally be provided within one week; more complex quotations as agreed directly with the customer.'
'Customer complaints will be acknowledged by telephone within 24 hours of receipt, and resolved (ie to the customer's satisfaction) within 10 days.'

Almost invariably, the service customers most want has to do with *time*. They do not want to wait in a queue for service, they do not want their product tomorrow, they want it now. They hate delays, and they simply do not care about explanations for delays. This is especially true when companies have created firm expectations in the customer's mind by making promises. For example, a company gives a delivery date but does not deliver. The most common form of written promise is timetables – they are not only in writing, they are made public. That is why people get extremely upset when trains or planes are late – the customer has a strong expectation that the train will actually leave and arrive on time, and they make firm arrangements with others on that basis, so they are much less forgiving of failure.

World class organizations have written service standards in place. A good example is that of Lands End, an American company, now also selling its traditional casual clothing in European markets:

We accept any return, for any reason, at any time. Our products are guaranteed. No fine print. No arguments. We mean exactly what we say. In one word. GUARANTEED.

You can count on us for quality, value, and always, always service. We're not out just to make a sale to you. We're out to build a relationship. You have our word on that too. It's the same single word. GUARANTEED.

Such a standard is bold and will keep the competition gasping. It is also clear to both employees and customers. That is a company you could do business with. However, if you set such a standard, be sure you can deliver!

'Complaints seen as an opportunity to create improvements'

It is difficult for staff not to feel offended when people complain. The natural response to blame is to defend oneself by quoting extenuating circumstances or getting aggressive. That does not help the customer. They pay you back by taking their custom elsewhere. So staff have to be taught to treat complaints as a genuine opportunity to improve. After all, if no one ever tells you, how will you know where you could do better? In fact, it might be a good idea to give a special 'thank you' card to those customers who alert you to problems . . .

What the customer expects is that you will put the problem right, and (given what we know about the importance of time) that you will do it immediately. Also, in these circumstances, just correcting the problem may not be enough. Since you have effectively offended the customer, you now may have to do something exceptional to compensate, ie to bring them back to a neutral position.

There is of course one key purpose behind taking all this trouble, and that is: to get the customer to buy from you again. That is where all employees' salaries are, both now and in the future. And the good news is that customers do buy from you again the more trouble you take. TARP (Technical Assistance Research Programs) of Washington, DC have conducted customer research for many years. An important study they conducted for the US White House Office of Consumer Affairs produced the following findings:

1. 96% of irritated customers do not bother to complain.
   Of those who do complain:
2. If you handle the complaint well: 95% of little complainers come back, 82% of large ones.
3. If you handle the complaint at all: 70% of the little complainers come back, 54% of the large ones.
4. If you fail to deal with the complaint satisfactorily: 46% of the small complainers return, 19% of the large ones.
5. Of those who were irritated but did not complain, 37% of the small complainers return, 9% of the large ones.
6. Unhappy customers tell three times as many people about their experiences as do happy customers.
7. One customer is lost for every 50 who hear negative word-of-mouth advertising.

Note the key findings: points 2, 3 and 4 above only apply to the 4 per cent who did complain.

• The percentage of customers who come back rises if you allow customers to talk to you at all about their complaint (compare point 5 with point 4).

In other words, get them to tell you . . . and listen. There is money in knowing about the complaint (rather than avoiding it), and even more money if you go out of your way to handle it well.

- Customers all have two legs and a mouth. They are either walking adverts for you or against you. And they love telling their friends how bad you are (point 6).
- Some potential customers never use you because they have heard bad stories in advance (point 7).

'At least 90 per cent of orders delivered in full and on time'

An increasing number of companies who deliver multi-item orders to their customers use the OTIF (on time in full) measure of their delivery performance. It is an excellent measure but can be interpreted in several ways.

First of all, what does 'on time' mean? Three ways have been described on pages 36–37. Initially, companies normally set their own delivery dates, ie the ones they think they can actually manage. If they cannot achieve that, they will not be able to get off the ground on the journey to world class. Once companies can manage this, they may mutually agree dates between themselves and the customer. By sticking with these two levels, companies can effectively keep control of the dates they have to meet, and that makes a huge difference to their measured performance.

Second, there are at least two interpretations of OTIF. At the first level, what gets measured is *how many items* on the order you were able to deliver on time, eg 83 per cent or 77.5 per cent, etc. At the second level, if you do not deliver 'in full' (ie every item on the customer order list) that is counted as zero even it was delivered on time. That is really tough, as it can often result in very low OTIF scores, and the people concerned feel demotivated or stop trying.

It is advisable to start at the first level of OTIF and to measure the second level alongside. That is because you may keep getting first level OTIF scores in the nineties but literally never delivering *everything* to anybody on time. Gradually then you can concentrate on raising the 'in full' score. The figure applied at Level 3 of the Ladders is over 90 per cent OTIF on the toughest measure, ie more than 90 per cent of orders delivered on time with no items missing.

One of the tough problems that comes up about OTIF is salespeople promising dates to customers that are unachievable. This destroys a company's credibility, until eventually customers do not believe a word you say. Customers would much rather give their business to companies they can rely on. This will mean doing two things to get this right, ie telling the customer the truth (a tough call for some companies) and making actual lead times and delivery times truly competitive.

The latter may take some time. For example, the company may be dependent on suppliers for crucial parts. Companies often make the mistake of playing one supplier off against the other to get better prices or delivery dates. But the supplier companies have no loyalty to such customers. They know their customer could drop them any time for another, and therefore do not want to give that customer special treatment. What companies need to do is to 'get into bed' with one or two of their most reliable suppliers, ie guarantee them more of the business in return for better delivery dates. This is not only advantageous for both parties but takes them ahead of their old-fashioned competition.

There are other advantages too:

1. You have fewer suppliers to deal with, fewer phone calls, simplified paperwork, fewer files to keep, etc.
2. You get to know your suppliers better, they get to know your requirements better, they treat you as one of their 'special' customers, etc. In these cases, they're also more likely to 'pull out the stops' to help you when you're in trouble.
3. Over time, you can help your suppliers improve their quality, make minor changes just to suit your special requirements, etc. You can also help them reduce their costs, and hence their price to you. A typical deal is to tell the customer you expect a reduction of 2% a year in the price of ongoing products as a result of improving productivity. You may think this is tough, but it happens in the car industry all the time.
4. Suppliers can also plan ahead, in deciding to make capital investments, which could be to your advantage, when they know they can rely on your business. In this connection, it is a good idea to take your key suppliers into your confidence about your forward plans just for this reason.

LEVEL 4

'Customer data discussed regularly at Board meetings'

Some companies profess that the customer is the most important person in their business, but surprisingly few directors or managers not in sales know who their customers are. Most board meetings are full of internally focused agenda items, such as accounts, financial plans, capital spend projects, departmental reports, product development, etc. Very few put customer service or customer complaints on the list regularly.

This is not so at Rank Xerox. They have learned the hard way. Falling from a share of about 70 per cent of the photocopying market in the 1970s to under 18 per cent in the 1980s, they realized they had to change. At one point the Japanese could land a better machine in the United States and charge a price to the customer that was lower than their manufacturing cost! Whereas Rank had prided themselves on the rapid service they gave customers who rented their machines, users found the Japanese machines did not actually need engineers as they did not break down half so often.

Rank started bench-marking themselves against the best (they are now regarded as experts in the bench-marking field), and started putting customer service score data on their board meeting agendas. In the United Kingdom, the top 200 executives had performance bonuses tied to customer service targets. It started at 4 per cent of salary, now it is 18 per cent of salary. Customer service comes top of their board meeting agendas all the time now!

'Service standards met and exceeded across the company'

This implies that:

- service standards exist in every department;
- performance is constantly measured;
- the measures are visibly displayed and understandable to all;
- targets and performance continuously improve.

'Cycle time, order to delivery, reduced by 50 per cent'

This means from its original starting point. By 'cycle time' is meant the elapsed time between an order arriving in the company and being despatched complete. This may not be as simple as it sounds. Some products are more complex than others. Some 'orders' may be a long list of disparate items that all have different cycle times, etc.

However, the main drive behind this item is to distinguish between the *added value* time and the actual overall cycle time. By 'added value' we mean the time actually spent working on the material to produce the final product. The time spent waiting between processes, being transported into and out of stores, waiting in inspection, hanging around waiting for bits, etc, is all 'waste' and does not count. (See Ladder 6 for more on waste elimination.) In practice you will find that the added value time may be less than 5 per cent of the total operational cycle time! Conducting this exercise with managers often astonishes (and shames) them. But it also shows how much room there is for improvement.

Companies will often call this 'lead time', and surprisingly just accept it without question. A South African manufacturing company told us they had to forecast in advance, because they quoted their customers a lead time of eight weeks on certain products, while they themselves had to wait 12 weeks for key component items. In this case, what was actually happening was that their supplier kept their order in his in-basket for 11 weeks and then actually made the product during the twelfth week! (In practice, the supplier may himself have to order raw materials from his suppliers etc, but the thrust of the point is largely true.) This company decided to 'get into bed' with a few reliable suppliers, and the first supplier approached reduced its lead time from 12 to 4 weeks and agreed to produce emergency items (not too often of course) in 48 hours. That is what is meant by 'reduced by 50 per cent' from where a company starts. Cycle time can generally be dramatically reduced by simply challenging long-held assumptions.

Cycle times in administrative organizations often have even less added value time in their processes than manufacturing companies. By the time you discount putting things in the internal mail, delays in getting information from others, waiting for signatures and authorizations from absent managers, etc, the added value time versus the elapsed time may be as low as 1 per cent! Here very dramatic improvements can be made (again, see Ladder 6).

'At least 95 per cent of orders delivered in full and on time'

In any relatively complex business, when the company gets to this level, you can take it the company has spent years getting a lot of things co-ordinated and made right first time.

LEVEL 5

'Regular surveys and focus groups keep company "in touch"'

Questionnaire-type surveys are largely quantitative in nature (30 per cent think this, 74 per cent think that), whereas focus groups are primarily qualitative, ie they give participants the freedom to say what they feel in their own words, to make suggestions, etc. Focus groups are very useful in providing nuances on answers, to explain the 'why' behind answers, to provide leads on other questions to be asked, or suggestions on developments the company might consider for the future.

Consumer companies like Mars Confectionery and their advertising agencies often use focus groups. Normally, a group of supermarket shoppers are asked to take part in a focus group (for a fee or a small gift), and are brought into a pleasant room where refreshments etc, are available. They are told that the big glass wall on one side of the room is in fact one-way glass, ie executives from the company are observing the respondents' views and conversation. Mars uses these discussions to find out what consumers think of their latest product, how it looks, how it tastes, the colour of the packaging, the price, etc. They might then bring in alternative forms of packaging to test reaction one against the other. Or they may show the group competitor products, and see what they think the merits of each are.

Generally, the proceedings are recorded (so that the discussion can be typed up and read), and so that you do not have to take furious notes at the time. If you are doing a report on a focus group, you may have a lot of material to plough through. However, one of the greatest benefits of recording is that you can let executives who were not there at the time actually hear respondents talking. At times the participants are not very complimentary. Whereas managers will often handle the information in a report with aplomb, actually hearing customers telling you what they think can have a major impact.

'Visible service improvements made year on year'

A client company now has this stated policy: 'Every month, in every department, we aim to make improvements which are visible to the customer.' Customers cannot give you any credit for improvements they are not aware of. Therefore, either choose to make those improvements that are visible to the customer, or make the customer aware of the improvements that you have actually made. Don't just hope they'll find out.

'Cycle time, order to delivery, reduced by 80 per cent'

The best lead time in the world is none, ie you get your product right away. But that means you have to be able to provide everything off-the-shelf, which in turn means keeping prohibitive levels of stock. The answer is to make only to order, and for your lead time to be next door to instant.

That may seem superhuman to some, but consider these two Level 5 examples. Aisin Seiki in Japan make 750 different types of mattress, which are offered for sale in some 2,000 Japanese stores. But their undertaking to customers is: whatever mattress you order today will be delivered to your home tomorrow if you live within 100 kilometres of our Anjo plant. Yet their stock level is only 1.8 days! Motorola's Pager Division in the United States operates on the following basis. Their salespeople enter the specific services wanted by clients in their pagers into their hand-held terminals at the client's premises. That information is then sent directly by modem across to the manufacturing plant, where work is started on the order within 17 minutes! The first pagers are ready to go within 24 hours!

'Complaints under 0.5 per cent, and at an all-time low'

No company is likely to achieve this level if it has not been working at 'right first time' in every area of the company for a number of years. Remember that customer complaints are not the way to judge overall performance (TARP results showed that only 1 in 25 irritated customers actually complain). Positives of service as well as the negatives have to be measured. However, when you get service right, complaints disappear too.

'100 per cent of orders delivered in full and on time'

What a marvellous thing!

IDEAS AND TECHNIQUES YOU CAN USE

Contents of this section:

- characteristics of companies with distinctive service;
- product differentiation;
- customer surveys;
- managing customer expectations.

Characteristics of companies with distinctive service

1. They find out, and respond to, the changing needs of their customers (see the section on surveys).
2. They have good products (see Ladder 5).
3. They make it easy for customers to do business with them.
4. They establish clear, actionable service goals.
5. They ensure customer service is important to everyone in the business, from top to bottom (see Ladder 1).
6. They establish concrete standards of performance and regularly measure themselves against those standards (see Ladder 4).
7. They recruit good people, then train and empower them to serve the customer well (see Ladder 9).
8. They make sure employees have the skill, knowledge and systems to meet their service standards (see Ladders 3, 5, 6, 7 and 12).
9. They treat their people well, knowing they will then be more inclined to treat customers well.
10. They reward achievement, and celebrate those who go the extra mile to please their customers (see Ladder 10).

Customer focus is not a subject that can be treated in isolation. It involves virtually all areas in the business. That's what makes the Ladders an eminently useful framework both to co-ordinate improvement efforts within a company, and to plan changes that will be both visible and appreciated by the customer.

Product differentiation

Some years ago former Harvard Business Professor Theodore Levitt published an article entitled 'Marketing Myopia', partly lamenting the fact that so few companies seemed to spend enough time seeking new ways to differentiate their products from the competition. The original key points he made then still make valid questions today. If you confine yourself to marketing what are essentially 'core products', then the only differentiation customers care about is price. That can make yours a cut-throat business. Examples of 'core products' in this sense would be sugar, petrol or electricity. It is only by creating *added value* (see Figure 2.3) that the customer both perceives and appreciates that you can distinguish yourself from the competition – and charge higher prices.

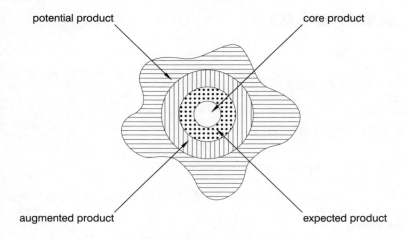

potential product

core product

augmented product

expected product

Figure 2.3 Creating added value to a product

However, if pretty well everybody is adding the same type of value, then in the customer's mind that simply becomes the 'expected product'. For example, 30 years ago, Marks and Spencer was one of the first retailers to guarantee the quality of their goods by promising a full money refund or exchange for any goods not found to be 'suitable'. Now that facility is a commonplace – it's 'expected'.

Cars are now following each other closely in terms of the technology they deliver. That's why car manufacturers have to be constantly looking at 'augmented service' to attract customers. Today they may offer free insurance for a year, free servicing on top of a three-year guarantee, a courtesy car when yours is being serviced, etc. And that's exactly the type of initiative most companies need to be thinking of to stay fresh and keep their customers loyal.

Finally, there's the charm of the 'potential product'. This is the product that responds to the question: 'Wouldn't it be nice if we could have the product do this?' They are the products that even the customers haven't thought of. When Akio Morita of Sony asked his technical people to produce a small, light tape player that he could listen to as he walked about, they told him it would never sell if it didn't record. They were so wrong. Walkmans are seen all round the world today. Looking for 'potential products' is almost a religion at the 3M's company. But even they didn't think there was a market for adhesives that would not stick. Neither did their customers. But it was just their culture of innovation that produced Post-it Notes. Their customers didn't know they wanted them, but now many just can't manage without them.

Very few organizations focus regularly on what would give their customers augmented service and even fewer on searching for that elusive 'potential product' that not only makes life exciting but keeps the competition in second place. Our advice is not to get too locked into the things you already know, but to avoid 'marketing myopia' by making innovation and 'stretching the envelope' part of the culture of your business.

Customer surveys

Example 1 Car Dealership Questionnaire

Name ———————————————— Business Telephone Number ————————————

1. Service provided (tick the appropriate box):
    - ❏ Supplied parts or accessories
    - ❏ Undertook engine service
    - ❏ Undertook work under warranty
    - ❏ Undertook repairs

2. Name and address of dealer:

3. Make of vehicle: Model:

4. How did the dealer rate on the following:

	Excellent	Good	Average	Poor	Unsatisfactory
* Giving you prompt and courteous attention	❏	❏	❏	❏	❏
* Giving you a fair estimate of the work required where requested before the work was started	❏	❏	❏	❏	❏
* Making clear who would be responsible for the work carried out on your vehicle	❏	❏	❏	❏	❏
* Having the work completed on time	❏	❏	❏	❏	❏
* Charging a final price in line with the estimate	❏	❏	❏	❏	❏
* Making available any parts removed from your vehicle for your inspection, where requested	❏	❏	❏	❏	❏
* Treating your vehicle with care and doing the work in a clean and tidy fashion	❏	❏	❏	❏	❏
* Overall, how would you rate the service your received from the dealer?	❏	❏	❏	❏	❏

	Definitely	Likely	Not sure	Unlikely	Definitely not
6. Based on this experience, would you use us again?	❏	❏	❏	❏	❏

7. We want to give you the best service we can. Please make any further comments you think will be of help.

———

———

———

When you have completed the questionnaire, please send it to us in the pre-paid envelope.
There is no need for a stamp. Thank you again for your help.

Example 2 Hotel Questionnaire

Name   Telephone Number

Please rate the following areas by ticking the appropriate box:

	Disappointed	Below expectation	Above expectation	Delighted

Reception

1. Were you pleased with the efficiency and speed of service? ☐ ☐ ☐ ☐

2. Were you satisfied with the accuracy of the bill? ☐ ☐ ☐ ☐

Room

3. Was your room ready and cleaned to your satisfaction? ☐ ☐ ☐ ☐

4. Were you pleased with your room in terms of comfort and appearance? ☐ ☐ ☐ ☐

5. Were you satisfied with the bedroom supplies? ☐ ☐ ☐ ☐

Restaurant and Bar

6. Did you enjoy the decor and atmosphere of the bar? ☐ ☐ ☐ ☐

7. Did you enjoy your restaurant meal? ☐ ☐ ☐ ☐

General Impression

8. Were you comfortable with our overall security measures? ☐ ☐ ☐ ☐

9. If you had any problems during your stay were you satisfied with the way they were dealt with? ☐ ☐ ☐ ☐

Did you find our staff helpful, friendly and professional?

10. In reception. ☐ ☐ ☐ ☐

11. In the bar. ☐ ☐ ☐ ☐

12. In the restaurant. ☐ ☐ ☐ ☐

13. In other areas. ☐ ☐ ☐ ☐

14. We would be pleased to hear your comments and ideas for improvement

_____
_____
_____
_____

Figure 2.4 Customer surveys

Managing customer expectations

Many companies understand the need to meet customers' expectations if they are to achieve regular customer satisfaction. Some even claim always to exceed the customer's expectations, which, we have to admit, often leaves us sceptical from the start. What we hear many fewer companies talk about, however, is the need to *manage* the customer's expectations. And we believe this is a crucial factor in achieving consistent customer satisfaction and trust.

Customers' expectations are created from a whole variety of sources. These include:

- your product offer;
- what the competition offers;
- your and others' marketing hype;
- the customer's personal experience (of you and others);
- friends' and colleagues' stories;
- the company's past image;
- hearsay;
- articles in the press or items on TV;
- experiences of related businesses.

There's no way to meet or exceed the customers' expectations unless you know exactly what these are before the event. Here are some key points to consider as you establish your customers' expectations and seek to meet and beat them:

- *You do not really know what your customers want until you ask them.* The organization can only find out what the customer's expectations are by asking him. Customer surveys (as shown in Figure 2.4, above) is one way of obtaining this information. In the end, quality is what the customer says it is.
- *You get positive responses only when you meet or beat the customer's expectations.* The least you can do to keep the customer satisfied is to deliver what he expects. The more you fall below his expectations the more he will become upset, irritated and angry.

Exercise

You can increase customer focus throughout your organization by having staff identify their customers, both internal and external, and then list specifically what they believe they would specifically have to do to meet and exceed their expectations. Try repeating the exercise at regular intervals.

- *The more you exceed customer expectations, the more they will be delighted.* Meeting the customer's expectation is enough to get satisfaction. The more you exceed his expectations the more pleased and delighted he will become. The opposite is, however, also true. The more you fall below the customer's expectations, the more upset you make him.

- *Where a customer faces a negative event (eg an expensive repair), he will still be pleased if what you deliver is better than his worst expectations.*
- *Relative perceived product quality is the most important factor in ensuring your organization's success with your customers.* Customers can only judge your company by what they see. That is all they have to go on. They make up their mind by all the signals they pick up in their dealings with you. Signals are anything that the customer experiences that gives him an *impression* of what you are like.

The Chairman of one big US airline put it this way: 'Coffee stains on the flip-down trays in the aeroplane mean to the passengers that we don't do our maintenance properly.' Of course this may be quite untrue and totally unfair. But passengers say to themselves: 'If this is how careless they are about the things we do see, how careless are they about the things we do not see?' If you care about your company's reputation you have to be careful about all the signals you give. You cannot take everyone down to the maintenance shops to show them how marvellous they are. Customers can only judge you by the signals they actually see.

In the air travel business the customer does not know what complex and expensive electronic equipment is used in the plane, whether the pilot has had long and intensive training, etc. He judges by much more mundane measures. Did the plane leave on time? Did the seats allow him enough room? Were the stewardesses pleasant and helpful? Was the food edible? Did he have to wait long for his luggage? How does the airline compare with other airlines? And many more. The airline gets no credit for all the hard work and effort that may have been made behind the scenes – the customer does not see that. He judges first and foremost by what affects him.

Exercise

Ask yourself: What signals are we giving our customers? For example, when customers visit, are the premises pleasant, clean and well cared for? Do we answer the telephones promptly? Do we respond to customer requests promptly, courteously and efficiently? What kind of impression does our delivery person create? Do the sales people make promises that the company cannot deliver? Is the paperwork (eg invoicing) easy to understand? How helpful are employees when customers complain?

In the eyes of the customer it all adds up to 'how you are', as he sees it. If you are going to impress the customer you have to stand in his shoes and think about how you look from his viewpoint. Reality about your company is simply what he perceives it to be. If you dismiss that out of hand because it's not 'the truth', then you are not going to meet or beat his expectations, and you are not going to deliver that superservice you are aiming at.

In conclusion, we can't resist this quote from the book *A Passion for Excellence* by Tom Peters and Nancy Austin:

> Markets do not buy products. Customers do. A 'market' has never been observed paying a bill. Customers do that. Ultimately it all boils down to perceived, and appreciated, consistently delivered service and quality to customers.

Three

Organizing the Workplace

LEVELS	MEASURES
Level 1	Scrap items, litter and tools are left scattered around. Walls, windows, floors and machines are dirty. The yard, car park and outside areas are untidy. Employees are sloppily dressed; desks and workstations are untidy.
Level 2	The floors and windows are clean. No un-needed items present in the workplace. Needed items are easy to find and easy to put back. The yard, car park and storage areas are tidy. Employees are neatly dressed. Desks and workstations are tidy: you can find whatever you want in 10 seconds.
Level 3	Equipment is cleaned up – it looks like new. Pathways are clear and without obstruction. The workplace is bright (painted). Tools and materials in well-marked, easily accessible places.
Level 4	Daily operator inspections keep equipment clean and maintained in good condition. Storage areas and materials are so clearly labelled even new employees can find them. Employees can retrieve what they need within three seconds. Any filed item can be retrieved in one minute.
Level 5	The workplace is *habitually* clean and well organized. Work areas and the flow of operations are easy to see. Storage sites and quantities are clearly marked. Staff know automatically when to re-order. Teams earn top scores even during surprise inspections.

INTRODUCTION

Many companies remain reluctant about getting the workplace clean and organized, irrespective of the introduction of the ISO standards. Inevitably, the claim is: 'Let's get the job done, rather than waste time cleaning and organizing the workplace.' But getting to world class standard takes discipline. If a company cannot succeed in keeping the everyday work areas clean and tidy, there is little chance of doing anything more complicated. This chapter describes the steps to developing an organized and effective workplace, one of the foundation stones of companies aspiring to reach world class standards.

The Japanese have named this simple but fundamental discipline the '5 S's':

- *seiri* – organization;
- *seiton* – orderliness;
- *shitsuke* – discipline;
- *seisa* – cleanliness;
- *seiketsu* – standardized clean-up.

The five S's are not just about conducting an occasional blitz on cleaning and tidying. They're about maintaining the standards, making it into a way of life.

LEVEL 1

'Scrap items, litter and tools are left scattered around'

'Walls, windows, floors and machines are dirty'

'The yard, car park and outside areas are untidy'

'Employees are sloppily dressed; desks and workstations are untidy'

The state of a factory or an office is reflective of how it is managed, and how much respect employees have for it. If you wouldn't want to associate with it, neither would employees. The immediate or direct consequence of such an environment may be an increase in levels of absenteeism, with no one having any great enthusiasm for coming to work.

A Level 1 operation is easy to identify: a quick walk around the premises, assessing the amount of litter lying around, the general look of the yard, car park and buildings and the appearance of employees will immediately signal the extent to which the company cares. And obviously, with customers and visitors you don't get a second chance to make a first impression.

In a large foundry where we have done some work, the management team agreed to stop production for a day to 'clean up and organize'. Each function produced a plan as to what they were going to store, scrap or sell. Everybody arrived in their overalls, front-end loaders were brought in and the place generally cleaned up. There were two notable consequences: the shop steward, on arriving at work the next day, said that it was the first time he had felt proud to come to his place of work in 10 years. With the change in attitudes scrap started coming down, and after two months hit an all-time low. The operations manager conceded that the amount of scrap found during the clean-up exercise had more than paid for the day's lost production.

LEVEL 2

Organizing

The start-point in creating a disciplined workplace is in fact 'organizing'. By that we mean:

- moving out of the work area all the clutter and items not actually needed to do the everyday job;
- organizing your workplace or desktop layout so that the things you use most are closest to hand, avoiding excessive bending, stretching or twisting;
- making it easy to pick up and use the items needed, and to put them back where they will be easy to find again;
- organizing your information, materials and equipment to make it easy to do the job 'right first time'.

In other words, it's all just plain and simple common sense. And simple cleanliness has several real benefits, namely:

- most people much prefer to work in a clean environment than a dirty one;
- clean parts and equipment mean less contamination of product and incidence of quality faults;
- clean floors, tools, indicator dials and equipment mean fewer safety hazards and accidents;
- regular cleanliness introduces a discipline of good habits, which is frankly essential to any company aspiring to world class status.

When starting out, we recommend that any problems identified with organizing the workplace be addressed one at a time, as this makes the process more manageable. It is important that employees identify with the initial campaign, so they need to be involved. One way to achieve this is to allocate specific responsibilities to every person, eg each to have specific responsibilities or be in charge of a certain area. Implementation of such a project must be preceded by a meeting with employees so they fully understand the reasons for the change.

'The floors and windows are clean'

'No un-needed items present in the workplace'

'Needed items are easy to find and easy to put back'

'The yard, car park and storage areas are tidy. Employees are neatly dressed'

These signals show progress is being made. Disposal of unneeded items is achieved through a process known as 'red-tagging'. This is the start-point of organizing, ie discarding items from the workplace that are not immediately required for the daily work. This is implemented by placing a red tag (see Ideas and Techniques You Can Use section) on everything that has not been used in the last month and will not be used in the next month, and removing it from the factory floor or office and finding storage for it. What is kept on the floor or in the office should be items that will be used for work during the month. Those items that are used regularly should be kept where they are easily accessible to users or operators. There are three ways of dealing with the red-tagged items:

1. Sell or lend out.
2. Dispose of as garbage.
3. Store where you will know where to find it, properly labelled.

Teams that are assigned red-tagging should not be from the same work area. Because of sentimental attachments, people in a work area often find it difficult to dispose of things even if they are obsolete. So it is useful that a team allocated the responsibility of red-tagging should come from a different section of the targeted area. A host of red tags on items makes a strong visual impact on people in the area, and importantly it makes everyone begin to think seriously about what they really need for the job, and how they have got themselves organized.

'Desks and workstations are tidy: you can find whatever you want in 10 seconds'

Some managers will protest: 'Oh, it may look a shambles, but I know where everything is.' If there are piles of any size on their desks, it is improbable that their claim is true. However, most managers agree that it would not only be easier for them to be more organized, but others (including their secretaries) would be able to find things more easily when they are out!

As with factories, the first stage is to 'red-tag' and have only those items they currently need to hand. Thereafter, designate a 'home for everything', and start labelling so that anyone (including newcomers) would know where to find things, and where to put them back. Remember that this takes time.

Do not criticize staff for not being perfect to start with. They have to start somewhere. Gradually they will get better.

Employees do not need to hoard pens, pencils, files, writing pads, etc in their desks and cupboards but they do. An exercise carried out in one company revealed un-needed items in desks equivalent to three times what was in the stores!

LEVEL 3

'Equipment is cleaned up – it looks like new'

In manufacturing plants this is the start of Total Productive Maintenance (TPM), ie cleaning up the equipment used to look like it was just newly installed. The eventual aim of TPM is to achieve zero breakdowns, and to maximize the availability time of the operating equipment to production. This can only be achieved by using the eyes and ears of the people who are using the equipment daily, ie operators. The basic principle is that operators take responsibility for their equipment and carrying out routine mainte- nance, and technical staff are called in only if the problem is beyond the operator's capacity.

There are seven maintenance functions that production operators can readily perform with training:

1. Five-minute equipment clean-ups every day.
2. Using daily checklists to ensure equipment stays in good condition.
3. Making minor adjustments, eg tightening loose screws and bolts.
4. Doing regular scheduled lubrication.
5. Replacing consumables, eg paper, ink, cartridges, blades.
6. Giving early warnings before abnormalities become breakdowns, eg noting overheating, vibrations, unusual noises.
7. Recording performance data on the equipment they are operating.

It is rather like the patient–doctor relationship, ie the individual looking after his own health and taking an aspirin or cough mixture for minor ailments, but calling in the qualified doctor when problems are beyond his capability.

We generally advise companies to organize an 'Operation Clean-up' day as an initial blitz to clean equipment. When this exercise has taken place, the immediate change makes a big visual impact, and helps convince everyone that things are beginning to change for the better. And if the company stops production for a day to do it, it has even more impact, sending a strong signal to everyone that the company is serious about improvement.

'Pathways are clear and without obstruction'

'The workplace is bright (painted)'

After the Red-tagging and the Cleaning Phases comes the Painting Phase. It is obvious that if the workplace is bright and cheerful, it will be a more welcoming place to come to work. And you don't have to employ professional painters to do it. With supervision employees are generally quite capable of handling a paint brush, but do not let them use ladders etc. Let them do what they can reach by standing on the floor. Also, pay attention to that part of the environment that staff see every day, but which is not part of the work areas, ie their tea rooms and toilets. They are a daily unspoken signal of the concern their company has for them, so make them bright, clean and cheerful.

When it comes to painting work areas with dividing lines, Table 3.1 shows some suggestions for implementation. The colour you use for different purposes may vary. The important thing is to be consistent in what the colours mean.

It is important that people can tell at a glance what belongs where, and what the different colours mean, eg green for operational areas, yellow for walkways (where no obstruction is allowed under any circumstances), white for place markers, red for scrap, and so on. Figures 3.1 and 3.2 show a couple of useful examples. Note the safety line showing the opening arc of doors etc.

Table 3.1 Divider lines

Category	Subcategory	Colour	Width	Comments
	Operation area	Green	10 cm	Solid line
Floors	Walkway	Yellow	10 cm	Solid line
	Rest area	Blue	10 cm	Solid line
	Area divider lines	Green	10 cm	Solid line
	Entrance and exit lines	White	10 cm	Broken line
	Door-range lines	White	10 cm	Broken line
Lines	Direction lines	Yellow		Arrow
	Place markers (for in-process inventory)	White	5 cm	Solid line
	Place markers (for operations)	White	5 cm	Corner lines
	Place markers (for defective goods)	Red	5 cm	Solid line

Source: Hirano

Figure 3.1 Trolley place markers

Figure 3.2 Door travel markers

'Tools and materials are in well-marked, easily accessible places'

When shop-floor employees first get involved in the cleaning and organizing process, it is useful to start by focusing on how to make the job *easier*. Since employees often fear the worst (that they will be told they must work harder, their jobs may be in jeopardy, etc) this can come as a pleasant surprise. It is crucially important that their first association with any change programme is positive, as this naturally provides a sound base to work from. That's why we first talk to them about doing things:

- easier: less stretching, bending, twisting and straining;
- better: improving quality, reducing defects and scrap;
- cheaper: streamlining processes, cutting delays;
- faster: improving output and productivity;
- safer: removing hazards likely to cause injury.

(Note: we only ask them to work faster when we have worked on the 'better' bit first, ie we don't want to speed up making more garbage!)

You will find practical ideas on tools and making the job easier in the section on ideas and techniques you can use later.

LEVEL 4

At this stage the ground rules are clear, and cleaning and organizing procedures have become routine and sophisticated.

'Daily operator inspections keep equipment clean and maintained in good condition'

These are the five steps we recommend in setting up cleaning procedures:

1. Specify the cleaning targets.
2. Allocate cleaning responsibilities.
3. Decide on cleaning methods.
4. Organize cleaning materials.
5. Implement the procedures!

Specify the cleaning targets

These include:

- equipment: machines, tools, measuring instruments, worktables, desks, chairs, computers, etc;
- materials: raw materials, semi-finished products, finished products, packaging, paper, files, consumable items, etc;
- spaces: floors, work areas, walkways, walls, windows, ceilings, shelves, cupboards, cabinets, rooms, and lights.

Allocate cleaning responsibilities

First, make clear that cleanliness is the responsibility of everyone who works in the company. Then, using a map of the work space, first allocate areas to managers, who in turn should allocate items and sub-areas to supervisors, and finally to individuals. The map should show all the cleaning areas, and the person responsible for them.

A schedule is also needed for the things that get done daily, weekly, monthly, etc, and by whom. People only treat it seriously when you get down to this detail. There may be designated persons who clean offices and toilets daily. Otherwise, everyone should take responsibility for their own assignments, and 'take their turn' on common items. In appropriate cases it is a good idea is to use a cleaning 'tag' that gets passed on to the next person, so that employees do not forget when it is their turn.

Decide on cleaning methods

Five-minute clean-ups are a good habit to establish and maintain. The first cleaning blitz may get equipment looking like new, but the trick is to keep it that way! That's where five-minute clean-ups come in. Doing it for five minutes either first thing in the morning or last thing at night soon becomes a habit, and is just the behaviour that should be encouraged. Also, as the operators are running their hands over the machinery in the process, they notice things that are not quite right (for example, oil drips, loose screws, etc), and can take action early before a breakdown occurs.

People need to be shown exactly what is meant by 'cleaning'. For example, if the operator is in charge of a cutting machine, you can divide the machine into sections, eg cutting section, saw table, hydraulic section, control board, overall exterior, surrounding floor area and local storage sites, and decide what each should look like when cleaned. Then make a simple checklist schedule with daily, weekly, and monthly routines.

Organize cleaning materials

Normally this will be brushes, rags, dusters and the like, but may have to include special cleaning agents, degreasers, etc. Don't spend great amounts on this: use simple materials that will keep costs down. Decide what these items are to be, where they are to be obtained, how often renewed, and where they are to be stored. Above all, decide where waste bins are to be located, make them big enough, and decide how often and where they are to be emptied, and by whom.

This may sound like a lot of work, but you only have to do it once. And once the system is in place, it will run by itself. How well it all works in practice will be directly proportional to the trouble you took to prepare in the first place!

Implement the procedures

This is the hardest bit. At first, people are quite enthusiastic and get into it. In week two they omit things or do things cursorily, either because they cannot be bothered or are trying you out. React immediately when you see anything undone. Do not wait, but do not get aggressive. Gentle reminders and nudges will suffice. But also, do not put up with compromises. Tell employees what the standard is, and that the standard is now 'part of the job'.

What employees give you in the first three weeks is what you are going to get thereafter – that is the test period. If you can keep the process going for two months, then you will have changed habits. Thereafter the process will be routine and only occasional reminders may be necessary. Discipline can be maintained by conducting regular, and sometimes random, inspections. Suggestions on inspections appear later in this section, under Level 5.

'Storage areas are so clearly labelled even new employees can find them'

The third element in the organizing process is the Labelling Phase. The basic idea behind good labelling is:

- time is not wasted scrambling around looking for items unnecessarily;
- because items are always stored in the same place, everyone knows where to find them, and where to put them back;
- the time spent labelling is a fraction of the time spent searching later when things are not labelled.

We show a number of examples of good labelling practice later in Ideas and Techniques You Can Use section.

'Employees can retrieve what they need within three seconds'

The three seconds refers to parts, materials and tools operators and staff need to do the everyday, ongoing job. Keep these within the 'maximum working area' shown in the later section.

'Any filed item can be retrieved in one minute'

This may sound a bit difficult, but it can certainly be done. Here are some tips that will help get you there:

1. Get managers to write in the top right-hand corner of their documents (circled to make it stand out) where they want the document filed. That way, both manager and secretary will know where the item is – and the boss will know where to find the document even when the secretary is out!
2. Where different people use the same files and these are regularly taken out, put an A4 sized card in the empty file. This should show: who's got it; when they took it. Those who take any files out must fill in the card. The last entry is obviously who's got it now.
3. Where you are not sure where to file something, or it could be put in more than one file, make a photo-copy and put one in each file. Or put in a

sheet in several files that tells you where the original documents are. Take the trouble: it saves a lot of frustration and time later!

4. Make the file categories obvious. The test should be: file drawers, shelves or cupboards are so clearly labelled even a new person could find what they need without help. And equally, they would see how to put things back correctly.
5. It's a good idea to have rules for discarding documents too, otherwise files get fat and unmanageable. Now that much is kept on computer, then most documents more than one year old should be consigned to the waste bin. Conduct a red-tagging exercise at least every year.

LEVEL 5

'The workplace is habitually clean and well organized'

'Work areas and the flow of operations is easy to see'

'Storage sites and quantities are clearly marked'

'Staff know automatically when to re-order'

Level 5 represents world class.

'Teams earn top scores even during surprise inspections'

Companies operating at this level have regular inspections to ensure that discipline does not deteriorate. Here are some guidelines for carrying out inspections:

1. *Make a checklist of the items to be inspected.* Make the definitions as unambiguous as possible. That way the 'inspected' know what to keep tidy to get good scores, and the inspectors know exactly what they are looking for, and how they will judge it.
2. *Get an independent person to do the inspections.* People are not as sentimental when they have nothing to do with the section concerned. It may be even better if you use an office-based person to do the shop floor inspections. First, they are generally used to cleaner office conditions and are less tolerant. Second, the interaction teaches office-based people how different/difficult things can be in other departments.
3. *Do spot check surprise inspections as well as regular ones.* That way, you get the message across that cleanliness and organization are meant for every day, not just the end of the month. Even better, get a Director or the MD to do it from time to time. It raises the importance of cleaning and organizing, and Directors stay in touch with reality!
4. *Agree the items to be inspected and the standards with the staff up-front.* Staff then know what will be inspected, and once agreed they tend to be more

committed to the process. They also feel more guilty when they have left something undone. Do not minimize the power of guilt to motivate!

5. *Get members of staff to conduct random inspections of their own area from time to time.* Having done a few *inspections* on their own, staff become much more sensitive to keeping up the standards themselves as a result.

6. *Use a scoring system in the inspections.* It is best to use a score out of 100, broken down into sections for ease of use. That way, teams can see whether they are improving overall (part of continuous improvement), and to which items they need to pay special attention.

7. *Set targets.* It is best if these are agreed between the team leader and team members themselves, as employees then accept 'ownership' of the process. The team leader should challenge the team to go for improvements.

8. *Recognize good performance.* Some companies give awards (such as winner's shields) to the best team in the area. It is preferable to give awards based on meeting standards, ie bronze, silver and gold standards and to display these in the area. That makes the exercise less of a win/lose contest, but encourages achieving (and maintaining!) high standards.

When embarking on a cleaning and organizing programme in any company, it is important not to try to reach perfection immediately. People get discouraged by the amount of work involved, they start questioning the value of supporting the programme, and senior management often expect too much too soon by way of improvement. Just get started, that's all. Use a simple programme (see Ideas and Techniques You Can Use). Leave enough time to get things done. If people see early results, they will be much more inclined to continue.

IDEAS AND TECHNIQUES YOU CAN USE

In this section the following processes will be dealt with:

- red-tagging;
- organizing in the office;
- labelling;
- performance improvement through 'making the job easier';
- use of a promotion schedules.

Red-tagging

Use the following procedure when undertaking red-tagging:

1. Decide on the criteria for red-tagging before starting the exercise, eg it could be red-tagging items not needed next month, or during the next week, not actually used during the last month, etc.

2. Decide on the targets, eg how many areas will be affected? what areas? offices too?

3. Appoint an overall Red-tagging Team (RTT) who designs the red tags, controls who does what when, decides how items are to be disposed of, sorts out differences of opinion, etc.
4. The tagging process should be carried out by small teams (for mutual support) appointed or organized by the RTT. Each member of the team should receive at least four red tags – otherwise they tend to pussy-foot.
5. The red-tagging needs to take place in one day. Stretching it out tends to turn people off.
6. Everyone needs to be educated/informed of what is being done and why before the event.
7. Make it fun, not a witch-hunt

ORGANIZING IN THE OFFICE

When it comes to organizing your desk, a good idea is to have all the items and equipment you need regularly readily at hand. Figure 3.3 represents a desk layout example.

Hirano (1990) lists five keys to orderliness in the office, namely:

1. *Eliminate wasting time searching for things.*
2. *Make things easier to find and use.* Put the things you use all the time in easy-to-see, easy-to-reach places.
3. *Make things easy to put back.* In a factory, parts and materials generally get built into a product. In the office, many items get used over and over again. So making things easy to find and easy to put back becomes the key to orderliness in the office.

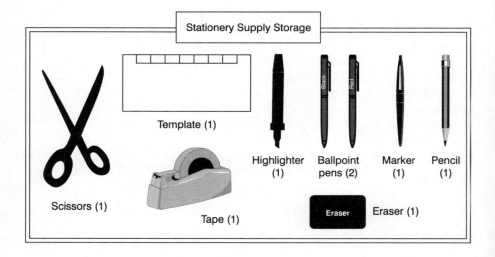

Figure 3.3 Desktop organizer

4. *Make things understandable at a glance.* Make it so obvious where things go in drawers, files and cupboards that even new or temporary staff will know where to find things, and put them back correctly.
5. *Avoid private collections.* Documents, papers and tools generally belong to the company. Company property and know-how are things to be shared by everyone rather than harboured by any one individual.

Labelling

Figure 3.4 shows the three categories of items that need to be labelled, ie spaces (areas), equipment and inventory items.
Let's examine each in turn.

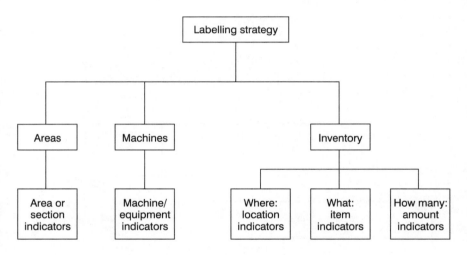

Figure 3.4 Labelling categories

Areas

Use signs to indicate the department or area, eg Personnel Department, Can-making, Line 1, etc. Make the notices big, legible, and put them in locations that can be seen easily, ie on doors, walls or hanging from the roof. Use signs at right angles rather than parallel (see Figure 3.5).

Machines and equipment

Designate the machine name, the process name, acquisition date, and name of the person in charge. Then hang the sign on or above the machine (see Figure 3.6).

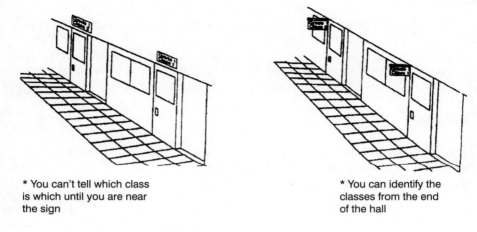

* You can't tell which class is which until you are near the sign

* You can identify the classes from the end of the hall

Figure 3.5 Place signs

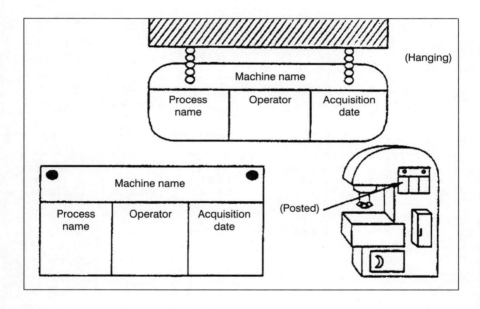

Figure 3.6 Sign above machine

Inventory

As indicated in Figure 3.7 and Figure 3.8, there are three specifics of visual orderliness:

1 Specific places – specify where things go via location indicators.
2. Specific items – specify what things via item indicators.
3. Specific amounts – specify how many via amount indicators.

Location should be modelled after the postal system. No matter where in the world a letter is sent, if the return address is on it, it will come right back without getting lost. The factory's address system should be at least as good as the post. Normally the factory system should have 'country', 'town', and 'street' addresses that indicate where any item belongs. Then a map and an address system is all anyone should need to find anything in the factory.

Figure 3.7 gives an illustration of location indicators. It's even better when items are labelled to match their locations (see Figure 3.8).

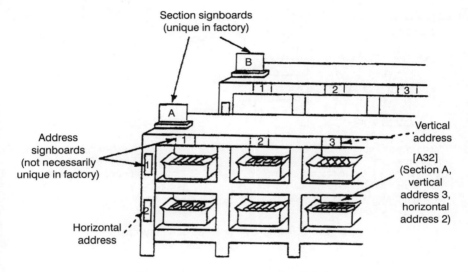

Figure 3.7 Location indicators

Source: Hirano (1990)

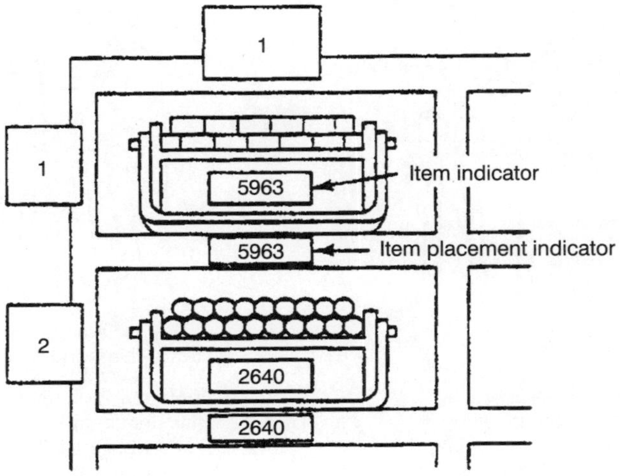

Figure 3.8 Item indicators

Source: Hirano (1990)

Performance improvement by 'making the job easier'

In manufacturing situations watch what employees have to handle all the time, eg materials or products they have to regularly move, lift, stack, store,

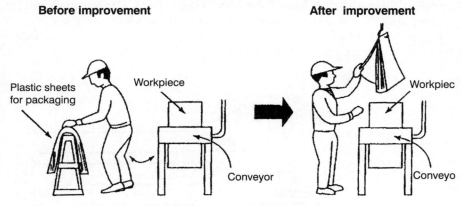

Before improvement

Plastic sheets for packaging

Workpiece

Conveyor

* Plastic sheets kept on rack behind the operator
* Operator forced to turn around each time he needed a plastic sheet
* Turning motion required four seconds

After improvement

Workpiec

Conveyo

* Now plastic sheets are hung on hook in front of operator
* The operator does not have to turn around
* Four seconds of motion waste eliminated

Figure 3.9 Improvement in parts layout
Source: Hirano (1990)

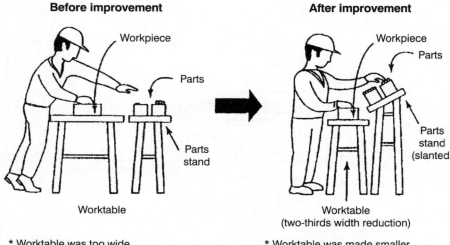

Before improvement

Workpiece

Parts

Parts stand

Worktable

* Worktable was too wide
* Parts stand was too far away
* Parts were laid out horizontally, making them hard to see and reach

After improvement

Workpiece

Parts

Parts stand (slanted

Worktable
(two-thirds width reduction)

* Worktable was made smaller (two-thirds width reduction)
* Parts were put within closer reach
* Parts were laid out on a slant, making them easier to see and reach

Figure 3.10 Improvement in parts pick-up
Source: Hirano (1990)

etc, and make it easy to do. The basic rule is: keep everything between knee and eye level, ie no bending or stretching beyond these limits. Try to eliminate repeated stretching, twisting and turning. Figures 3.9 and 3.10 show two examples.

Bring all tools and materials within a sensible work area (see Figure 3.11). It's best when things are within the 'standard' work area, ie elbows close to the body, but if you cannot manage that, keep them within the non-stretch maximum area.

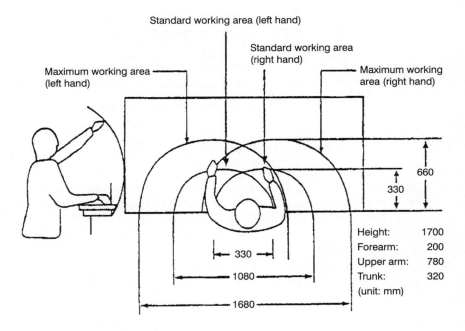

Figure 3.11 Working area

Here are some principles to follow in making the job easier:

1. *Start and end each motion with both hands moving at once.*
2. *Both arms should move symmetrically and in opposite directions.* The brain copes with that better, and it is less tiring.
3. *Keep trunk motions to a minimum.* Ideally keep all parts directly in front of operators, slightly to their right and left sides. That makes the work easiest to do. Watch worker movements from the side and you will easily see what movements are being used to do the work.
4. *Use gravity instead of muscle power.* Let parts slide down a roller conveyor towards the operator rather than having to shove or pull them. Do the same with finished parts.
5. *Move with a steady rhythm.* Avoid zig-zagging motions and sudden changes of direction. Motions should be continuous, gentle and flowing.

6. *Maintain a comfortable posture.* Operators should be seated or standing at a comfortable, relaxed height relative to the worktable or machinery.
7. *Use the feet.* Some motions are made easier with a foot switch, particularly when the hands are already occupied.
8. *Arrange materials and tools in their order of use.* See Figure 3.12.

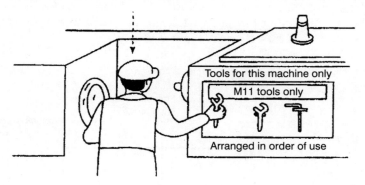

Figure 3.12 Tools kept close at hand
Source: Hirano (1990)

9. *Make handles and grips in efficient and easy-to-use shapes and positions.* In theory, operator motions should add value to the product. In practice, only a small percentage of motions actually do. The goal then is to reduce the number of non-value-adding motions (see Ladder 6, Waste Elimination) as well as making the work easy to do.
10. *Use two-handed movements.* Switching to two-handed operation in the example below raised productivity by 37%. See Figure 3.13.

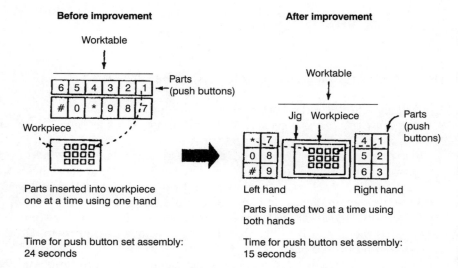

Figure 3.13 Improvement from one-handed to two-handed work
Source: Hirano (1990)

11. *Make things easy to see and read.* See Figure 3.14. This is especially important where safety is concerned.
12. *Use colour coding for identification.* It makes things easier to see and leads to fewer errors. See Figure 3.15.

Before improvement   **After improvement**

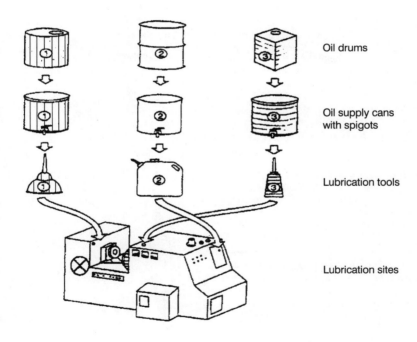

* Gauge readings checked against   * Gauge readings checked against
  standards in manual   standards indicated on gauge diplays

Figure 3.14 Eliminating the need to check for manual standards
Source: Hirano (1990)

Oil drums

Oil supply cans
with spigots

Lubrication tools

Lubrication sites

Figure 3.15 Colour-coding for fault-free lubrication
Source: Hirano (1990)

13. *Eliminate the need for special tools.* It is quite common for work and parts to be held in place by a whole variety of fastening devices, eg slotted screws, Philips head screws, bolts, nuts, Allen key screws, circlips, jubilee clips, etc, all having different sizes, head shapes, thread patterns, etc. One often gets the impression engineers want to show how smart they are, or how difficult they can make it when they really try!

There is actually no need for all that. Indeed, world class companies now try to make fastenings on any piece of equipment workable with only one spanner or tool. And engineers can get very creative when you challenge them to do just that. Clearly, it makes things easier for both operators and engineers if you do. Even better, however, is to have fastenings that don't need any tools at all. You can use wing nuts, handles, grips, clamps, etc. A couple of examples are shown in Figure 3.16.

'How can we eliminate the need for this wrench?'

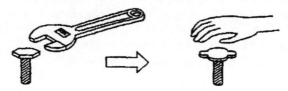

'How can we eliminate the need for this hex wrench?'

Figure 3.16 Ways to eliminate the need for tools
Source: Hirano (1990)

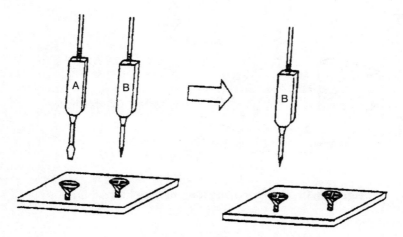

Figure 3.17 Standardizing tools
Source: Hirano (1990)

14. *Unify tools wherever you can.* In other words, use one pattern of screwhead all the time, and, if possible, which need only one size of screwdriver. Or use only one or two sizes of bolt or nut, which require only one spanner to tighten. The point here is to *standardize* and to avoid variety and complexity. See Figure 3.17.
15. *Maintain a worker-friendly environment.* In other words, make it a pleasant place to work. Keep lighting, ventilation, heating, etc, at levels where the work can be done reasonably comfortably. Avoid noise, fumes and smells too. The simple test is: would you be happy to work in these conditions every day? If not, make improvements.

Don't make it hard for operators to do a good job. Productivity and quality increase where the work area is clean and well organized; where equipment is regularly and well maintained; where materials are neatly stored, labelled and close to hand; where the work is made easy to do and get 'right first time'. And involving employees themselves in the daily cleaning and maintenance routines brings a regular discipline to the workplace that makes good habits commonplace throughout the company.

Use of a promotion schedule

Table 3.2 shows a simple example of a calendarized promotion schedule. In each case 'D' means Start Date. In our view, keeping things simple is one of the key features of world class performance.

Table 3.2 Promotion schedule

No	Activity	Scheduled date
1	Training and lectures about organizing the workplace	D+10
2	Organizing area promotion teams Drafting a calendar plan	D+15
3	Red-tagging exercises	D+20
4	Organizing needed items in work areas	D+30
5	Designating storage sites	D+30
6	Posting signboards and attaching labels	D+45
7	Improvement activities	D+45 on
8	Evaluation	D+60

CONCLUSION

Organizing and cleaning can have a major visual impact on a company. First, it is quick visible evidence to managers and staff that they are beginning to make real positive changes. Second, that kind of early visible impact greatly enhances the company's reputation with clients, when they see the company literally 'cleaning up its act'. Organizing is an activity within every management's control. It helps to bring discipline and order. That is why it is such a valuable element to focus on early in the journey to world class performance.

F o u r

Visible Measurement Systems

LEVELS	MEASURES
Level 1	Only general company-wide measures used. Departments tend to keep performance measures to themselves. Lack of hard data means much has to be done on 'gut feel'. Some departments think their work is not measurable.
Level 2	Key performance measures decided on and publicly displayed. Measures show performance meeting the standards set. Budgets agreed by department and monthly data fed back. Plenty of data but often in different formats and places.
Level 3	Performance measures publicly displayed in every department, and simple enough to be understood by all. Data shows performance continuously improving. Standards clear for every machine and every job-holder. Each manager agrees own budget and gets regular feedback.
Level 4	Team members themselves produce the performance charts and graphs and update the displayed data. Visible management systems instantly make clear deviations from normal performance in production areas. One-page management in operation, ie data on key measures fed back monthly/weekly to each individual manager.
Level 5	Company realizes that measurement is the only way to sustain continuous improvement. Senior management or visitors are able to tell from displayed data how any department is performing at any time.

INTRODUCTION

As one of the ladders to world class performance, visible measurement systems are an essential component of improving the organization's output. However, it is not in itself a guarantee of success. For example, Florida Power & Light, which won the coveted Deming Prize in November 1989 (one of the most valued icons of world class performance), found itself in difficulties a few years thereafter, a clear warning that even world class performers can have their problems.

The benefit of world class performance lies in providing the cost, quality and service advantages that sets one organization apart from its competitors. This is only possible if effective measurement techniques and systems, capable of providing accurate performance data, are in place. Measurement can be a complex issue, so let's just consider some principles before embarking upon the explanation of the levels.

A COMMENT ON MEASUREMENT

Measurement is both the way to discover the facts about what is actually happening, and the means of exercising a degree of control over the results. Control has several elements, each of which is commonplace to most organizations:

1. *Post-facto control*, where what has been done is reported on and analysed to ensure the mistakes of the past are not repeated.
2. *Operational control*, in which steps are taken to ensure that known or anticipated problems do not occur.
3. *Design control*, in which the preparation of plan scenarios is done in such a way as to ensure that the eventual results are confined within planned parameters.

The three are listed in the order of the frequency in which they are found in most organizations.

Measurement plays a key role in each of these elements and in the pursuit of world class performance, none more so than in design control. The first two elements contain a subsidiary process that requires that a mistake must first be made before it can be corrected. Design control, on the other hand, takes place before any tangible evidence is available. Adequate design control means getting it right the first time (a frequently-used synonym for productivity) and helping the organization achieve the desired organizational result quicker than its competitors.

DEFINITION OF VISIBLE MEASUREMENT SYSTEMS

The principal requirements of measurement are that it should be *appropriate*, *accurate* and *objective*:

- *appropriate*: If the measure is achieved (actual against standard or objective), the organization will have achieved the organizational result it wants.
- *accurate*: The measure is believable and preferably quantifiable. While complete accuracy is a possibility there is usually a trade-off between accuracy and speedy reporting. The rule-of-thumb is that a measurement be sufficiently accurate to engender the right response in time to effect a better organizational result.
- *objective*: The final requirement is that the measure be objective. The presence of subjectivity inevitably raises dissent with the outcome of the measure, which may in turn lead to ambivalent or ineffectual responses to actual problem situations.

The visibility component of measurement is a facet of organizational communication policy. When an individual is made responsible for a result without knowing the facts, he is effectively robbed of both control and responsibility. The fact that someone more senior in the organizational hierarchy knows the full situation means that the responsible individual must be continually supervised, which defeats the whole purpose of delegating responsibility. Visibility requires that the individual be continuously aware of the consequence of his actions and it is the responsibility of the organization to provide the individual with the means to gain this awareness.

Measurement has invaluable benefits:

1. Measurement is the real test of your good management. It is the acid test.
2. Measurement means you can manage by fact, not by opinion.
3. Measurement creates importance. The things that we measure become important, and what gets measured tends to get done.
4. Measurement makes you think. It makes you ask questions like: What are the critical success factors on this job? What do we most want to improve? What really makes a difference?
5. Measurement urges correction and improvement. When you start to get data on your performance, it's very difficult to remain indifferent. One is naturally drawn to investigate causes, to try things that will make the numbers improve. The urge is almost irresistible.
6. Finally: if you can't measure it, you can't manage it! If you want to improve, you need to know where you are now. Only with measurement can you check if you are actually making progress.

LEVEL 1

'Only general, company-wide measures are used'

At this level, reporting will normally focus on the most obviously measurable things, eg production output, profit, costs, sales, overtime, gross margins, etc, and will be largely financial in nature. What is often lacking is something valid to measure performance against – a budget, for example – and a clear trail pointing out the causes of the results reported. Key performance measures by department or by individual are also generally lacking. The company is unlikely to use, say, statistical process control (SPC), on time in full delivery, or to have known and accepted standards for customer complaint resolution, time scales for answering letters, safety targets, etc.

Little integrated reporting (and hence measurement) at the divisional and departmental levels within the organization takes place. By integrated measurement is meant the production of information directly related to the company-wide measures already in place. The key issues on a daily basis will be those such as revenue and production (sometimes quality) although the sources of information may often be of variable credibility. The measures are not often directly meaningful to middle management and their perspective on what needs to be done to improve matters is normally provided to them by their superiors, who themselves usually receive data once a month.

'Departments tend to keep performance measures to themselves'

Often departments will keep their own information because they don't trust information from any other department, or they want specific items included that are missing from the original, or they prefer different layout formats, etc.

Differently constructed measures are often used by individuals to justify a particular result. As a defensive tool they may cause more problems than they solve. In addition, these records, not being part of a company-wide system, may meet the needs of the record-keeper but not the organization as a whole, and as such may be treated with suspicion. Similar (but never identical) data being kept on the same subject in different areas of the company leads to much time-wasting, not only in collecting and assembling different data, but in discussions and arguments between departments about just whose data is correct.

'Lack of hard data means much has to be done on "gut feel"'

Generally in these cases, managers have to take decisions on 'gut feel' because the data either does not exist, or it is not stored in a format that helps decision-making. For example, overtime costs may be totalled, but not subdivided by department or individual. Or it is stored as a total cost (base rate plus premium) but not as actual hours worked. Again, total production costs may be measured but not broken down by product (some may be so complex to make, they are actually making a loss). The Marketing Manager may know what each client buys in total, but doesn't know which products sell better by region or season, etc.

At other times, managers don't take the trouble to check out the data because they actually prefer 'gut feel' and don't want their emotional inclinations contradicted by the facts. One thing you can say for sure: hard data plus 'gut feel' produce consistently better results than 'gut feel' alone.

'Some departments think their work is not measurable'

Often departments such as Personnel, Public Relations, Research and Development, Pensions, Industrial Relations, etc, will claim their work is not really measurable. If that is so, we have to ask 'What is the company actually paying for?' When you identify the answer, that is what is measurable and what should be measured to keep staff focused on the value they need to deliver.

In other cases, the 'not measurable' claim is symptomatic of those who prefer not to have to answer for their performance. Teachers, academics and politicians often have difficulty with hard measurement. There is a distinct tendency where targets are not set and measures do not exist for subsequent performance to be both haphazard and mediocre. Realistic targets and objective measures are essential to any organization aspiring to climb the ladders to world class performance.

LEVEL 2

'Key performance targets decided on and publicly displayed'

At this stage, every department has decided what the key measures of its performance are, how to collect the data required, who will collect the data, and how it will be organized and communicated. Preferably, departments need to confine themselves to a set of three or four performance measures and practise getting these right over a period of time. After all, the measures are not there for decoration, they are about focusing energies on the key priorities and thereby improving actual performance. Looking spectacular by tracking 10 different measures, at least initially, leads to a diffusion of attention and variable performance.

In this context, it is important to set modest targets initially. Going for bold targets might make teams look good at the outset, but later failure only serves to demoralize the group, often leads to carping by other departments, and can put teams off the idea of measuring at all. It is critically important to set realistic targets – as a rule of thumb giving the team an 80 per cent chance of success. When teams experience the glow of success, they are encouraged to continue to improve still further. Early success is a great fuel to use on the journey to excellence.

'Measures show performance meeting the standards set'

When performance is seen to be meeting the standards set, it implies that the company, or the department and its staff, are actually paying attention to the measures and succeeding in meeting them. The behavioural change that staff have to undergo is to treat meeting the measures as a necessary part of working life. Having measures is all very well, but meeting them is what it's all about.

The easiest way of doing this is to agree the measures with the staff beforehand, allowing them to gain ownership of the process by being involved from the outset. Of course the manager himself has to act in a way that will indicate to his subordinates that the measures are serious. The people doing the work need to know that their manager is as committed as they are – or even more so.

Exercise

To test how serious a department is about measures and meeting them, ask individual members of a department what its performance measures actually are. How readily they answer will be a measure of how seriously they regard the matter. If they fumble to find the performance data, chances are it is not taken all that seriously. Another test is to ask how the performance targets and measures were decided upon or agreed. We believe that employees will be more committed if they were involved by the manager in *agreeing* these measures and standards.

It is relatively straightforward for manufacturing companies to set the production objectives that they want to achieve. In service companies, however, it is more likely that they will call these objectives 'standards'. By 'standards' are meant objectives that have to be met on an ongoing basis, eg reply to telephone calls within five rings, no one waiting at the bar more than three minutes to get a drink, getting responses to customer queries out within 24 hours, etc.

'Budgets agreed by department and monthly data fed back'

Budgets are one of the most common financial tools used in business and it is rare to find departments operating without some form of budget. A good budget will have the following characteristics:

- It will have been constructed and agreed by those responsible for the results.
- It will be based on operational realities, not on hopes.
- Each sub-department will have its own sub-budget.
- The people involved will have free access to the ongoing results of their endeavours.

'Plenty of data but often in different formats and places'

This is symptomatic of one of the more modern organizational problems: 'masses of data and very little information'. Widespread use of computers has enabled the average organization to produce more data than the average manager can assimilate. The result is that the critical elements of that data may get swamped by all the nice-to-have stuff.

One GPM consultant recalls conducting an interview with the operations director of a large company. Midway through, a member of staff entered and placed a 10-inch stack of computer print-out in his in-tray. While conversing, the director took the stack and moved it straight into his out-tray. The consultant asked what the item was. The director said he didn't know, but the lady brought it in every Thursday!

In another company that had installed an elaborate MRP II (Manufacturing Resources Planning) system, each week the computer produced an 'exceptions' list (items not produced that week as scheduled). Eventually, the list became so long it took five hours to print and made up a stack more than three feet deep! At that point, the company was using human production controllers to run around the production areas superseding the computer with hand-written lists.

A company that has plenty of data, but in an uncollated form, is probably the clearest definition of a company at Level 2. This is frequently associated with the problem of different computer systems not being able to 'talk' to one another or producing irreconcilable information. This situation contains within it the hope that the appropriate information can be yielded from the available data. In moving forward on the journey, however, a fairly ruthless approach to eliminating the unnecessary may have to be adopted.

LEVEL 3

'Performance measures publicly displayed in every department, and simple enough to be understood by all'

There are several assumptions here: first, the performance measures appropriate to the department have been decided; second, the measures have been agreed by all the departmental staff; and finally, the measures accurately reflect the performance of the department in a timely fashion.

Perhaps the question of visibility needs some explanation. It does not mean that electronic scoreboards are flashing coloured lights above each department. It must be seen in the context of the user. For an accountant, visibility may mean 10 pages of computer printout instead of the normal 3 inch stack. For an employee on the shop floor, visibility may mean easy-to-read data on his section's communications board. The individual being able to clearly understand the status of the department's performance without having to search it out and without having to have someone explain it is the important issue.

Given that the employees will want to achieve or exceed the standards, the frequency with which the information is updated is governed by the extent to which the employee can alter his work behaviour to affect the degree to which the standard is being met.

There are a number of reasons why we recommend that departments not only choose performance measures but also display them publicly, namely:

1. It is important to decide what are the key measures that will gauge the

performance of the department. This not only makes people think, but it also gets them to focus on what their real contribution is.

2. A decision has to be taken on how the data required to produce the measurement is going to be collected, ie by whom, from where, and how often.

3. The next step is to decide how the data is going to be presented, ie in the form of a table, graph, pie chart, etc. The display should be big enough to be readable from six feet and simple enough for any visitor to understand. Hand-produced charts should not be ridiculed, by the way, since the act of completing charts by hand produces a strong sense of ownership on the part of the responsible individual(s).

4. Using the data published on their communications board, we would want team members to be continuously reminded of what they need to focus on and what constitutes success. This is especially important for people engaged in repetitive work.

5. Charts containing performance information have a positive subliminal and reinforcing effect when placed close to employees' workplaces or where they see them every day. Even more so when they are colourful too.

6. The public display of target and performance data has a distinct motivational effect: people love the emotional strokes that the evidence of success gives, but just as important, people hate publicly being seen to fail.

'Data shows performance continuously improving'

Level 2 requires that the measures show that performance is *meeting* the standard. At Level 3 the requirement is that the performance is gradually *moving the standard upwards*. This does not detract from management's responsibility for adjusting the standards to match the capability and ambitions of the organization. It does, however, presume that there is a culture in the department that strives for improvement, and one that does not rely solely on management to provide the impetus for the journey to world class performance.

'Standards clear for every machine and for every job-holder'

In practice, in a manufacturing environment, visible information should be posted on each machine, containing the following: history, maintenance requirements and performance. For example, the machine should carry a label with its name, date purchased and name of the operator in charge. It should also have a list of its maintenance requirements on a daily, weekly and monthly basis; its cleaning schedule and checklist; process control graphs that are regularly filled out by the operator of the machine to show how it has been performing, and what the trend of its performance is; and clear instructions on how the machine should be operated, ie Best Operating Practice (see Ladder 7).

Standards should also be clear to every job-holder. Everyone should know what the unique contributions of his job are and how to measure each aspect of his performance (see Ladder 9 on Staff Empowerment). In service industries standards will often take the form of reminder check-lists. For example, Walt Disney World in Florida reminds employees each day that they are 'on stage' when they meet Guests. Employees are called 'cast members'. Their guidelines are:

1. Make eye contact and smile.
2. Greet and welcome each and every Guest.
3. Seek out contact with Guests.
4. Provide immediate service recovery.
5. Display appropriate body language at all times.
6. Preserve the magical Guest experience.
7. Thank each and every Guest.

One of the reasons Disney consistently delights its customers is that they don't leave anything to chance. They spell everything out in detail. They have rules on dress and grooming that cover items such as: aftershave, deodorant, costumes, hair colouring, pins and decorations, sunglasses, hairstyle, moustaches, beards and sideburns, tattoos, fingernails, jewellery, etc. What they find is that when the standards are made clear and simple, employees generally conform with goodwill and energy.

'Each manager agrees own budget and gets regular feedback'

Part of the standard in Level 2 was that each department should have its own budget. Here the requirement is that each manager should have budgetary responsibilities. In other words, every person responsible for managing people should have access to and responsibility for independent expenditure, one of the tools necessary for quick reaction to changing circumstances.

LEVEL 4

'Team members themselves produce the performance charts and graphs and update the displayed data'

At this stage not only is visible measurement an integral part of the accepted culture, but the team members themselves (not their managers) produce and update the performance measures. As simple as it sounds, this is quite a far-reaching step; it presumes that the routine of measuring is perceived as a natural part of each person's job. Better results will be obtained if the team members have been involved in setting the targets and parameters in the first place, to encourage their involvement, ownership and commitment.

'Visible management systems instantly make clear deviations from normal performance in production areas'

Here the subtle shift from 'visible *measurement* systems' to 'visible *management* systems' is made. By this is meant: setting up systems that make it visually clear to everyone when there is a deviation from normal expected performance, allowing the taking of immediate action. For example, in Ladder 3 (Cleaning and Organizing) we advised painting the factory walkway lines with yellow boundary lines. This not only reminds staff to keep these transport ways clear, but managers can cover large areas visually and tell at a glance whether any items have been placed out of line. They can also take immediate action to have moved anything stored 'temporarily' that is causing obstruction or a safety hazard.

Here are a few other practical examples of simple, but effective, visual management:

1. The use of a set of traffic lights at each work station. When work is going smoothly the green light is lit. When an operator *anticipates* a problem shortly he lights the amber light. That calls for outside help within, say, 30 minutes. When something has happened that stops the job altogether, eg running out of materials, or a machine breakdown, etc, then the red light is lit. The red light calls for immediate action by the supervisor and the whole team.
2. Deluxe Check of Minneapolis produce cheques for use in all sorts of banking and other organizations. For years they have had as a company standard that all orders should be despatched no later than the day after they are received. To help them fulfil that obligation, they use order slips of a different colour every day. Since Tuesday's colour is green, managers make sure there are no green orders left on the work floor by 4.30 on Wednesday. It is an extremely simple, but efficient system.
3. Statistical process control charts attached to machines, which are filled out at regular intervals by machine operators, indicate at a glance whether any process is staying within its upper and lower control limits.
4. Painting shadows of tools on a toolboard lets you know at a glance whether all the tools have been put back in their right place.
5. Kanban squares painted on the work floor indicate how many pallets or boxes should be stored between processes at any time. At a glance both operators and supervisors can tell whether the kanban squares are up to date with stock, and make sure no excess stock has inadvertently been placed in the area.
6. White lines painted on the floor with the names of the item to be stored within the boundary urge operators to put carts and other mobile items in their appropriate place. It also becomes obvious very quickly when items that should be there are missing.
7. The use of communication boards is discussed in Ladder 11 on Purposeful Communication. Suffice to say here the kind of useful information that can be posted on workplace communication boards:

- quality information – daily, weekly, monthly quality figures and trend charts;
- productivity figures versus targets;
- cost information versus targets;
- delivery information – production versus customer requirements;
- machine downtime figures and targets;
- suggestions submitted;
- quality circle activities etc.

'One-page management is in operation, ie data on key measures fed back weekly/monthly to each individual manager'

As we mentioned in our descriptions of Level 2, many companies produce a plethora of information, but much of it in different places and in different formats. As a result, managers are forced to compile the information that is important to them personally from a variety of different sources. That takes time and effort, and when managers are under time pressure, the job may be relegated in their priorities, or may not get done at all. We feel it is *essential* for managers to know how they are doing on their key measures without having to scramble through a whole jungle of information.

The fundamental idea behind 'one-page management' is for the chosen measures to appear every month (or at defined intervals) for every manager on one page. If the data suggests further investigation is needed, then the manager should know exactly where to go for the back-up detail that produced the 'top-line' figures he sees. But he never fails to see the key data every month on one master page.

For each managerial position there are usually between 6 and 12 key measures. Recorded on a single page, the information should be capable of giving the manager an at-a-glance report on the status of his operation. The frequency of the report is a function of the key reporting requirements of the position: a managing director reporting to a board of directors annually will probably need the information monthly, while a front-line supervisor faced with a weekly review meeting would need his report weekly, or even daily.

This is a methodology that can actually be applied at every level of the business. Figure 4.1 is an example of one-page data for the salesperson of a business selling insurance products. The measures are designated down the left of the figure. Each month, in the 'This month' boxes, the salesperson will see just how they did, and be able to compare that with the standards set alongside.

In the company in which this is used, this becomes a very important and useful document. First, salespeople know in advance what 'good' and 'outstanding' performance looks like. They can quickly see each month just how they're doing. The document is also used as a standard for the design of salesperson training, and in recruitment situations to show potential employees what will be required of them. With training and good coaching, the company wants all their new recruits to succeed, but if with help they repeatedly cannot achieve the minimum level, then they are helped to find a more suitable job.

	This month	Minimum	Good	Outstanding
New business each month		£4,000	£7,000	£10,000
New business 3-month average		£5,000	£6,000	£7,500
Renewals cumulative %		78%	85%	90%
Number of orders		1	5	8
Initial appointments		54	60	72
Full presentations		18	20	24
Documentation errors/returns		1	0	0
Visits to each existing client		2	3	3

Figure 4.1 Salesperson key success measures: monthly target levels

LEVEL 5

'Company realizes that measurement is the only way to sustain continuous improvement'

At this level, management realize that hard results are the only sure evidence that things are improving. And on the road to world class, that kind of evidence is absolutely essential. In addition, even when you have won the gold medal, you know that the world standard will keep improving, so you need these measures to make sure continuous improvement doesn't stop. It is truly a forever job.

There is a danger at this level too. People can keep so many measures they can literally drown in them. The antidote is to keep all the key measures on one page (without changing the font size!). Keep as many other 'interesting' measures as you choose, but never lose focus on the essentials.

'Senior management or visitors are able to tell from displayed data how any department is performing at any time'

This represents the pinnacle of transparency: the results of any part of the operation are immediately visible to any member of the management team. Organizational control is almost entirely based on results and the credit due to any manager is objectively located in performance. The plant manager at Premier Exhausts who won the best factory in Britain title in 1994 said: 'This year I want to be able to walk through the plant and be able to tell what every department is doing without having to ask anyone at all.' The visible measures should tell him everything he wants to know.

At this stage teams everywhere know exactly what to focus on, they know what counts, and that's what they work on every day. That makes management significantly simpler. And when the managing director 'manages by walking around' they know he'll ask questions about the numbers that are showing problems. But they also know he'll congratulate them when they are winning.

IDEAS AND TECHNIQUES YOU CAN USE

The following issues are discussed in this section:

- guidelines for making visible measurement systems work;
- visible management systems examples;
- types of measurement tools.

Guidelines for making visible measurement systems work

We recommend the following guidelines to making visible measurement systems work:

1. *Measurement charts must be placed prominently at the place of work.* These measurement charts are meant to remind the working team every day of the most important elements of their work. That is why they need to be in the open, where everyone will see them, and not kept in the team leader's desk drawers. The measures are important for the whole team. Also, for any manager or company visitor who is passing, the work and performance of the team are shown right in the work area.

   We favour using a Communications Board (you may choose to use a different name) approximately five feet wide by three feet deep. That size can't be missed, and makes it look important (which it is!). It also gives you room to attach a number of charts of easily readable size.
2. *Measurement charts should be easily readable from a distance.* By readable from a distance we mean 'readable easily at six feet'. Don't make chart legends (explanations of what the symbols or lines mean) so small that people have to peer to read them. The meaning of the chart ought to hit you as you pass.
3. *Charts should be easily understood by employees and visitors without explanation.* If the chart or graph needs to be explained, it's too complicated. Keep it simple.
4. *Each chart should show target limits, or targets for improvement over time.* Data without targets or standards does not mean very much. It means so much more to everyone to see if you are succeeding (meeting or beating the target), or improving.

   We recommend using the same colours for the same purpose, eg target lines are always red, and actual achievement lines are shown in green. That way, everyone knows what each line means on any chart throughout the company. We also encourage teams to put target lines on their charts that suggest steady but continuous improvement.

5. *Data should be marked up by team members.* If the manager or team leader marks up the data, the charts and the data are his. When the charts are updated by team members themselves, ownership and responsibility for performance are shared by the whole team.
6. *The data should be constantly referred to by the team leader and team members.* If the team leader conducts a 10-minute 'start-of-day' team meeting every day (as we advise in Ladder 11 on Purposeful Communication), we recommend he holds it close to the Communications Board, so that the performance information can be constantly referred to, and brought to the forefront of team members' minds.
7. *Performance charts should foster the twin goals of teamwork and continuous improvement.* Visible performance charts keep team members' minds focused on results. They help make teamwork and continuous improvement a habit, part of the ongoing culture of the business.

Visible management systems

The philosophy behind encouraging visibility in both measurement and management systems is twofold:

1. We want to encourage an open information system where nothing is kept in the manager's desk.
2. The second key principle of visual management is to make problems obvious when they occur. For example, if a machine is set up to stop whenever it produces a reject, the stopped machine makes the problem obvious. Or if the lines of transport lanes are clearly painted on a production floor, you can obviously see when material is wrongly stored in the transport lane. The visibility brings problems to notice enabling the team to take immediate action to correct problems.

In his book *Gemba Kaizen*, Masaaki Imai puts it this way: 'Management must manage the 5 M's: manpower, machines, materials, methods, and measurements. Any abnormality related to the 5 M's must be displayed visually.' Imai lists a series of questions you can ask yourself to test whether you have the necessary visibility in these key measures. Here they are:

Manpower

How is worker morale? This can be measured by the number of suggestions made, the extent of participation in quality circles, and figures on absenteeism. How do you know who is absent from the line today and who is taking their place? These items should be made visible at *gemba* (the workplace).

How do you know people's skill level? A display board in the workplace can show who is trained to do what tasks, and who needs additional training.

How do you know that the operator is doing the job right? Standards that show the right way to do the job . . . must be displayed.

Machines

How do you know that the machine is producing good quality products? If automatic stop and fail-safe devices are attached, the machine stops immediately when something goes wrong. When we see a machine stopped, we have to know why. Has it stopped because of scheduled down time? Changeover and set-up? Quality problems? Machine breakdown? Preventive repair?

Lubrication levels, the frequency of exchange, and the type of lubricant must be indicated. Metal housings should be replaced by transparent covers so that the operator can see when a malfunction occurs inside the machine.

Materials

How do you know the materials are flowing smoothly? How do you know whether you have more materials than you can handle and whether you are producing more products than you should? When a minimum stock level is specified and *kanban* – attaching a note to a batch of work in process as a means of communicating orders between processes – is used, such anomalies become visible.

The address where materials are stored must be shown, together with the stock level and parts numbers. Different colours should be used to prevent mistakes. Use signal lamps and audio signs to highlight abnormalities such as supply shortages.

Methods

How does a supervisor know when people are doing their jobs right? This is made clear by standard worksheets posted at each work station. The worksheets should show sequence of work, cycle time, safety items, quality checkpoints, and what to do when variability occurs.

Measurements

How do you check whether the process is running smoothly? Gauges must be clearly marked to show safe operating ranges. Temperature sensing tapes must be attached to motors to show whether they are generating excess heat.

How do you know whether an improvement has been made and whether you are on the way to reaching the target? How do you find out whether precision equipment is properly gauged?

Trend charts should be displayed in the workplace to show the number of suggestions, production schedules, targets for quality improvement, productivity improvement, set-up time reduction, and reduction in industrial accidents.

Types of measurement tools

It is important to choose the right type of table or chart to show your performance data most effectively. Here for your information are some of the alternatives:

- Pareto chart;
- fishbone chart;
- tree diagram;
- pie chart;
- histogram;
- run chart;
- control chart;
- radar chart.

Pareto Chart																	
Fault Description	1	2	3	4	5	6	7	8	9	10	11	12	13	14	15	16	17	18
Paper jam	✗	✗																
Machine cut-out	✗	✗	✗	✗	✗	✗	✗	✗	✗	✗	✗	✗						
Mis-feed	✗	✗	✗	✗														
Label sticking	✗	✗																
No glue	✗																	
Etc																		

Figure 4.2 Pareto chart

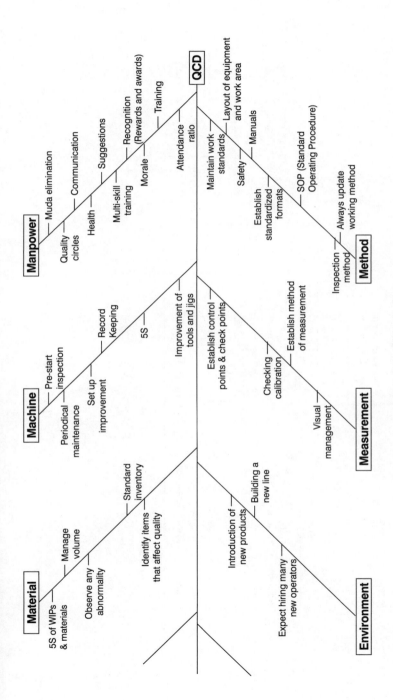

Figure 4.3 Fishbone chart

See Ladder 6, Managing for Quality, for more on the fishbone chart.

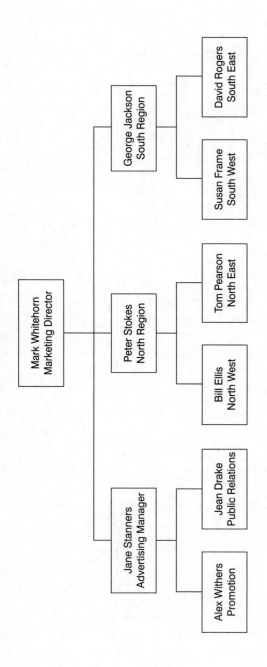

Figure 4.4 Tree diagram

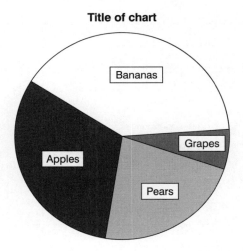

Figure 4.5 Pie chart

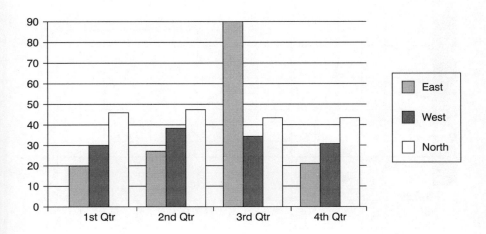

Figure 4.6 Histogram

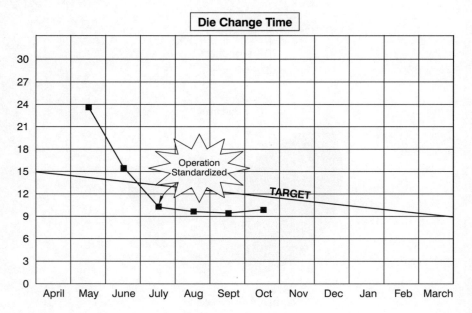

Figure 4.7 Run chart

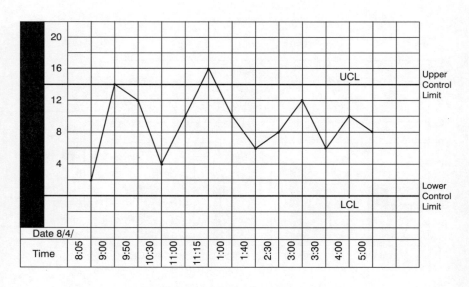

Figure 4.8 Control chart
Note: Percentage items defective

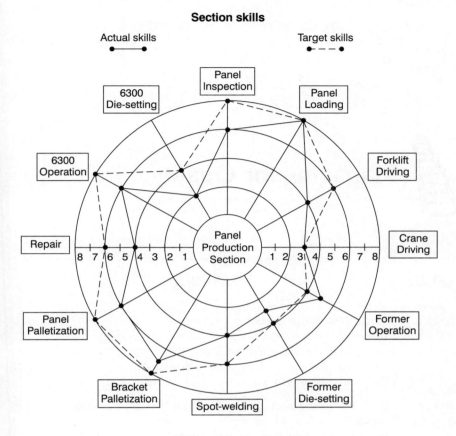

Figure 4.9 Radar chart

CONCLUSION

In concept, the journey up the ladder to world class performance in visible measurement is relatively simple:

- know the key measurables in the business;
- install an organization-wide culture of measurement in the workplace;
- extend the system to cover every key measurable at every level in the organization;
- extend the culture to one of management by measurement at the level of the individual.

F i v e

Managing for Quality

LEVELS	MEASURES
Level 1	People think that production is everything. They think it is the operator's job to make products and someone else's job (the inspector's) to catch mistakes. Pay systems emphasize quantity rather than quality. The primary drive is to 'get stuff out of the door'.
Level 2	The company has made the key mind-shift from quality defect detection to active prevention. Staff are now responsible for inspecting their own work and know exactly the standards they have to meet. Customer service measures actively measure fulfilment of service standards.
Level 3	Corrective action taken immediately on discovered defects. Staff use the '5 Why's' technique to solve problems. The defect rate has been reduced by at least half. Customer service measures show distinct improvements.
Level 4	Mistake-proofing devices are being implemented. Two-point inspection is now established. The defect rate is less than 0.5%. Customer service quality is measured at an all-time high.
Level 5	The abnormality rate is tracked, ie deviations from normal rather than the defect rate. The entire company has installed mistake-proofing devices. The abnormality rate is down to 0.1%. Customer complaints are down to zero.

LEVEL 1

'People think that production is everything'

There is a strong tendency for manufacturing companies to be obsessed with production figures. Often, when one asks managers what they are judged on, they will readily tell you that the most important thing is reaching the output numbers required either by the end of the week, or by the end of the month. These are the numbers that get invoiced to customers, these are the numbers that appear in the accounts, and these are the numbers that Boards look at most critically and most regularly. So managers respond – in their own best interests. They would rather argue with the Quality Manager than have to explain to their boss at the end of the week why they 'didn't make the numbers'. Companies that stay in this mode are always going to be Level 1 when it comes to managing quality.

Another strong indicator that quality comes second is the prevalence of a 'month-end rush', generally accompanied by a surge in overtime work. In a situation like this, operators will often take things more slowly at the beginning of a month hoping they might thereby create the opportunity for extra overtime earnings later. Towards the end of the month, as panic rises, managers cut corners and make compromises to make sure that at all costs they 'hit the numbers'. Arguments often develop between production and quality people about what is OK to ship and what is not OK. Relations become strained, and even the most senior management will put pressure on the quality people to relax standards to make sure end-of-month targets are met.

Companies who are locked into this kind of habit find it most difficult to stop. They are too busy pedalling to take the time out to decide how they are going to change. In fact they often take a secret pride in showing how by rushing around they achieved their target yet again against 'impossible' odds. That kind of company will always be stuck at Level 1.

There's only one solution, in our view. And that is to say: 'From next month on, quality means meeting agreed customer requirements. No compromises.' You may have to refuse to let some non-conforming product go in the first month to make the point (and prepare for that). That's the penalty you'll have to pay. But the long-term benefits to your quality, your customers, and your profits will be enormous.

'They think it is the operator's job to make products and someone else's job (the inspector's) to catch mistakes'

This is the fundamental quality flaw in many companies, ie that they separate the people who make, from the inspectors or checkers who 'make sure' that things are right before they go out the door. The unspoken signal this gives is that the responsibility for quality rests with inspectors, not the producers. Is it any wonder that production people don't treat their responsibility for quality anything like as seriously as their inspector colleagues? The inescapable implication also is that you can trust someone who is called 'inspector' but you cannot really trust anyone else. The idea is obviously quite ridiculous.

There is only one cure. You have to put responsibility where the control actually lies. And that is with the front-line member of staff who is making the product or delivering the service. Quality is not achieved after the event – it is *built in* as the product is being made, or as the service is being delivered *at the time*.

Our recommendation is to treat every member of staff like a mature adult, and to expect them to behave like mature adults. First, that means training staff not only to do the job right, but to know precisely what a good job looks like. But having done that we would then *expect* them to do the job right without any further checking or supervision. And when you give more responsibility to front-line staff they do not get more irresponsible: on the contrary, they act more responsibly than ever before. That's when you'll see your quality starting to improve. The companies that we see achieving the best and most consistent quality are companies who do not have independent armies of inspectors.

There are half a dozen additional serious problems that go along with using inspectors to check quality:

1. The people who are producing the work simply see the inspector as a hurdle to get over. Even worse, they do not think of the end customer who is going to receive their work. Their focus is only to do the job well enough so that the inspector will not send it back. This leads to people only doing a 'good enough' job rather than an excellent job.
2. Inspectors cannot normally examine everything. They usually work on a sample, say, 5%. Inspectors obviously cannot find all the defects when inspecting only samples. Therefore, there are bound to be defective products in the unchecked 95% that goes out to the customer. The inspector can act as a goal-keeper, but he cannot assure his customer that faulty goods will not get out.
3. Conflict inevitably occurs between production and quality inspection staff. They argue about what is OK and what is not OK, and opinions abound. Not only do both production and quality people dislike the conflict, but the person who actually suffers is in fact the end customer. As an example, we can recall the quality audit manager at a large UK engineering concern, where product safety was critically important to the customer, telling us that he spent two-thirds of his week arguing about concessions, ie compromises to quality standards to allow the product to leave the building. That is the reality in companies where production and quality are separated. Built-in conflict will never get people acting as one team intent on producing good quality.
4. Inspection happens after the work process is complete. That's too late. All you can do if you detect a fault is to send the product for rework or scrap. As Deming, quality guru *extraordinaire* (1986), said: discovering defects and eliminating them is fine, but that just gets you back to where you

were before. What counts is tracing back to its source what caused the defect in the first place and curing it forever. Work primarily on improving the process, not on detecting the faults.

The old way: inspect bad quality out.

The new way: build good quality in.

5. Inspection is not about improvement. As Shigeo Shingo, widely acknowledged as the architect of 'zero defects' (1990), said: 'No matter how accurately and thoroughly inspection is performed, it can in no way contribute to lowering the defect rate in the plant itself. This inspection method is therefore of no value whatsoever if one wants to bring down the defect rate within plants.'
6. It costs more. An inspector may do his job conscientiously, but that doesn't add value to the product in any way. It only adds cost. Every pound or dollar spent on inspection comes off the profit line of that product. It can't come from anywhere else. Teaching employees to produce 'right-first-time' quality results not only in a better product, it costs less too.

'Pay systems emphasize quantity rather than quality'

'The primary drive is to "get stuff out of the door"'

This is particularly true in companies that operate on the basis of piece work, ie the more you produce, the more you get paid. We have seen such pay systems in a whole variety of industries, including garment-making, hosiery, shoes, pottery-making and the docks. Managers say: 'We wouldn't get the output if we didn't have piece work.' But when the pressure is constantly on output, people inevitably cut corners and quality takes a back seat. Sometimes operators will work at a very high pace in order to have time at the end of the work period, such as before lunch or before the end of a shift, when they are idle. This is often a signal of being more concerned with getting the job done than maintaining quality. In service companies, such as insurance, for example, staff may have a tendency to get rid of work by getting it off their desk or passing it on to another department. In such cases they are less concerned about delivering what the customer wants, and more about being free of the work.

Companies operating on a piece work basis will never be world class when it comes to quality. They are likely to stay at Level 1. This is principally why we advise companies to remove piece work and to establish new quality-supporting payment systems. Managers are often scared to touch the payment system in case productivity slumps and they can't get it back, but we have seen departments reach all-time high levels of productivity when piece work systems were removed. (See Ladder 10, Rewards and Recognition, for more on this.)

LEVEL 2

'The company has made the key mind-shift from quality defect detection to active prevention'

This may sound like a small move, but it is fundamental. The critical concept is to build a process that gets the product or service 'right first time', where faults are unlikely to occur, or indeed *cannot* occur (more of this in Level 4). One of the good reasons is that it costs so much to get it wrong! Philip Crosby (1979) argues that the Costs of Quality (COQ) may be as high as 25–30 per cent of sales in companies who haven't yet started seriously working on quality. Savings on these costs would naturally all fall on companies' profit bottom line. Hence his assertion: Quality is Free.

It's well worth doing the exercise in your own organization to see what your own costs of quality are. Here are the factors you should take into account:

Scrap	Engineering/technical changes
Rework	Purchase order changes
Warranty costs/returns	Material shortages/delays
Service repairs /failures in service	Customer complaint handling
Quality control costs	Computer problems/software etc
Inspection labour	Breakdown costs and delays
Test equipment costs	Inter-department problems
Sales information deficiencies	Making up for other 'things gone wrong'

It may take as much as six months to collect all this data. Prepare to be shocked when you add it all up. But don't despair. Rather than see it as a huge problem, see it as a great mountain of improvement you can dig into, a pile of money you can add to the bottom line. Crosby says reasonable expenditure for quality costs should be no more than 2.5 per cent of sales value, made up as follows:

Scrap	0.25%
Rework	0.25%
Warranty/service	0.2%
Quality control costs	1.8%

Don't expect to get there in a year, or even three. But make solid plans to improve measurably every year, and involve every member of the company in doing it.

When companies first start to focus on quality defect prevention, they find they have to go right back to the beginning, to deliberately plan for quality right from where the product is first designed. And here are the questions they need to ask themselves:

- *Is this product what our customers want? Will it excite them? Is it at least as good, or better, value for money versus what our competition offer?*

  These are *marketing* questions. You have to have a product that really fulfils a real customer want before they will part with their money. If it does it in an innovative way or at less cost than the competition, then even better.
- *Can we meet our promises?*

  This is critical. Marketing advertising may hype the product and raise customer expectations to the point where you cannot deliver consistently any more. So in fulfilling these promises you also need to ask:
  - Will the product or service we offer do what is claimed?
  - Can we do it consistently?
  - Are the process, systems and equipment we use capable of making exactly to specification every time?
  - If we make it right, will it be reliable in the customer's hands?
  - Can we actually deliver on the dates our salespeople promise?
  - Have we built in zero defect checks at each stage of our process?
  - Have our people been trained well enough to do it right every time?

All of these are questions about *quality*. And quality is never simply down to the performance of front-line staff. Publishing platitudes like 'Quality is Everybody's Business' will have no perceptible effect on quality at all. Quality has to be designed in at every stage of the process. . . and the authority for that belongs firmly in the hands of management. Indeed, when Deming strongly contends that responsibility for quality rests 85 per cent with management and only some 15 per cent with front-line people, we wouldn't disagree. Only management has the authority to initiate the research and make things happen.

In manufacturing companies, Deming was a strong advocate of statistical process control (SPC) to determine the variability in current processes as a first step to bringing processes 'under control'. By plotting observed data you could see the natural variability present in all processes, and set upper and lower control limits round the mid-point value. If measures fell between these acceptable limits, then the process was 'in control' and should be left alone. Readings outside these limits indicated a special factor or 'assignable cause' at work. This should be investigated at once and actions taken to eliminate the root cause so that it never returned.

Having succeeded in creating a stable process over a period of time, then management should devote its time to narrowing the degree of variability in each process to make each product closer to its ideal specification. That is fundamentally the process Deming brought to Japanese industry in 1951, and which they have subsequently carried to world class levels ever since.

'Staff are now responsible for inspecting their own work and know exactly the standards they have to meet'

'Process capability', ie having processes in place capable of producing the product time after time consistently, is obviously essential to any company intent on producing good quality. But 'operator capability' is important too. For most companies that means having people not only with the right skills or capacity to learn, but a positive attitude as well. But is that enough? Not really. No matter how willing they are to co-operate and be flexible, it's difficult to deliver good quality without all the following things being in place too:

1. *A product design capable of right-every-time manufacture.* Often, over-enthusiastic designers, or designers who don't understand the production processes involved well enough, can create designs that may look beautiful, but are so complex to produce they cause persistent problems, high levels of scrap and soaring costs. It is at the design stage that quality truly begins. It is always a problem scrambling later to make up for design deficiencies.

2. *Process equipment capable of right-every-time manufacture.* Don't blame the operator if in fact the equipment is not capable of holding the quality parameters required.

3. *The right materials to do the job, delivered at the right time.* We once conducted an employee survey where 66% of employees in manufacturing complained they didn't have all the materials required to do a good job. That's a drastic situation, but it's one where action will obviously produce big improvements.

    Suppliers to internal customers need to supply them not only with what they need to do a good job, but in a sequence, time-scale and format they want. For example, in a production environment operators not only want the parts they are using to be of the right quality, but they may want their materials put in a particular place to make the job easier; they may also want them delivered in a layout that makes it convenient for them to use and in quantities and receptacles that are not too heavy to handle, etc.

4. *All the work-tools needed to do the job.* This may sound obvious, but it is surprisingly common to see staff struggling with inadequate tools.

5. *The right information at the right time.* This means detailed specifications, as well as what, when and how many.

6. *Standards to work to.* One of the simple ways of helping staff turn out a good job – and it is one neglected by over 90% of companies – is to give staff actual examples of what a good job looks like. In the case of office-based staff this would mean not only showing them the forms and paperwork they have to complete, but showing them models of completed examples. In the case of people making a physical product, it is good to put an example of what a good product looks like on the wall, close to each operation. Where this is slightly complex, an exploded view of the parts that compose the product with each of the components' names should be displayed (it is surprising how many operators call the same parts by different names leading to obvious confusion).

7. *Suitable measuring/test equipment.* Don't give the measuring equipment only to special 'inspectors'. Give it to the people actually doing the job.

Train them to fully understand, and take full responsibility for, their own quality.

8. *A Best Operating Practice method* (see Ladder 7). Best Operating Practice (BOP) sheets are designed to show step by step the process one has to fulfil if you are going to make a quality product or do a quality job. And having been properly trained, operators are expected to follow the BOP religiously. The author of the book *Kaizen* (1986), Masaaki Imai, is quite categoric on this subject: 'If management cannot get people to follow the established rules, nothing else it does will matter.' We wholeheartedly agree.

    That willingness to follow Best Operating Practice consistently is highly valued by companies like McDonald's and Mercedes. McDonald's detail *exactly* how food should be cooked and served and how customers should be greeted and served. It's why they get such consistent service round the world even using teenage staff. Mercedes test those who apply for shop floor jobs by asking them to follow instructions in fitting equipment to a Mercedes car. Those who rush or take short cuts are not those who get the job. It's those who implement to instruction. It's one of the key reasons Mercedes manage to produce such consistent quality.

9. *Training in the methods and process.* And here we mean: having not only been trained, but tested to verify both skills and knowledge.

10. *Contact with, and awareness of, their customer's requirements.* Meeting with customers to see how they actually use the product or use the information one produces, is much more motivational in producing consistent good quality than any money incentive.

With all that in place then performance is all down to the operator. What they have to do then is to implement to instruction (the BOP), and co-operate with their suppliers and customers in doing it. They may come up with a better idea for producing the product: if they do, incorporate it in the BOP. Until then, the message is clear: produce to instruction.

'Customer service measures actively measure fulfilment of service standards'

At Level 2 all staff know that they are part of a customer chain (as described in Ladder 2). Individual staff members are encouraged to make contact with their receiving customers and to make contracts across sections or departments. At their first meeting we suggest they just ask these three questions:

1. *What do we do now that you appreciate and want us to continue?* It's important for the internal customers to start by saying positive things. Otherwise, if individuals' first experience of the discussion with their customers is negative, they tend to resist continuing the relationship or making efforts to improve.

2. *What things do you think we could do that would improve our service to you?* Often people, when given the chance, will produce a long list of

complaints. To make the request manageable, staff members then ask question number three.

3. *If we were to confine ourselves to just two of these improvement items, which would be the most important for you?* This ensures that the request is manageable. It is also more likely that staff members will try to make these improvements quickly, and therefore please the customer. Customers are impressed by speedy responses. When the *supplier's* first experience in this process is also one of success, they are encouraged to develop the relationship with their customer further.

That's the very first step in measuring customer satisfaction: actually talking to them directly. It is surprising how many companies don't. The second step is to measure on a regular basis how well you're doing. Our advice is to start with the basics, ie the degree to which the product or service works first time every time, and how often you meet your promised delivery dates. Don't do anything more complicated until you have mastered that. That's what customers want first and foremost. And getting just that right often involves working through many details, changing systems, working with suppliers, training staff, ensuring salespeople don't make promises you can't keep, etc. It is seldom as easy as it first appears.

LEVEL 3

'Corrective action taken immediately on discovered defects'

Earlier we quoted Shigeo Shingo as saying that inspection itself contributes nothing to *lowering* the defect rate in a company. Even then, if there is a delay between actual production and quality checking, there will always be further defects created in the interval that could have been prevented. The answer is to feed back information with the least possible delay, and for corrective action to be taken *immediately*. To reinforce the point about quality first, Shingo advises shutting down lines until the source of the faults is removed – that grabs attention, makes everyone very conscious of not being the cause of stoppages, and, most importantly, thorough action tends to be taken on the source of the fault to ensure it does not occur again.

At first, production managers are horrified at the thought of stopping a whole line: 'We can't afford to lose all that production', they say. But that's a Level 1 attitude, ie never mind the quality as long as we're producing. No paying customer wants a defective product, so emphasize the point that you never want to produce any – at any stage. The loss may well be considerable the first time you stop a process. But the psychological impact will be great.

And eventually the stoppages will be shorter and will get less frequent. Those who are not willing to make the move have little chance of reaching Level 3 on quality. Today, not only is Toyota willing to stop its car production line if a fault occurs, every operator actually has a button at their work-station that allows them to stop the whole line if they can't complete their job defect-free in time. That's taking quality seriously. And far from damaging their ability to produce, Toyota is acknowledged as the most productive car manufacturer in the world.

Corrective action, when it is taken, should always be in the form of '*permafix*' solutions. By that we mean: don't dab ointment on problems, or merely apply Band-Aid-type corrections. Cure the disease. Take action that puts the problem to bed for ever, permanently, so that it never comes back. That means taking the trouble to get right back to the *source* of the problem, and taking action that not only means the problem will not recur, but *cannot* recur. That's where using techniques like the simple but effective '5 Why's' procedure can be very valuable.

'*Staff use the "5 Why's" technique to solve problems*'

The idea originated in Japan where companies were anxious to get to the root cause of a problem and cure it, rather than implement temporary quick-fix solutions. The technique looks disarmingly simple, but the fact that is still used throughout Japan after more than 30 years speaks volumes for its effectiveness. Here is an example:

1. Question: Why are you throwing sawdust on the floor?
   Answer: Because the floor is slippery and unsafe.
2. Question: Why is the floor slippery and unsafe?
   Answer: Because there is oil on it.
3. Question: Why is there oil on it?
   Answer: Because this machine is dripping.
4. Question: Why is it dripping?
   Answer: Because oil is leaking from this coupling.
5. Question: Why is it leaking?
   Answer: Because the rubber seal inside the coupling is worn out.

The point is very simple. Don't keep throwing sawdust on the floor in a 'that will do for now' fashion. Don't wait until an accident occurs before you take action. Fix the problem once and permanently. Remove the root cause of the problem: fit a new seal. That's the sensible 'permafix' solution.

Problems are not always so straightforward, of course. In more complex cases, two other techniques have proven their long-term worth in practice. The first is Pareto charting. Wilfredo Pareto (1848–1923), an Italian mathematician, conducted research that showed that in 19th-century Italy, 80 per cent of the wealth was held by 20 per cent of the population. Since known as the 80/20 rule, one can see a similar pattern in many aspects of life. For example, 80 per cent of sales in many companies come from 20 per cent of the product lines; 80 per cent of machine breakdowns often come from 20 per cent of the possible causes. Dr Joseph Juran, the quality guru, long ago felt the Pareto finding could be very useful in identifying the key causes of quality problems, ie in isolating what he called the 'vital few' from the 'trivial many'. In other words, by working first on the key cause one might remove 80 per cent of the quality faults. In practice it seldom works out exactly like that, but the principle is still valid.

The first step in composing a Pareto chart is to collect data. In other words, don't too readily jump into solution mode before you see the facts. In analysing the causes of accidents in one company, the Safety Officer found the following breakdown:

Handling/lifting/carrying	25
Contact with machinery	9
Slip/trip/fall	7
Struck against object	7
Struck by object (inc. doors)	6
Trapping of fingers	5
Exposure to dust or fire	5
Other causes	0–2

Examining the facts makes it obvious where to concentrate, in this case in terms of both education and work methods, if accidents are to be reduced. Pareto analysis helped this company halve its accident rate in three years, and cut its days lost though accidents by some 65 per cent over the same period. (See later in this chapter for more on Pareto charting.)

The second useful problem analysis technique is cause and effect diagrams (sometimes called fishbone diagrams). The origin of the technique is attributed to Kaoru Ishikawa, who was seeking to provide managers and their work-teams with a simple technique to break down quality problems into their component parts. The process generally examines the problems under five headings all starting with the letter M, ie Materials, Machinery, Manpower, Measurements, and Methods. Some companies add a sixth called Environment. The chart will then look something like Figure 5.1.

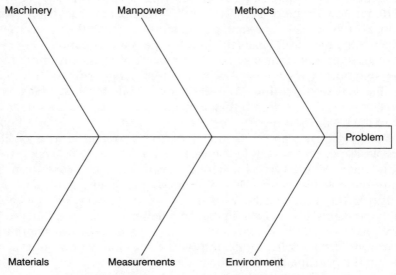

Figure 5.1 A cause and effect diagram

As the work-team analyses the causes of the problem (stated in the box on the right), they list the various items under their different heads. If the equipment being used has breakdown problems, that would be listed on the 'Machinery' leg; if some of the operators were new or had not been trained sufficiently, then that would be attached to the 'Manpower' leg, and so on. Eventually a picture is built up of the likely causes of the problem being examined.

One refinement of this technique is to issue each team member with Post-it Notes, coloured, say, pink and yellow. Team members then write possible causes on pink notes, and attach these to the left-hand side of the appropriate leg, whereas if they have a possible solution to a stated problem they write this on a yellow note, and attach that to the right-hand side of the respective leg. Physical involvement, we find, helps the process, and the build-up of yellow notes encourages optimistic problem-solving. In addition, you can change the titles of the legs if this makes the process more appropriate. For example, in analysing the cause of hospital waiting times, the legs might be named as Systems, Information, People, Procedures. Theses can be altered to suit, but in general the five M's are a useful model to keep in mind. (See the end of this chapter for a further example.)

'The defect rate has been reduced by at least half'

By the word 'defect' we don't just mean work that has been scrapped as unusable, but also work that has had to be rectified, re-worked, or done again to make it right. In manufacturing situations that means both scrap and rework. In office situations that means anything having to be done twice or more (and often that is quite a lot!).

One of the problems in cutting the defect rate is that managers and employees often accept the current defect rate as inevitable or 'normal', and are not motivated to do anything about it until it exceeds the already accepted standard rate. We have worked in companies where a scrap rate as high as 30 per cent was regarded as normal. But the great prize in such situations is that any cut in the rate results in all the savings falling directly to the bottom line. It's a prize worth pursuing not only in getting more 'right first time' for the customer, but in improving the cost base and the profitability of the company.

It's difficult to cut the defect rate just by exhorting and shouting. What works better is team commitments to goals and using visible measurement systems (see Ladder 4 for a full discussion). Consider this story from Masaaki Imai in his book *Gemba Kaizen* (1986):

Suppose that external requirements have prompted the plant to reduce the set-up time of a particular press within six months. In such a case, a display board is set up next to the machine. First the current set-up (for example, six hours as of January) is plotted on a graph. Next, the target value (one half hour by June) is plotted. Then a straight line is drawn between the points, showing the target to aim for each month. Every time the press is set up, the time is measured and is plotted on the board. Special training must be provided to help the workers reach the targets. Over time, something incredible takes place. The usual set-up time on the graph starts to follow the target line! This happens because the operators become conscious of the target, and realize that management expects them to reach it. Whenever the number jumps above the target, they know that an abnormality (missing tools etc) has arisen, and take action to avoid such a mishap in the future. This is one of the most powerful effects of visual management. Numbers alone are not enough to motivate people: without targets, numbers are dead.

'Customer service measures show distinct improvements'

We illustrated in Ladder 2 (Customer Focus) how it is impossible to know whether your service to customers is improving without actually measuring customer reactions on a regular basis. It is interesting to note that Avis, the car rental company, actually coined their slogan 'We try harder' way back in 1963. But they didn't actually start measuring customer service until 1989, 25 years later! And the experience was both surprising and salutary. They found they were working on things the customers never mentioned; but they also found when they paid attention to what the customers did mention, their scores started to improve markedly.

After clients rent an Avis car, a customer service form asks them various questions about the company's service. These include:

- waiting time to get the car;
- availability of the car asked for;
- type of car the customer was given;
- cleanliness of the car;
- mechanical condition of the car;
- professionalism of Avis personnel;
- personalized service by the staff;
- accuracy of the bill.

Customers are asked to rank their opinions on each item in five categories from 'Very Satisfied' to 'Very Dissatisfied'. All this data, including a total 'Customer Satisfaction Index', is then fed back to every Avis rental station every month. It looks like Table 5.1.

That's giving data back where it belongs – to the people who are dealing with the customers face-to-face. Companies measure what's important to them. But it's also true that what gets measured becomes important. That's exactly what Avis found – customer service was given a whole new importance throughout the company.

Table 5.1 Customer satisfaction index

	3-month	Current	12-month
Customer satisfaction index			
Station	94	82	84
District	91	80	83
Country	85	84	81
Waiting time to get car			
Station	95	100	97
District	95	96	95
Country	94	95	92
Availability of car group asked for			
Station	91	96	88
District	89	91	88
Country	87	85	86
Type of car given			
Station	92	96	88
District	93	95	89
Country	90	90	87

LEVEL 4

'Mistake-proofing devices are being implemented'

For a long time following the influence of Deming and others, the Japanese were married to SPC (Statistical Process Control) as the best means of assuring good product quality. Shigeo Shingo was a convinced advocate of the technique, until he began to realize that SPC fundamentally accepts that there are always going to be faults, but that SPC will help you detect and control them. He often wondered: isn't there a way to prevent defects from happening altogether? The idea originated with Mr Toyoda, founder of the Toyota company, who engineered his original weaving machines to stop production immediately should either the warp or woof thread break. In other words he prevented faults from happening altogether.

Shingo developed the idea to other situations using the term '*Baka-Yoke*' meaning fool-proofing. First introduced into a car seat making plant, one of the ladies who had been there for years burst into tears when told that fool-proofing devices were being introduced because operators kept mixing up right and left-hand parts. She was absent the following day and when her manager went to see her she asked him: 'Have I been such a fool all these years?' He explained they didn't think she was a fool, but that everyone tended to make inadvertent errors from time to time. The experience persuaded Shingo to change the name from *Baka-Yoke* to *Poka-Yoke* (pronounced poka-yokay), the latter meaning mistake-proofing. It just shows how easy it is to upset your best allies if you are not careful!

Mistake-proofing devices can either be of the warning-type or control-type. The warning-type calls operators' attention to abnormalities by sounding a buzzer or flashing a light. This 'warns' the operator to take corrective action. The control-type device actually shuts down the machine or immediately halts operations when abnormalities occur. Control methods are far more effective than warning methods, so control-type devices should be used wherever possible.

Poka-Yoke devices do not need to be complicated or expensive. Here are two examples to illustrate the point. In assembling a control panel with on-off buttons, operators would sometimes forget to put a spring under one of the buttons. To prevent this from happening a small tray between the box containing the springs and the operator was introduced. The operator was then told to take two springs out of the supply box and put them in the intermediate tray. That way, at the end of the operation, they could always see whether they had put a spring under each of the two buttons. As a result, defects disappeared.

In another case, a small ball valve had to be inserted into a carburettor before a cap was installed. Sometimes workers forgot to insert the ball valve before putting on the caps. To eliminate the problem a photo-electric beam was put in front of the ball valve supply. This was connected to the parts box containing the caps. As a result, only if the operator's hand had moved through the photo-electric beam to fetch a ball valve would the shutter on the caps box open, ie a cap could not be removed without first taking out a ball valve. Not a single instance of missing ball valves occurred in the years following these improvements. The fundamental idea behind *Poka-Yoke* is to make it as near to impossible to do the wrong thing.

'Two-point inspection is now established'

In seeking forever to improve his error-prevention techniques, Shingo was much impressed in 1977 when he discovered that one department assembling drain pipes for the Matsushita washing machine company, despite handling some 30,000 units per month, had achieved a whole month's production with *zero defects*. Secretly he thought this was impossible, but on investigation discovered it had been achieved by the use of:

- source inspections;
- self-checks by operators;
- successive checks;
- the installation of effective *Poka-Yoke* devices.

Source inspections are making sure that your supplier supplies you with the correct raw materials or information, without omission or defect. In the case of outside suppliers, that may mean getting him to correct material received which has been causing problems, introducing supplier classification systems where in-house inspections are gradually reduced to zero depending on their improvement and reliability, or arranging visits to the supplier to help him improve in specific areas.

Self-checks means that the operators check the material, product or information *before they use* it; then perform their own value-added operation; and finally check their work is right *before passing it on* to the next process.

Successive checks means that the receiving person, ie the customer who is next in line in the process, also checks the material as he receives it, and immediately feeds back information to the previous process, should they discover any quality problems. That is what is called 'two-point inspection'. In a simple process, the pattern then looks like Figure 5.2.

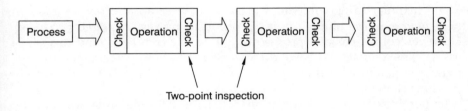

Two-point inspection

Figure 5.2 Two-point inspection

Shingo says that in his experience: 'The implementation of a successive check system leads without exception to a lowering of the defect rate to one fifth or one tenth of the previous value in the space of a single month.'

If you are intent on planning for zero defects, then bear these key points in mind:

1. *Use source inspections*. That means two things. First, it means going back to the source of faults and eliminating the causes permanently, not making up for defects after they have been created. Second, it means working with suppliers to ensure you start in the first place with the right materials and information to enable a zero-defect job to be done.
2. *Use 100% inspections rather than sampling inspections*. However well statistical process control is executed, it will only test a statistically significant sample of the items produced. That means defects will get out, ie in the products passed but not examined. However, you don't have to add an army of inspectors. All you have to do is to make sure operators do their own checks as the products are being produced, and that someone *independent* of each operator makes a check immediately afterwards. That does not need to be an inspector – it can just as easily be the next person in the process line. That means you don't add any extra costs or people, but quality becomes the daily responsibility of the people doing the job.

And it also means they check every item, so you have an infinitely better chance of achieving the goal of zero defects.

3. *Minimize the time between the discovery of any defect and taking corrective action.* Don't wait till you have a batch. Act to put things right immediately as soon as any defect is discovered.

4. *Set up Poka-Yoke devices and systems.* The general experience in setting up 'warning-type' devices is that 80% of the previous faults disappear within a few weeks. However, 'control-type' devices (where the equipment actually stops as soon as an abnormality occurs) means 100% of the previous defects disappear. We make a distinction here between *errors* and *defects*. Errors are always likely to happen, either caused by humans or machinery. But if you get immediate feedback and action at the error stage (ie the machine stops), then you can always correct the item before it moves on in the process. In other words, *errors* don't turn into *defects*.

'The defect rate is less than 0.5 per cent'

Many manufacturing companies measure their scrap and rework rates in percentages, ie the number of scrap products in every hundred produced. However, companies that proceed to the 0.5 per cent level (and this is not easy) will eventually go beyond measuring defects in percentages. Indeed, today companies who are world class in product quality measure defects in parts per million.

In our Introduction we mentioned that in 1982 Motorola was already reaching a 0.5 per cent defect rate. But they were still getting complaints about quality from their customers. Why? Well, look at what 0.5 per cent actually means:

Number produced	Number of defects
1,000	5
10,000	50
100,000	500
1,000,000	5,000

Since they do make millions of bits, that's an awful lot of defects being sent out to customers. Motorola decided to launch out on a never-ending quest for better quality. By 1992 the company was able to set a standard of no more than 3.4 defects per million parts produced. Astonishing as it may seem, this is more than a thousand times better than those companies at Level 4 achieving less than 0.5 per cent scrap. Now that is world class! The fact is, by continuing on the journey you get to levels of performance you previously thought were just impossible.

'Customer service quality is measured at an all-time high'

At this level, we would expect that less than 1 per cent of the customers served or the transactions completed result in a customer complaint. There are generally so many things to go wrong in serving customers well, that getting to this level takes years of effort, having excellent systems in place, and staff who are not only well trained but empowered to 'do the right thing for the customer at the time'. It pays also to measure the right things, and that may not just be the product you deliver.

For example, one company for whom we worked is a leader and much admired in its industry. Although complaints about the products were very low and the company rightly thought they were achieving high customer service quality, we discovered that as much as 25 per cent of customers raised queries or problems with the invoices they received! Now that's really a complaint. The fact that the customer has had to telephone because the invoice is not simple or clear enough simply adds unneeded time and cost for both the customer and the manufacturer – it adds no extra value at all. The objective needs to be: get it so right the first time round that the customer has no need to make an unnecessary phone call. Of course, getting all that right may mean looking at systems and habits in the sales force, manufacturing, despatch, finance, etc, and taking the time to co-ordinate and streamline it all. But in the long term it will not only reduce costs, it will visibly improve customer service.

LEVEL 5

'The abnormality rate is tracked, ie deviations from normal rather than the defect rate'

The abnormality rate is a much tougher measure than the scrap rate or the level of customer complaints, and is generally only used by companies who have already reached a very high level of right-first-time quality. If a customer complains, or a product has to be reworked, that is normally just recorded as one complaint or one reworked product. What the abnormality rate records is *how many times* a product had to be reworked, or a customer complaint handled before it was put right. In other words, if a product was reworked at two different stages in its manufacture, that is recorded as two fault points. If it takes three letters, or attention from three escalating levels in the company before a customer complaint is finally resolved, that is recorded as three fault points.

We like to emphasize the value of 'right first time' in companies for several reasons:

1. It costs less to get it right first time. Correcting mistakes merely adds cost and no extra value.
2. The habit brings a valuable discipline to companies. People in manufacturing get used to checking that their set-up, equipment and materials are all right before they launch into producing. In other words, they think *prevention* before correction. And that same attitude of mind can apply everywhere, whether you're issuing a ticket, typing a letter, making pho-

tocopies, compiling accounts, producing china or even manufacturing aeroplanes.

3. Reworked items are seldom as good as those got right the first time. In an exercise that Ford in the United States conducted on problem gear boxes, it was found that they were almost exclusively units that had been rectified after faults had been discovered on the line. Very few customer complaints were received about gear boxes that had been made right first time. The fact is that products made right first time not only cost less to make, they perform better for the customer too.

'The entire company has installed mistake-proofing devices'

Mistake-proofing devices have been conducted in administration areas for years. For example, double entry bookkeeping has been used for years to make sure that books balance, but that's simply a means of squeezing errors out of the system. Using computers today, form filling can be devised that does not allow the form to be completed unless there are entries against every key item. Although this can cause problems at times (where there is not enough flexibility), it does ensure that people do not forget to enter important information at the data entry stage. Also, computer systems that allow different information to be withdrawn, or different calculations to be made from the same raw data entered only once, means that there are likely to be fewer discrepancies between departments in the calculations they make and in the conclusions they draw. Therefore, one should not think that mistake-proofing devices only apply to manufacturing companies. They apply everywhere.

'The abnormality rate is down to 0.1 per cent'

Some companies have managed, after years of effort, to get themselves to a defect rate of only 0.1 per cent. But the *abnormality rate* (as explained above) could well be 10 times this level. Many people ask us the question: 'Don't you get to the end in looking for further improvements in your defect rate?' The answer is: definitely not! Reaching a defect level of 0.1 per cent is outstanding, but don't forget that the equivalent defect rate for Motorola is 0.001 per cent! There are always new places to go.

'Customer complaints are down to zero'

In service companies, there is generally no opportunity for an inspector to stand around to ensure the customer only gets perfect service. The experience the customer has with the staff they actually meet face-to-face is what determines quality. The service is delivered in millions of 'moments of truth'. You can of course teach front-line staff a standard way of delivering good service. The problem comes when staff are asked to deal with non-standard situations. That is where employees need to be empowered '*to do the right thing for the customer at the time'* (see Ladder 9 on Staff Empowerment). That means sometimes giving employees the authority to act without reference.

And far from being irresponsible, our experience is that non-managers take their responsibility very seriously when empowered to act. For example, when Avis empowered front-line staff to do it right for the customer at the time, a number of directors were afraid they might 'give away the shop'. In practice they found that it was directors who were more likely to 'give away the shop'. One company who really accepts the point, the Ritz-Carlton Hotel chain, gives every employee the authority to spend up to $2,000 if they need to, to make sure any customer problems are resolved at the time. That is truly taking customer service seriously. And it is only when you do that, that customer complaints will eventually come down to zero.

IDEAS AND TECHNIQUES YOU CAN USE

This section covers several quality improvement and problem-solving procedures real companies have found work well in practice. They are:

- check-lists;
- Pareto charts;
- fishbone diagrams;
- Customer Partnership Analysis;
- structured brainstorming.

Check-lists

One of the easiest – and most neglected – ways of ensuring everything is in place before starting work, ie *preventing* errors, is to compose and use simple check-lists. One of the reasons it is safer to travel on aeroplanes than any other form of transport, is that pilots, no matter how experienced they are, religiously go through their pre-take-off check-lists before they start flying. It is the most basic form of discipline any company can use who is serious about safety or quality.

You can apply check-lists to virtually anything. Figure 5.3 is an example of an equipment cleaning check-list.

Quality is made by the good habits people get into every day. Check-lists simply encourage the use of good habits that can make good quality commonplace in your company. We would say: don't move on to anything more complicated if you aren't already using check-lists.

Pareto charts

As we explained earlier in this chapter, the 80/20 rule Pareto discovered applies to a lot of things. Often 80 per cent of a company's profits come from 20 per cent of its customers; and similarly 60–80 per cent of defects are often

No	Checkpoint	Tick
1	Have you removed all dust and oil from around the equipment?	☐
2	Have you removed dirt, oil and rubbish from underneath the equipment?	☐
3	Have you removed dirt, oil and rubbish from on top of the equipment?	☐
4	Have you removed dirt, from oil level displays, pressure gauges, etc?	☐
5	Have you removed equipment covers and removed all the dirt inside?	☐
6	Have you removed dirt and oil from pneumatic tubes, electrical wiring, etc?	☐
7	Have you removed dirt and dust from light bulbs and tubes?	☐
8	Have you removed dirt, oil and swarf from jigs and cutting tools?	☐
9	Have you removed dirt and oil from all measuring instruments?	☐
10	Have you removed dirt, dust and oil from the machine control panel?	☐

Figure 5.3 An equipment cleaning checklist

Labelling Machine No 1																		
Fault Description	1	2	3	4	5	6	7	8	9	10	11	12	13	14	15	16	17	18
Paper jam	✗	✗																
Machine cutting out	✗	✗	✗	✗	✗	✗	✗	✗	✗	✗	✗	✗	✗					
Mis-feed	✗	✗	✗	✗														
Label sticking	✗	✗																
No glue	✗																	
Etc																		

Figure 5.4 Pareto chart for problems on a bottle-labelling machine

sourced to one or two causes. If you want to isolate these causes, a Pareto chart can be a simple and effective tool to use.

Figure 5.4 is one version of a Pareto chart, used to isolate the causes of problems on a bottle-labelling machine. To start with, record the faults you think will occur in the 'Fault Description' column (use proper descriptions rather than numbers). Then, as each fault turns up, put a cross in the appropriate row. Use a reasonable time interval to record the information before you come to conclusions – several days, or a week, is usually about right. Then you'll be able to see what is causing most of the trouble.

When you do find a fault, always try to find 'permafix' solutions. That means finding a cure for the problem so it never comes back. For example, when an operator at Nissan Cars put brake fluid into radiators instead of anti-freeze, they had to undo the radiators on 45 cars, flush them out and refit them all before the cars could go out. To make sure the problem never occurred again, they put different hose fittings on the anti-freeze and brake fluid tanks so, no matter who was doing the job, they could only work one way – the right way. Don't use temporary 'Band-aid' solutions if you can help it. Put the problem to bed forever.

Fishbone diagrams

We explained the basics of this technique earlier in the chapter. Figure 5.5 is another used to identify the causes of cuts and injuries occurring in a factory producing cold meat products.

Having identified the likely causes of problems, the next step is to examine which of these most frequently gives rise to cuts and injuries, eg by examining the first aid or medical records. Thereafter, by concentrating on the most frequent first, the task is to suggest ways of overcoming the problems best, ie simply, cost-effectively, and permanently. This is where it's best to involve the working team in the process. Not only do they treat safety more seriously afterwards, they encourage their fellows to make work the ideas they themselves come up with to resolve the problems.

Customer Partnership Analysis

Serving internal customers well in the steps of any complex process is essential if in the end external customers' needs are to be consistently met. Customer Partnership Analysis (CPA) is a simple but powerful method of enabling internal suppliers to:

- clarify and agree the needs of their internal customers;
- measure the degree to which they consistently meet these needs;
- respond in a positive way to the changing needs of their customers in an organized and systematic way.

Customer Partnership Analysis is normally conducted between work-teams who act as suppliers and customers to each other, and involves six steps:

1. Identify the *customers* the team actually serves, ie those who get the result of their work. Decide what measurable outputs each of these are dependent on the team to provide. Estimate how well they believe they are doing on each of these.
2. Identify the *suppliers* to the team, ie those on whom they are dependent to be able to do a good job. This may be for materials, information, technical advice, etc. Decide what improvements in key areas they would like to see from whom, if the team were to materially improve their own performance.

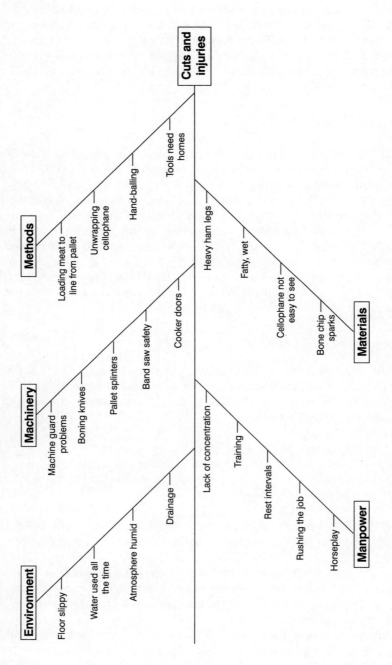

Figure 5.5 Fishbone diagram of causes of cuts and injuries in a cold meat factory

3. Appoint team members (or the Team Leader) to visit named customers, using the following outline script:

> We've been thinking about how we could improve our service to you, and we'd be grateful for your constructive input.

> What do we do well now that you appreciate and would want us to continue?

> What would you most like us to try to improve?

> If we were to concentrate on just two of your suggestions, which would be most important to you?

Note: Don't make promises or raise expectations at this stage. Simply indicate that you are grateful for their input, you will discuss their ideas with the team, and will come back to them within a defined timescale.

4. Have the Team Leader visit the team's suppliers, in order of importance, to make requests for change that would help the team improve their performance. Make deals. Don't ask for too much. Confine yourself to, say, an important two items, just as you are doing with your customers.
5. Discuss the results with the team. Decide which requests from customers you can actually deliver. Get team members to revisit the same customers to confirm the points that are to be implemented. (Note: You have to deliver on the first things you promise, otherwise your customers will never believe anything else you say. So only accept actions you can safely manage first time round.) The Team Leader should also report what 'deals' he has been able to make with the team's suppliers. Again, these should be confirmed at a second meeting.
6. Set up measures to make sure you are delivering on your customer promises. After a couple of months, repeat the exercise. Repeat every two months. That way you will be aware of changing customer requirements, and you will successfully establish a culture of continuous improvement. Later, you can hold Customer Partnership TOMs (see Ladder 1 for a discussion on the TOM process), in which two departments hold a joint session to agree more deeply on how they can work more effectively together.

Structured brainstorming

Brainstorming – as the name implies – is a technique designed to generate a large number of ideas from a group in a relatively short time. Used in a structured way, it is an effective problem-solving technique that can be used in many contexts, not only to solve problems with quality. For example:

- to produce creative ideas for new products, new services, etc;
- to identify the causes of problems;

- to produce ideas for solutions;
- to identify possible problems in implementing solutions.

Here's how to brainstorm:

1. *Show the rules of brainstorming on a flip chart:*

   (a) quantity first;
   (b) suspend judgement;
   (c) free wheel;
   (d) cross-fertilize.

   Explain what each rule means: *quantity first* = generate large numbers of ideas, quality will come from later selection; *suspend judgement* = no evaluation or criticism, ask for explanations, if necessary, but don't kill first ideas with scornful comments; *free wheel* = let go of inhibitions, have fun; *cross-fertilize* = build on others' ideas.
2. *Conduct a warm-up session.* This is especially useful if team members have not been involved in a brainstorming session before. Conduct a brainstorm session for example on: 'All the other uses for a . . .', eg a brick, glass, saucer, etc. And have a bit of fun.
3. *Conduct the brainstorm session.* You can use one of two ways to seek ideas. Either go repeatedly round the room asking each team member for one idea (that ensures everyone gets involved early). Or take ideas from anyone in any order. Write all the ideas on a flip chart. Post up each flip chart separately. Ensure each page can be viewed by the group throughout the session. Number each item. It will help later to identify specific ideas and also motivate the group. For example, if you have 83 ideas, the comment 'Only 17 more ideas and we've got a century' will virtually always get you to 100.
4. *Sift and prioritize.* With the team's help, try organizing the ideas into groups or categories. With a bit of structure, the ideas are better understood. Discuss the value and practicality of the ideas listed, whether some could be used effectively together, etc. Then give everyone three votes to vote for three ideas they think will have most impact in resolving the problem they are considering. Put red tick marks against each person's choices. You will usually find the votes agglomerate round the same items. It is a very simple procedure but very effective in narrowing down the choices with all-round agreement of the group.
5. *Actions and dates.* Agree which actions should be taken first. Allocate Prime Contractors and agreed completion dates. Draw up a matrix calendar of events, showing people responsible on one axis and dates on the other. Ensure there is a logical sequence to the actions. Build in interim reviews when appropriate on specific dates.

CONCLUSION

Managing for Quality starts right at the design stage in any company, whether it is the design of a product or a service. Steps need to be taken right at the beginning to ensure the product will fit the identified customer want, to do it reliably, cost-effectively, attractively, and to do it better than the competition. Since complexity is the enemy of reliable quality, companies should attempt at this stage to make the product and processes as simple as they can. Then they have to ensure they have the capacity, capability and trained staff to deliver. All this is not easy, but building in quality in the initial stages is crucial.

In quality-conscious companies, they don't give quality responsibility to anyone other than those doing the job. All are trained to recognize what a good job looks like. They know their customer is the next person in the process. When they do discover defects, they act immediately. They use the 5 Why's technique to get right back to the source of the problem, and implement 'permafix' solutions, ie they don't dab ointment, they cure the problem once for all.

Quality First companies design their systems to fit their drive for quality. They don't continue with pay systems that only focus on output. They teach staff to identify their internal customers and to make 'contracts' with them; staff know that quality is not what the producer says it is, it is what the customer says it is. They install two-point inspection and mistake-proofing devices. They strive for zero defect quality and know it is actually achievable.

S i x

Eliminating Waste

LEVELS	MEASURES
Level 1	Managers think that being busy means they are being productive. Things are rushed, people turn up late at meetings, etc. When you talk to them about improving the systems they use, they say 'We're too busy working for all that!'
Level 2	People understand that all activities that do not add value to the product or service are waste. Managers realize that operators watching machines working is not work, it's waste. Teams start to use Business Process Improvement charts to identify waste. Managers use time management techniques to improve their time utilization.
Level 3	Process waste reduced by at least 20%, eg scrap, rework, order cycle time, process steps, transport, etc. Process Mapping used everywhere. Operators look after two or more jobs or machines. Study groups meet to discuss how to reduce waste using the SPECS procedure.
Level 4	Process waste reduced by at least 50%. The overall actual work ratio has reached 75% or higher. Operators manage whole groups of machines. Managers plan what specific value they will add every day. Equipment breakdowns are virtually eliminated.
Level 5	The actual work ratio is at least 85%. The whole company is purposely organized to minimize waste. Stock-holding – of raw materials, in-process work, and finished goods – is the lowest in the industry. Even new employees can follow procedures easily. New processes are designed to maximize added-value activity.

INTRODUCTION

The most telling characteristic of 'waste' is that people aren't aware of it. To most people waste has to do with material waste, scrap, rejects and things that are thrown away. That is not how waste is defined in this chapter and in world class companies. Waste is any activity that does not add value. 'Adding value' means: *changing the product or information in some way that is of value to the customer*. The customer in this case may be an external customer (the end user of the information or product) or it may be an internal customer, ie the next person in the process.

For example, in the washing machine factory, they may first bend the metal sheets to form the shapes of the top, bottom and sides of the machine. That's 'adding value', ie changing the material in some way that will be of value to the later operators who assemble the machine. The shaped metal parts then go to the paint spray booth. If some of these metal shapes were split or damaged before they entered the spray booth, they will have to be discarded on exit. That's waste – and not just for the cost of the metal and the paint – but for the time spent loading and unloading useless parts, storing them somewhere using valuable space, having them collected, transported and discarded, feeding back information to the press shop about the problems they are causing, etc. It costs five times as much to rectify a problem as to get it right first time.

It may look different in the office, but waste is there just the same. In the finance department, all the information may not have come in on time from the various departments, so office staff have to phone up to remind them. That's waste. The data only comes through at the last minute, so staff have to work overtime. That's waste. Sales people have submitted their sales orders to calculate their commissions, but data is missing or is illegible. Staff have to contact salespeople to verify information. That's waste. Some of them are uncontactable, so delays are inevitable, and additional phone calls have to be made. That's all waste.

It has been said that factories and offices are virtual storehouses of waste. The Japanese have a word for it. It's *muda*. This is how they list 'the seven sins of *muda*':

1. Making mistakes.
2. Duplication.
3. Waiting, delay.
4. Excessive transport or motion.
5. Overproduction.
6. Overstocking.
7. Run-outs.

The good news is: it takes time and effort, but it's all preventable. And the even better news is: every £ or $ saved falls right to the company's bottom line. If there is anything to explain the Japanese ability to land products in countries abroad at a cost lower than home countries can make themselves, it has been their assiduous attention to eliminating waste. That is what this Ladder is all about.

LEVEL 1

Walking into the warehouse to check on stock in most instances would be considered as *adding value*, whereas in truth it is either duplication or distrusting a system that already makes mistakes! In many factories the perception is that provided people have got their heads down they must be working hard and therefore being productive. Managers don't have time for meetings, are too busy to consider improvements and are more concerned with *activity* than *output*.

When customer surveys are conducted internally, employees generally don't know who the company's major customers are, they don't know what their service levels criteria are, and they have absolutely no idea that adding value is what the customer pays for.

'Managers think that being busy means they are being productive'

This is a sure sign of a Level 1 company. Typical signs are: managers' desks are laden with paper, some appear a shambles; managers' diaries are so full they find difficulty getting anything more in; at a late date and *ad hoc*, managers will move a meeting they have already fixed, causing everyone to scramble to rearrange things at the last minute; senior managers feel it is their privilege to do so, and the frustration cascades down the organization; everything appears to be urgent; managers give you the impression that they are overburdened with work; they take work home as it is the only place where they can get the necessary peace and quiet.

'Things are rushed, people turn up late at meetings, etc'

Again, there are typical examples: meetings do not start on time; people will come late to meetings keeping everyone else waiting, and appear to think nothing of it. The 'month end rush' is another example, ie everybody works frantic overtime in the last week of the month to achieve the figures and the despatches, compromising quality on the way. This is followed by a 'relaxation period' in the first two weeks of the month as staff and managers 'catch their breath'. Far from worrying about the bad habits they get into as a result, managers may even take a macho pride in how they 'did it again'.

Unfortunately, overtime becomes the ready answer to every problem, which in turn encourages the tendency never to deliver anything on time. And as it builds up, overtime can often amount to 40 per cent or more of employees' work time. That's a financial and human cost any company can do without.

'When you talk to them about improving the systems they use, they say "We're too busy working for all that!"'

The great fallacy here is that managers think that being busy is being effective. In fact, there is a strong correlation between ineffectiveness and 'busyness'. When you suggest stopping the merry-go-round to stand back and take a look at the systems they use, typical comments are: 'We can't take two days out of the working week to think about how we work together, or about our strategy. We're all too busy.' Or 'The place would fall apart if I weren't here for two days.'

What seems to persuade managers that the last remark is true is the number of times subordinates bring everyday operating problems to them for a quick answer (a safe one!). All that tells you is how poorly trained or trusted that manager's staff are, or how he needs the repeated strokes of appearing to be needed. All that rushing about and waiting around for answers adds no value to the product at all, just extra cost. Managers who manage daily in this rush and butterfly mode are definitely Level 1.

LEVEL 2

'People understand that all activities that do not add value to the product or service are waste'

Level 2 companies are those where employees have been taught in simple, everyday language what creates value and what makes waste. The definition of added value is 'any change in the material or information that is of value to the customer'. For example, in a garment factory, cutting out the dress shapes correctly from rolls of material adds value as it allows the seamstress next in line to sew a fault-free dress. In the office, taking all the order information from buyers and turning it into a work schedule adds value as it tells work staff just what to make and how many. In a multi-step process, the customer is the next person in the line, ie the person who receives the output of your work. The most important customer is the end user, ie the customer who pays everybody's salary. It is important to teach employees that everything that happens inside the business only adds cost; and that the only real income comes from customers outside the business.

It comes as quite a shock to managers and staff to realize that so much of what they do is actually waste, ie if you define work only as that which adds value for the customer. For example, virtually every company uses inspection of some kind, yet this does not change the product in any way, and therefore is classified as waste. (The alternative obviously is for the person doing the job to be responsible for their own quality and to do it right the first time, as was discussed in Ladder 5 on Managing for Quality). Companies transport things back and forth on their premises; they take things out of store and put them on the floor, they transport them between departments, they transport them back to the store, etc. Transport does not change the product at all, ie it adds no value. The customer does not care how many times material has been transported around your premises; he is not willing to pay any more for that.

Then again, *people* go back and forth between departments, to the store, to see others, to check things, etc. None of this changes the product either in any way. Again, this adds cost but no extra value. Sometimes companies store huge amounts of stock, eg many months' worth, some of which may be obsolescent or obsolete, all of which costs money to house and keep in good condition. All that storage again only adds costs and no extra value. Re-work is often seen as a good thing, ie it changes our non-saleable product into saleable product. But since the product should have been made right the first time, all the extra work is additional cost that cannot be recovered from the customer.

Managers and staff often feel taken aback when confronted with these examples. We see this exercise as giving them a pair of 'waste glasses' – suddenly they see waste everywhere. This is a bit like the hypnotist who tells his subject that when they put on his 'special' glasses, the people they look at will have no clothes on. Soon they start giggling because they can see things they couldn't see before. That's just how it should be when staff are educated about waste. They will see opportunities everywhere.

'Managers realize that operators watching machines working is not work, it's waste'

Toyota originally highlighted the fact that often their machines were written down in the books to a zero balance, and therefore cost only a pittance to run (ie the electricity and on-going maintenance costs). Whereas the cost of running machines kept falling each year, the cost of employing people kept going up as a result of pay rises etc. Toyota reckoned on average that it was costing five times as much per hour to employ a person than to run a machine. As a result, they stopped trying to occupy their machine capacity all day and concentrated more on getting added value work from their employees all day.

This led them to have operators operate more than one machine. To help this process they developed a U-shaped machine layout rather than a straight-line configuration so that operators could more readily move from machine to machine. The fact is that on average today an operator in the Toyota car works operates five machines.

In many Western manufacturing companies managers appear to find nothing wrong in their skilled personnel standing watching their machines working. This is anathema to companies intent on removing waste. There is also a tendency among Western management to feel that idle maintenance staff is a good thing, ie the machines must then all be working. Under the eliminating waste scenario we never expect skilled maintenance people to be idle. When there are no machines broken down needing their attention, we expect them to be doing project work, ie finding solutions and modifications to eliminate recurrent faults, to be teaching operators how to do extended routine maintenance, to be undertaking projects to help machines deliver more consistent quality, etc. We need to find ways of using skilled staff's time as productively as possible.

'Teams start to use Business Process Improvement charts to identify waste'

A useful way of demonstrating to managers and staff where all the waste occurs in the company is to use the technique known as 'Process Mapping'. Staff are taught the six symbols used for mapping a process, and to distinguish between those that add value and those that add waste. Figure 6.1 shows the symbols and their meanings. Table 6.1 shows that only one category adds value. Everything else is waste.

Operation	○	Any value-adding step that moves the process forward
Transport	⇨	Any step that moves objects, information or people
Delay	D	Any unplanned delay to material, information or authorizing decisions
Inspection	□	Includes inspections, checks or signatures
Storage	▽	Planned delay to materials or products
Rework	Ⓡ	Any unnecessary or repeated operational step

Figure 6.1 Business process improvement symbols

Table 6.1 Symbol classification

		Added value	Waste
Operation	○	✖	
Transport	⇨		✖
Delay (unscheduled)	D		✖
Inspection	□		✖
Storage (scheduled)	▽		✖
Re-work	Ⓡ		✖

Source: Harbour (1994)

In training sessions the basics of Process Mapping should be taught with examples and exercises, and then an actual process should be mapped. Start with a relatively short process (see the simple example of filling out a purchase requisition shown in Table 6.4 on page 140, for instance), and only then move to more complicated ones.

Note that streamlining processes often involves cutting out steps and delegating authority, and managers can sometimes find this difficult. For example, operators may have been given full responsibility for quality but managers still feel awkward not sending products to 'inspection' – just in case. Administrative staff may be required to make their own decisions, but managers can feel uncomfortable about not having signatures as a way of checking before goods are dispatched, items bought, or letters sent. Thus, process improvement often requires changing the mind-sets of those in positions of authority. But the basic idea still comes down to concentrating only on the actions that add value, and cutting out those which don't.

Exercise

A key way to test how much waste is involved in a process is by examining how long the *elapsed time* is between an order being placed, and finally being delivered to the customer. Compare that with the time actually spent in activities that add value. We often find this ratio to be 8:1 or more, ie an order may actually take one week of added value operating time to produce, but the customer is quoted an eight-week delivery date. This technique – comparing elapsed time with added value time – is an excellent way to highlight the opportunities that exist for saving waste in any company

---

'Managers use time management techniques to improve their time utilization'

Managers often say they could arrange their time much better if it weren't for other people – they are the real problem. They send you letters that need replies, they call you to meetings, they phone at the most inconvenient times, and generally disrupt your day. But managers need to accept that much of their day will be taken up with reacting to other people's requirements. That we term 'reactive time'. That's part of managers' everyday life. However, the in-basket should not control the manager's life completely. They have to spend at least part of every day devoted to doing the important parts of their job, those where they can make a *unique contribution* – that we call 'proactive time'.

So, what should the proportions be exactly? That depends on the job. If you are a manager with a number of subordinates or colleagues with whom you have to interact, then perhaps less than 50 per cent of your time can be put in the 'proactive' category. The more senior you are, the less likely you are able to control the amount of proactive time you can deliver. Then again, if you are serving customers face to face, more than 80 per cent of your time may be spent 'reacting' to their needs.

Normally, any manager should be able to devote two hours or more each day to the major objectives of the job, ie on the positive tasks that will make a difference to the performance of their department or the business. That may depend on getting enough uninterrupted time to get something worthwhile done. That is a common management problem. The only way managers can regularly get some UDT (undisturbed time) is to make agreements with their boss, colleagues and subordinates. Here's what one group of managers decided to do to get over the problem.

They agreed that they would take their UDT in chunks of one and a half hours. Why one and a half hours? Because you can get something useful done in an hour and a half. And there is seldom anything so urgent that a colleague can't wait for that length of time without any real problem. They also agreed that UDT would be taken between the hours of 11.00 and 12.30 pm and between 2.00 and 3.30 pm. That way, they knew that they could interact on small matters three times a day (before 11.00; between 12.30 and 2.00; and after 3.30). But they all knew they could have some useful undisturbed time without having to leave the building!

There is a great tendency for the urgent to crowd out the important all the time. Effective managers know they have to manage their scarcest resource – their time – in a positive way to get important things done.

LEVEL 3

'Process waste reduced by at least 20 per cent, for example scrap, re-work, order cycle time, process steps, transport, etc'

'Process Mapping used everywhere'

At this stage employees have started with Process Mapping and have reduced waste by at least 20 per cent, ie scrap, re-work, order cycle time, the number of process steps, inspection, transport, storage, etc. In their teams workers are now looking after two or more machines. They meet in their Team Meeting Areas to discuss how waste can be reduced as part of an overall improvement process.

When they look at their own work processes in detail, they use the following basic rules on each of the process steps they identify. The aim is to:

- *eliminate*: but if that's not possible, then
- *reduce*;
- *simplify*: in fact, see how simple you can make it;
- *combine*: ie with another step or function.

Not only are there benefits in each such exercise, but there are even more benefits in getting the participants into a frame of mind where they are continuously thinking about which process steps they can now either simplify, reduce, combine or eliminate. Getting that new mind-set is absolutely crucial.

And with practice they get very good at it. Don't leave it all to managers, we say. Get every brain and pair of eyes working on the task every day.

Here are some other words of advice:

1. *Reducing order cycle time.* Companies should set bold targets. For example, at one pottery company, although the sales force quoted customers an eight-week delivery time, the fact was that 70% of their customers were receiving their goods between 9 and 12 weeks later. In this context, companies are encouraged to set themselves bold goals, eg 'within six months, no export order will take longer to deliver from the date of order than six weeks maximum'. It needs to be a bold goal to get people to sit up and think 'out of the box'. Furthermore, such a bold goal is appropriate when, as in this case, there is no product in the company that actually takes longer than five days to make! The rest is all turbulence and delay caused by the current systems and processes. Setting bold goals starts attacking waste at its root, and can make a real difference to the company's business.

2. *Reducing transport.* As an example, in conducting one Process Mapping exercise at one manufacturing company, we discovered that there was only one fork-lift truck between two groups who worked 300 yards away from each other. As a result much time and effort was wasted moving up and down to fetch the fork-lift truck – it never seemed to be where it needed to be at the right time! Transporting raw materials, work-in-progress and finished goods all adds cost – and no value. It is also worth looking into how the company stores its products. For example, one cosmetics manufacturing company we know used about seven warehouses for their finished goods, which they then moved back and forth at great expense to try to satisfy customer demand.

3. *Scrap and re-work.* There is a tendency for production managers to regard only scrap as waste. As can be seen from the seven sins of *muda* (described in more detail in Ideas and Techniques You Can Use section) this is far from the truth. However, some companies have become so good at reducing scrap that instead of measuring this in percentages (ie parts per hundred) they now have so little that they have to measure it in parts per million! Note that companies who get down to this level in measuring scrap may be around a thousand times better than their counterparts who are still measuring in percentages! When people say 'I don't think there is much more we can do to improve in this area', we remind them that the ability to improve is forever and close to infinite.

'Operators look after two or more jobs or machines'

This implies that staff have been involved in multi-skills training to improve their value to both the company and themselves (see Ladder 12 on Continuous Learning for more on this). That kind of versatility has particular advantages:

1. Staff can cover for their colleagues when they are off sick or on training courses.
2. No critical process need be held up for want of skilled staff.
3. Staff will be occupied more of the time doing productive added-value work.

'Study groups meet to discuss how to reduce waste using the SPECS procedure'

In the same way as we encourage staff to put on their 'waste glasses' when looking around them, so we like them to use the five-step SPECS procedure to tackle the business of making improvements systematically. This is what SPECS means:

Study the problem.
Plan your improvement.
Execute your plan.
Check you get the planned improvements in practice.
Standardize the new procedure.

1. *Study the problem.* By that we mean: don't jump into solution mode before you have analysed the causes of the problem. Collect hard data. Study the data to see what it is telling you. Often the data points out a cure.
2. *Plan your improvement.* Decide who is going to do what, when. Sometimes it's simple and straightforward. If it's more complicated, produce an action sequence calendar.
3. *Execute your plan.*
4. *Check you get the planned improvements in practice.* That means collecting hard data as before, to make sure the improvements you anticipated actually materialize. If they do. . .
5. *Standardize the new procedure.* Once you have found the best way you have yet devised, make sure you tell everyone involved, and that they adopt the new method. Don't let it escape; capture it for ever. In other words, put it in the BOP manual! (See Ladder 7 on Best Operating Practices.)

LEVEL 4

'Process waste reduced by at least 50 per cent'

A company has reached the heights of Level 4 when it has reduced its original level of waste by more than 50 per cent. It may well take a number of years to get there. First, the company will have taught every one of its employees what waste looks like. They will all understand the seven sins of *muda* (see ideas and techniques you can use), and know that transport, storage, unplanned delays, inspections, etc all add time and cost but no value as far as the customer is concerned. Any company who has managed to reduce its waste by more than 50 per cent will have educated all its people and involved them in the task. It cannot be done by confining the job to management alone.

'The overall actual work ratio has reached 75 per cent or higher'

This indicates that the added-value steps in each process amount to 75 per cent or more of the total time taken to do the work. This is a level that can take years of continuous improvement to achieve. One way that helps is to ensure that no *new* processes are installed that don't exceed the 75 per cent added-value hurdle. Then gradually the older processes can be improved and streamlined – or be entirely revamped – to come up to the new standard. One of the secrets is to be patient, to keep making small improvements, but to stay at it forever.

'Managers plan what specific value they will add every day'

When managers have established the unique contributions of their job (detailed in Ladder 9 on Staff Empowerment and Involvement), they know the specific outputs required of their job and how their performance will be measured. However, they realize they have to allocate their time sensibly between working alone and working effectively with others.

It's next to impossible for a manager to spend all of his time 'proactively'. But it's unsatisfactory for the manager to spend all of his time merely 'reacting' to what comes over the telephone and into the in-basket. These are the days when managers say 'Well, I've been rushing about all day, but I don't seem to have *done* anything.' The key job of the manager is not to keep himself busy, but to get the *right things* done, and his unique contributions list tells him exactly what that is.

The higher a position is in the organization, the harder it gets to use time 'proactively'. But it is essential. At junior level in specialist functions (like engineering or Research and Development) it may be possible to spend as much as 80 per cent of one's time on 'proactive' work. At senior management level, the figure may legitimately be only 20 per cent. So, managers should not fret about spending so much of their time 'reacting' to others – teamwork is an essential part of the job. But they should not go home any day without spending at least 20 per cent of their time making the specific contributions they are uniquely being paid for.

'Equipment breakdowns are virtually eliminated'

Part of Total Productive Maintenance (TPM) is to reach a point when there are no machine breakdowns at all! Yes, we really mean what we say. In Ladder 3 on Cleaning and Organizing it was suggested that operators become the army of the maintenance people, in doing daily checks of their machinery to note if there are any abnormalities, such as vibration, overheating, loose parts, etc. In other words, the idea is to make timely small adjustments where they can, but to *forewarn* the maintenance specialists and before abnormalities become breakdowns. Surprising as it may seem, it is actually possible to have no breakdowns at all!

LEVEL 5

'The actual work ratio is at least 85 per cent'

Achievement ratios are now at 85 per cent and over time the organization has developed a synergy of improvements in the other eleven Ladders. Layout improvements have resulted in a 75 per cent reduction in work-in-progress. The development of minor inventory stores between processes, and the virtual elimination of conveyance, have also helped boost the achievement ratio. By the time a company genuinely reaches Level 5, you can be sure they have been working at it for years!

'The whole company is purposely organized to minimize waste'

In manufacturing companies this means that the company has now laid out processes so that whole products or units of products can be made in the same area (with machinery often in U-shaped formations), with no transport, delays or stock-holding between the steps of the process, and in a way in which process operators can handle the work with ease. Kanban arrangements – where defined amounts only of product are made, and where operators know from the kanban cards exactly what they have to make, how much and when, and how and where their completed units are to be delivered – mean the required product, and only the required product, gets made in a timely fashion across the company.

In office-based companies, staff have been organized into units that can handle the client's needs in one area without time-consuming hand-overs to other departments, their computer data systems mean everything to do with the customer can be brought quickly up on-screen, they use one database from which everyone works, and they have short time standards for resolving customer problems, knowing that taking longer only irritates customers and adds cost. The company has reduced its cost base by flattening the hierarchical pyramid, and delegating responsibility to act so that staff can do it right for the customer *at the time*.

When companies have taken the time and effort to plan their recurrent processes with detailed care, and have squeezed waste out of their systems successively over the years, the everyday processes move along automatically, and the one-off exceptions become the minority of the business to be dealt with every day.

'Stock-holding – of raw materials, in-process work, and finished goods – is the lowest in the industry'

Holding stock costs money, so many companies apply a 'stock turns' measure to get themselves focused on reducing waste in this area. 'Stock turns' is arrived at by dividing the total value of stocks held – ie raw materials, in-process work, and already finished goods – into the company's total sales value. We have been in manufacturing companies where the stock turn figure is less than two (ie holding more than six month's stock) whereas the figure may be as high as 100 or more at world class level (ie two days' stock). Industries are different, so one cannot make hard and fast rules, but we would expect Level 5 manufacturing companies to achieve levels in excess of 25.

This is not easy to do, of course. But companies with low stock levels find they have much more space available, there is less to transport, less to label and keep records on, less paperwork, less obsolescence. And stock-taking takes less time, and they make fewer errors doing so. All this is waste-saving and cost-saving, and, importantly, the savings are permanent.

'Even new employees can follow procedures easily'

At Level 5 procedures have been simplified, it is visually easy to see how the process works, there are instructions on every single machine, Best Operating Practices have been written for every job (see Ladder 7), everything is labelled, there is a home for everything and everything is in its home, and tools and materials are in clearly marked places. Of course, new employees may have to develop skills, and that takes time. But their training should not depend on untapped secrets hiding in the heads of those currently doing the job.

'New processes are designed to maximize added-value activity'

When new processes are designed in the Level 5 company, those in charge use Process Mapping to make sure they only include activities that add value. They deliberately 'manage for quality' (see Ladder 5) at the outset. They build into the process at this design stage mistake-proofing devices; they avoid duplication and the likelihood of delays or hold-ups; they build in two-point inspection into sequential processes; they make cycle times as short as possible. And they get ownership from the people who will operate the process by involving the staff concerned (who have already been trained in added value and waste avoidance) in setting up the process to make it easy, reliable and cost-effective.

IDEAS AND TECHNIQUES YOU CAN USE

In this section, we will deal with the following:

- eliminating waste – goals and principles;
- Process Mapping – identifying areas of waste;
- the seven sins of *muda* – an explanation;
- the '5 Why's' – getting to the root of the problem.

Eliminating waste – goals and principles

As we indicated in Ladder 3, Cleaning and Organizing, the goals of eliminating waste and streamlining processes is to do the job:

- *easier*: less stretching, bending, twisting and straining;
- *better*: improving quality for the customer, reducing defects and scrap;
- *cheaper*: reducing costs, streamlining processes, cutting delays, using fewer resources;
- *faster*: improving throughput and productivity;
- *safer*: removing hazards likely to cause injury.

Note: we only do it faster when we have worked on the 'better' bit first, ie we don't want to speed up making more scrap!

In tackling problems and making process improvements, use the five-step SPECS procedure:

- **S**tudy the problem, ie collect hard data.
- **P**lan your improvement, ie who will do what, when.
- **E**xecute your plan.
- **C**heck you get the planned improvements in practice.
- **S**tandardize the new procedure, ie put it in the BOP!

Some basic rules to follow in making process improvements:

1. Eliminate waste altogether. If you can't do that, then do point 2.
2. Minimize waste.
3. Simplify everything. See how simple you can actually make it.
4. Combine process steps wherever possible.
5. Think parallel, not linear, ie do things concurrently where possible, rather than one after the other.
6. Collect data once, at its source.
7. Use technology to improve processes.
8. Let customers help in the process. Generally, they are most willing.

Process Mapping

Look back at Figure 6.1 (page 129) that shows the symbols used in Process Mapping and their meaning. Now look at Table 6.2 and ask yourself, 'What symbol would you place next to each process step?' The answers are shown in Table 6.3.

Table 6.2 Process analysis

No	Process step	Minutes	Process symbol					
			○	⟡	D	□	▽	®
1	Assembling two components							
2	Repeating a step in a process							
3	Searching for information							
4	Moving materials							
5	Checking a report							
6	Waiting for a meeting to begin							
7	Re-entering data a second time							
8	Walking to a stores area							
9	Faxing information							
10	Storing material in a warehouse							
11	Capturing data once at its source							
12	Performing a QC inspection							
13	Waiting for a print-out							
14	Signing a request for action							
15	Leaving a form in an in-basket							
16	Experiencing a scheduled delay							

Source: Harbour (1994)

Table 6.3 Process analysis answers

No	Process step	Minutes	Process symbol					
			○	◊	D	□	▽	®
1	Assembling two components		✔					
2	Repeating a step in a process							✔
3	Searching for information				✔			
4	Moving materials			✔				
5	Checking a report					✔		
6	Waiting for a meeting to begin				✔			
7	Re-entering data a second time							✔
8	Walking to a stores area			✔				
9	Faxing information			✔				
10	Storing material in a warehouse						✔	
11	Capturing data once at its source		✔					
12	Performing a QC inspection					✔		
13	Waiting for a print-out				✔			
14	Signing a request for action					✔		
15	Leaving a form in an in-basket				✔			
16	Experiencing a scheduled delay						✔	

Source: Harbour (1994)

Using the symbols and the tables given as an example, a process can readily be examined in terms of what elements add value and what elements are *waste*. Table 6.4 illustrates this, using the example of making a purchase via a simple requisition form process.

As can be seen, in this simple process only 28 minutes are identified as value-adding activities, and 2,457 minutes are designated as 'waste'. That means in the total cycle time of 2,485 minutes, less than 2 per cent is value-adding activity!

Table 6.4 Process analysis: purchase requisition

No	Process step	Minutes	○	◊	D	□	▽	®
					Process symbol			
1	Requisition form raised	10	✔					
2	Form put in post to boss (for authorizing signature)	720		✔				
3	Form sits in in-basket	75			✔			
4	Form reviewed and signed	12				✔		
5	Form sits in out-basket	90			✔			
6	Form put back in post to originator	720		✔				
7	Form sits in in-basket	45			✔			
8	Form put in post to Purchasing	720		✔				
9	Form sits in in-basket	75			✔			
10	Purchasing order items requested from supplier	18	✔					

Source: Harbour (1994)

These type of activities happen in many, many companies. The scope for waste-saving is quite enormous. In this case, if the originator was given the authority to purchase items for the job up to a certain value, and had been given a list of approved suppliers from which the item in question could be bought, then clearly all that work-stopping delay could be avoided. And it makes life simpler for three different people: the member of staff concerned does not have to write an explanatory justification; the person's boss is relieved of reading the explanation and signing the requisition; the buyer does not have to make the phone call or start phoning the member of staff back if there is a detailed problem, etc. Cutting waste simplifies life as well.

Waste: the seven sins of muda

1. *Making mistakes.* For example: mistakes that create rework and scrap. Having to do things twice, three, four times or more because the job wasn't done right the first time. Typically the worst examples of mistakes are those that exist between functions. For example: in a foundry the supervisor in the pattern shop supplies either a damaged or the wrong pattern to the foundry; the operator in the machine shop drills holes that are 1mm out before supplying the part to assembly; reservations supply the list of guests to the hotel a day late; the typist fails to spell check a document going to an important customer, etc.

2. *Duplication.* Here are some examples. People checking other people's work (where two people are doing the same thing, one is not required). Having to get several hierarchical signatures to get things done or approved. Keeping the same figures in different departments (because they can't trust each other). Duplication of facilities. Double handling. Typical of the duplication examples we see are: purchasing department checking the stores on a daily basis because they don't believe the computer; the sales representative being accompanied by the sales manager because 'it is important' for the sales manager to be there; a leave form having to be submitted to the applicant's manager, his manager, the regional manager, the human resources department and the salaries department.

3. *Waiting, delay.* For example: time wasted, space occupied (eg goods waiting) to no useful purpose. People holding their colleagues up by arriving late (eg for meetings), or not having work done when they said they would. Delayed decisions (generally from several levels up) preventing people from getting on with the job. Other typical examples: sales waiting on a pricing decision from finance to effect a sales promotion; a line manager having to wait on authority from a human resources officer to grant leave; products having to be left half-finished because vital parts have not arrived; insurance claimants having to wait because the key decision-making person is on holiday; etc.

4. *Excessive transport or motion.* Transport does not add value (ie make a change to the product or information) – it only adds cost. Therefore make transport lines as short as possible or eliminate them altogether. Shorten, simplify, or reduce the movements needed by operators to get the job done. Typical examples include: bad plant layout; equipment being 'shared' between departments; sending out incomplete loads or orders, requiring second shipments as a result.

5. *Overproduction.* Only produce what the customer needs when he needs it. Otherwise you only have to store it, transport it, double handle it, etc. All of which costs money that we cannot realize from the customer. Typical examples include: making for stock rather than to customer's order; keeping products in the store 'in case it's needed one day'; having significant obsolescence in product ranges; writing long reports to impress when short ones would do.

6. *Overstocking.* For example: overstocking of raw materials, work-in-progress, or finished goods. Every £ or $ of reduction is that amount of cost you don't have to finance, handling you can avoid, and space you don't have to use. And don't just look in the building named 'store'. Examine maintenance stores and office stores as well as production stocks. Examine departmental sub-stores too. If you do decide to go for smaller stocks, however, you have to have fail-safe procedures. Think it all through carefully first, then proceed step by step.

7. *Run-outs.* A typical 'run-out' is not having all the materials required to hand and on time to do the job. Worst of all is running out of the product the customer actually wants. Typical causes include: buyers forgetting to order; users forgetting to tell the buyer on time; displaying a product that is not in stock; promoting a product you haven't made yet; negotiating lead times that you know you can't meet.

The '5 Why's'

Often when people are tackling a problem, they will come up with a 'that will do for now' solution. We say: 'Don't dab ointment – cure the disease!' In other words, we always want to be looking for 'permafix' solutions, ie solving the problem once and for all so it never comes back.

The '5 Why's' is a very simple – but very effective – way of helping people get to the root cause of a problem. Here are some examples:

Example 1

1. Question   Why did the machine stop?
   Answer   Because the fuse blew due to an overload.
2. Question   Why was there an overload?
   Answer   Because the bearing lubrication was inadequate.
3. Question   Why was the lubrication inadequate?
   Answer   Because the lubrication pump wasn't working right.
4. Question   Why wasn't the lubrication pump working right?
   Answer   Because the pump axle was worn out.
5. Question   Why was it worn out?
   Answer   Because sludge got in.

Example 2

1. Question   Why do you have to do checking?
   Answer   Because I get mistakes.
2. Question   Why do you get mistakes?
   Answer   Because Jo inputs data inaccurately.
3. Question   Why does she input data inaccurately?
   Answer   Because the salesmen's writing is difficult to read.
4. Question   Why is their writing difficult to read?
   Answer   Because the space on the form is too small to fit their writing in.
5. Question   Why is the space on the form too small?
   Answer   Because it was originally designed for less information.

You may not have to ask five questions to get to the root cause. On the other hand, you may have to ask more questions. In the end, the purpose is to encourage employees not to put up with temporary solutions but to cure problems once and for all.

S e v e n

Best Operating Practices and Continuous Improvement

LEVELS	MEASURES
Level 1	Staff don't want to get involved in improvement activities. They say things like: 'Why should we?', 'What's in it for us?', or 'That's management's job.' Suggestion boxes are little used or ignored.
Level 2	Company realizes there is a 'best practitioner' for any job, and that it must capture this and make it standard practice. Company starts writing Best Operating Practices (BOPs). Employees contribute at least six improvement ideas a year. At least 50% of the ideas submitted are implemented. Teams are trained in improvement techniques.
Level 3	BOPs written for all routine jobs. Employees contribute at least one improvement idea a month. Two-thirds or more of employee ideas are implemented. Team problem-solving sessions take place regularly, and teams tackle at least two major projects a year.
Level 4	BOPs now written for all jobs, and by job-holders. Employees contribute at least two improvement ideas a month. More than 75% of employee ideas are implemented. Teams tackle three major projects a year. Benchmarking visits used to seek out and use best practice.
Level 5	Employees average more than four improvement ideas a month. More than 85% of employee ideas are implemented. Teams tackle more than four major projects a year. Benchmarking *visitors* show company among the 'best in class'.

INTRODUCTION

There are two fundamental points in this chapter. First, how to specify Best Operating Practices for every job, which means capturing who does it best *now* and making that standard practice; and, second, tapping into the brain power of everybody in the business to focus on constant step-by-step improvement.

Best Operating Practice (BOP) represents:

- the best, easiest and safest way to do a job;
- the best way to preserve in-house expertise;
- a basis for training;
- a means of preventing recurrent errors;
- a discipline to maintain standards of performance;
- a way to monitor and show when improvements are actually being made.

In a nutshell, it is *the best way* anybody knows how to do a specific job. In order to find out what the best way is to do a job, we use the person (employed by the company) who is currently best at doing the job as a benchmark. A fundamental principle of BOP is that it is not optional not to do the job the 'best way' once it is known.

LEVEL 1

'Staff don't want to get involved in improvement activities'

'They say things like: "Why should we?", "What's in it for us?", or "That's management's job"

That is generally the reaction of staff or employees when they are first approached about contributing ideas that might improve how things get done. They imply that they only come here to do work and take money home, and that everything else really is management's job. They also say things like: 'You're changing our contract if you want us to give lots of ideas, and that will mean we have to have an increase in pay.' Or they will quote some marvellous idea suggested by some other person in another company, which has saved literally millions and that the individual received a reward of thousands of pounds (an actual example from the Rover Car Company). The implication behind the story is that the company better be prepared to pay out large amounts if they want the employees to play ball.

These sort of initial reactions generally frighten management and they decide not to bother, or the scheme they do set up does not get any commitment or power put behind it. That is a mistake. Non-managers are generally the biggest untapped source of ideas and improvements right inside the walls of every company. It just takes know-how and patience to bring it out.

'Suggestion boxes are little used or ignored'

Many companies have launched suggestion schemes in their companies with great fanfare and initial enthusiasm, only to end up regretting they ever started. There are several reasons why formal suggestion schemes fail:

1. Generally 25% or fewer of staff ever make a suggestion under formal schemes. Obviously that means that the majority of people (in this case 75% or more) – the very people you are trying to motivate – never ever submit a suggestion. No suggestion scheme should be for the minority. Processes are needed that engage *everybody's* brain and get their regular contributions to improvement. That means building it into the front line manager's job to encourage ideas every week of the year, and building it into the established management systems, such as the appraisal process etc.

2. Most suggestion schemes work on the basis of offering financial rewards, often related to the percentage of the savings incurred. This is done with the best of intentions, ie to excite employees about the prospect of a reward and motivate them to make suggestions. However, the practice has three serious disadvantages.

   (a) First of all, it is often difficult to quantify any savings that might be made. For example, do you take savings as estimated over one year or more? Do you wait until the savings are actually realized, or will you make an award on the basis of projected savings (which in practice often don't materialize)? This can lead to problems and arguments and be demotivating to the suggestor rather than encouraging others.

   (b) Second, some suggestions are welcomed but they may not have many savings associated with them. For example, it is difficult to come up with large savings in the personnel department or in administration, but people in those departments still need to be encouraged to make positive improvement suggestions. As a result, many staff members get alienated from the process.

   (c) Third, and more seriously, the strong implication is that staff are only motivated by money (ie managers do not have any influence in motivating or encouraging staff). The unfortunate consequence then becomes an attitude of 'Don't help management with anything unless they pay you extra money for it.' That is a serious problem – the very opposite of the attitudes that should be encouraged.

3. Companies find it very difficult to set up systems where *responses* to suggestions can be made quickly. The evaluation team may only meet once a week or once a month, the suggestion may be complicated and need investigation, it may need several signatures to be approved, which inevitably all takes time. Delay in responding is one of the most common problems with suggestion schemes, and of course it discourages those who are making suggestions as they get tired of waiting for feedback.

4. It becomes very difficult to explain to suggestors why an idea has been

rejected. It may be because the company does not think the suggestion is viable, it may have been tried before and did not work, or some engineer is already working on the idea, etc. This not only discourages the suggestor, but virtually always they complain to their colleagues that the company's suggestion scheme is not worth a light. Their negative word-of-mouth advertising then discourages others from even trying.

5. Suggestion schemes carry a heavy administrative burden, ie recording who made what suggestion, when was it made, keeping track of where the suggestion has got to, persuading technical people to take time out of their busy schedule to assess another suggestion, getting all the people in the evaluation team to turn up to the meetings, feeding back to suggestors, arranging for awards to be made, etc.

We strongly favour improvement suggestions happening in *the workplace*, by the people who know the work, and decisions being taken as near to the work area as possible, ie by the team leader or front-line manager. There are many companies who succeed in getting continuous improvement suggestions from their staff without paying any extra money. They treat it as part of everyone's job. You get much more instant reaction, and it simplifies the process considerably.

LEVEL 2

'Company realizes there is a "best practitioner" for any job, and that it must capture this and make it standard practice'

Companies will often go off on benchmarking visits to see how other companies do things. There is nothing wrong with this. On the contrary, it is one of the best ways we know of exciting employees and motivating them to make pretty fundamental and immediate changes in their working practices. However, for years these same companies will have been accepting that different employees will do the same job somewhat differently, that the job is done differently on one shift versus another, etc. But there must be a 'best way', ie the way that produces the most consistent good quality, or is the most cost-effective way, or the easiest way of doing the job. And these 'best ways' are not outside somewhere, they are right inside the walls of the business!

The very first job of the front-line manager is to capture these best practices and make them standard practice. In other words we may use ideas from all sorts of people in describing best practice, but once we know what it is, *it will not be optional not to do the job the best way we know how*. That means the company may be democratic in arriving at a description of best practice, but it then needs to become autocratic about implementing it.

By way of example, an engineering company with a large rubber plant comprising 24 operators recorded that at least 15 per cent of the product needed to be re-worked every month. Upon closer questioning the foreman revealed that five of his operators actually produced flawless work month on month with no re-work requirements. The five operators were requested to describe 'best operating practice' in their area of responsibility, and the outcome was captured and put on paper. Work-teams were then formed with each one of these operators as a team leader, and the best practices were communicated to the rest of the operators. In a matter of three months re-work fell by some 80 per cent.

That is the prize of capturing and using the best operating practices right inside your own business. Not only does the company gain a benefit, employees feel proud to have contributed. The greatest compliment you can give your own employees is to listen.

'Company starts writing Best Operating Practices (BOPs)'

Many Japanese companies have used Standard Operating Procedures (SOPs) for years. These are often written up on standard operation sheets (SOSs), are placed at every process, and are used and updated regularly. However, because the word 'standard' appears to suggest 'ordinary', and the word 'procedure' seems to suggest something dull and boring, we prefer to name these Best Operating Practice or BOPs.

We think this has two implied advantages. Most people prefer to 'do their best' naturally, and this tells them just how to do that. 'Best' also implies that we have to keep striving, and like the Olympic standard, forever improving. 'Procedure' seems to describe 'what we should do', but for us 'Practice' means it's 'what we actually do'.

This is what the BOPs should include:

1. A description of the job to be done.
2. The material and equipment involved.
3. The method to be used, including particular key points to be watched.
4. A description of what a good job looks like. Here it is good to use diagrams or pictures whenever possible. We prefer to have a finished product in model form on the wall close to the job location, and, where required, an exploded version of the parts that make up the job, where each part has its own specific name. In an office situation we like to have 'model' completed forms to guide those who are using them.
5. The measurement methods (or tools) to be used, so that the job holder will know when a good job has been done.
6. The most common faults, and how to correct variability.
7. The name of the person who wrote the BOP, and the date when it was last updated.

'Employees contribute at least six improvement ideas a year'

We find few companies can actually say that on average each of their employees is contributing even one suggestion a year. If 90 per cent of the employees are non-managers, and that is the case in most companies, that is a vast untapped resource of brain power and improvement capacity. Normally, when we put it to management audiences, they accept that it would be reasonable to expect just one modest suggestion per person per month. The heading above (six improvement ideas a year) only implies making one suggestion every two months. That shouldn't be too difficult! However, even some of the best companies in the world have found it difficult to get started on this front.

For example, when Toyota started their request for suggestions in 1962, they got around 5,000 suggestions from 8,000 employees in the year. That amounts to only 0.6 of a suggestion per person per year! Worse than that, they only implemented 34 per cent of the suggestions they received, ie they discarded two-thirds of them! But 20 years later, in 1982, approximately the same size workforce produced 1,950,000 suggestions, a fifty-fold increase. Better than that, they implemented 90 per cent of them. The fact is employees have to learn to *think about* improvements before they start to make common sense practical suggestions. You not only have to use the brain power you have available, you have to *educate* the brain power to reach its full potential, and that involves time and hard work!

'At least 50 per cent of the ideas submitted are implemented'

As you can see from the story above, this may not be achieved in the first year of asking employees to make positive improvement suggestions. In other words, Level 2 is not easy to achieve. One way of giving employees a good impression from the start is to give feedback quickly and implement early, ie employees see evidence that you are actually listening. As a standard, feedback needs to be given within one to two weeks, no longer, and implementation should take place in the week following approval. People feel proud when they see something implemented that they have suggested. These are the very feelings we want to encourage. Once this happens, people cannot resist giving you even more suggestions.

'Teams are trained in improvement techniques'

When companies first suggest to employees that they need to be trained in 'improvement techniques', they often fear the worst. They take the implication to mean that somehow the company thinks they are 'not good enough' presently, or that they are going to have to work a lot harder. To dispel these fears, we like to start teaching staff about making the job easier. (This is part of our 'easier, better, cheaper, faster, safer' concept discussed in Ladder 3, Cleaning and Organizing.) We explain about bringing all the materials and equipment they use daily close to the job, in positions where they don't have to repeatedly bend, stretch and twist, where parts are easy to pick up, etc. We explain it is best if materials are delivered in units that are not too heavy to lift, between knee and eye height to avoid accidents and back strain, etc.

Having given a number of examples, we then go out to the workplace to see what we can improve. And teams always find a series of items they can either immediately change or work on. It is important that managers and team leaders in the area know about the training and expect such a visit, so that their attitude is positive and welcoming. If the team then find the company willing to immediately make the changes they suggest, they get a very positive view about the process right from the start. And that positive attitude among employees is crucially important.

We are very attached to using simple techniques. Some 80 per cent of problems and their solutions are essentially simple, and by teaching basic concepts to everyone you can have every brain and pair of eyes thinking about improvement every day of the year. We also find that when we have started with training that has actually made the job easier, employees are then much more willing to contribute to changes that will make the job better (ie improve quality), cheaper (ie cut costs), or faster (ie improve productivity). That is when, step by step, we introduce staff to other techniques and ideas. These are described in some detail in Ladder 5, Managing for Quality, and include the following:

- the seven sins of *muda;*
- the SPECS procedure;
- process mapping;
- Pareto charting;
- the '5 Why's';
- fishbone diagrams.

LEVEL 3

'BOPs written for all routine jobs'

The first BOPs to be written should be those covering jobs that are done most regularly, ie every day, every week or every month. To start with, these don't have to be complex and elaborate. They may simply be lists that act as reminders and guide staff into good habits.

Conservation Corporation Africa (CCA) operate luxurious game lodges in five different African countries. Their company ethos is: 'Care of the People, Care of the Land, Care of the Wildlife'. Dave Varty and his wife Shan who founded the business go to extraordinary lengths to make sure their visitors have the time of their life. And judging by their reactions and comments, that is exactly what happens. But in any hospitality operation there are so many things to go wrong that could irritate the guest or spoil their visit. The Vartys' goal is not just to please their guests, but to delight them. And they know that they have to spell out to their staff exactly what good practice looks like if they want it to happen faithfully every day. That's why they developed their own Best Operating Practices manual, covering everything from bedroom standards to bush dinners, from gate welcomes to children management.

The manual is not written in elaborate language. Rather it is written in practical terms that everyone can understand and put into practice. Here's just one excerpt from the bush dinner section to illustrate:

Rules for Management of Hot and Cold Boxes

- All bags scrubbed daily and spotlessly clean.
- All scuffed, dented and broken cooler boxes to be discarded.
- All containers inside hot box to be in perfect condition.
- All containers and contents to be according to CCA standard check-list.
- Secure and clean storeroom for hot and cold boxes.
- All cups/glasses to be washed and checked on return.
- All drinks from the cold box to be recorded.
- All drinks to be packed in containers so that they don't lose their labels.
- All boxes to have bottle openers.
- All containers in hot boxes to be cleaned and filled up every day.

To give customers outstanding service you have to pay attention to the detail every day. BOPs like these make the standards clear to everyone. Conservation Corporation believes their BOPs are one of the key reasons they keep getting 'Wonderful!', 'Marvellous!' and 'Truly outstanding!' on the customers' report cards.

'Employees contribute at least one improvement idea a month'

Ideas do not need to be earth-shattering, they can be as modest as you like. What is important is that every individual is *thinking* every month about how their job might be improved. The best place to organize that is with the immediate manager, right in the daily workplace. He can evaluate ideas on the spot, and if they make sense, implement them straight away. That is the pattern that makes continuous improvement part of everyday working life.

Some organizations introduce employee award schemes to encourage employees to contribute. One South African manufacturing concern developed a catalogue of awards in 'bronze, silver and gold' categories. The value of these gifts (ranging from £10 to £25) were classified as follows:

Bronze	R100.00 to R150.00
Silver	R150.00 to R200.00
Gold	R200.00 to R250.00

The gifts in the catalogue included company 'gear' (tracksuits, pens, bags, etc) as well as other useful-to-have items. The money involved is modest; the important thing about gifts is that they are a lasting reminder to the employee of a success they had at work (a feeling we like to encourage). Some organizations also have 'floating trophies' for the best improvement suggestion of the month.

Level 3 companies are those keen to develop a 'culture' of continuous improvement. By this time the language of Best Operating Practices (BOPs) is becoming common parlance, Team Meeting Areas are set up, and Communication Boards with visible measures are seen in every work area.

'Two-thirds or more of employee ideas implemented'

It takes a long time to get to this level, but when employees get here it is an indication that they have been making improvement suggestions for some time, and intuitively know how to make their ideas practical and effective. If by this stage employees are averaging one suggestion per person per month, then in a company of 500 people that means there are more than 330 *improvements* being implemented every month. That makes nearly 4,000 a year. That is exactly the kind of steady, whole-company progression that eventually takes businesses to world class performance.

'Team problem-solving sessions take place regularly, and teams tackle at least two major projects a year'

By a 'major project' is meant something that cannot readily be attempted by an individual, but is more complex and requires the participation of the whole work team, or even co-operation between departments. In this case our advice to front-line managers is to choose the problems they would like to see solved most, but we emphasize that they should not choose a 'whale' to start with, ie we would want managers to choose something they will definitely succeed at the first time. This is crucial, ie that the first time employees attempt such a project they experience the feeling of success. There is nothing like early success to motivate employees to want to participate again.

LEVEL 4

'BOPs now written for all jobs, and by job-holders'

By this time and at this level, BOPs have been written to cover all jobs, not just the routine. Furthermore, rather than have managers or front-line supervisors write the BOPs, they are written and modified by the job-holders themselves. There are two reasons for this: job-holders are the people who know most about the job (they do it every day); and they take ownership of the job when they produce the BOP themselves. That means they are more likely to see work problems as their problems and not that of the manager. Getting that sense of responsibility is vitally important.

'Employees contribute at least two improvement ideas a month'

'More than 75 per cent of employee ideas are implemented'

This implies a company who has been soliciting and using employee suggestions for some years. At this stage the whole business of using employees' brains as well as their hands has become truly established in the business.

'Teams tackle three major projects a year'

As teams become more skilled in problem-solving and team-working, so the number of projects they can tackle will rise.

'Benchmarking visits used to seek out and use best practice'

The fundamental idea behind benchmarking is to get managers and staff in any business to think 'out of the box' of their own experience in their own company, by visiting other 'admired' companies to see at first-hand new ideas and approaches that could benefit their own operation. A number of books have been written on the subject of benchmarking. This is the advice we would offer based on our own experience:

- Benchmarking visits generally have a major impact on those who make the visit. Pride often makes employees and managers initially sceptical that any other company can teach them much (after all they have been at their own business for years). But if you choose your target company carefully, and your visitors see systems in operation before their eyes that are well in advance of their own, there is often a quantum and immediate change of attitude.
- Decide in advance what you are going to look for, and what specific questions you want to ask. That way your visitors don't just wander around wasting time.
- Allocate specific responsibilities to either individuals or small groups of individuals, and have them report on their findings to a specially convened session back at work.
- Take front-line employees along to the visit (ie non-managers), especially those who are most cynical or have most influence at the workplace. If they get enthused, they will be powerful advocates for change with their colleagues.
- The companies to benchmark are not only those in the same industry as yourselves. Companies should seek out and visit those companies who are particularly good at one aspect of their business, eg achieving low stock levels, handling telephone sales, implementing total preventive maintenance, etc.
- One company that is already world class and continues to make benchmarking visits, insists that its people do not spend their time congratulating themselves on how much better they are at some particular aspect of work than the company they are visiting. On the contrary, they deliberately look past these deficiencies to see if each team member can discover just one new idea they can add to their already world class performance.

- Be prepared to receive visits when other companies want to visit you. Mr Matsushita, founder of Panasonic, when asked why he didn't mind sharing the company's best ideas with visitors, once said: 'Some of you will be enthusiastic now but will not actually implement anything back at your own company; some of you will implement but not follow through; it will take those of you who do implement a year or two to make it effective, and by that time we will be two years further on in our own programme of continuous improvement.'

LEVEL 5

'Employees average more than four improvement ideas a month'

'More than 85 per cent of employee ideas are implemented'

It always looks daunting to managers to imagine that employees could be *averaging* four new improvement ideas a month when currently the company may not be getting even one idea a month. But over time, as Toyota found, employees get better not only at coming up with ideas in the first place, but at coming up with practical ideas that can be readily implemented. It becomes a virtuous circle: the more practical the ideas become, the more they get implemented; the more employees' ideas get implemented, the more they want to contribute.

The Japanese company Pioneer, which makes electronic audio equipment, started off modestly with only one idea a month. Today every employee is *expected* to contribute seven ideas a month, and they regularly implement more than 80 per cent of them. The Pioneer plant is a company of around 1,000 employees, and to be conservative let's assume they only get five actual ideas a month. That's a total of 5,000 ideas, and implementing 80 per cent means 4,000 *improvements* every month. That makes a total of nearly 50,000 improvements every year! Would you want that kind of continuous improvement every year in your company? Well, it's never going to happen leaving it all to managers. You have to engage the talents and brain power of everybody in the business. That is a prerequisite for companies intent on reaching world class standards.

It also helps to reach Level 5 when every element of the organization is focused on improvement. New technology, automation, best operating practices, reward and recognition systems, employee skills, employee behaviour, are all needed to be supportive so that both internal and external customers really see the benefit of working with a world class organization.

'Teams tackle more than four major projects a year'

At this stage, it is commonplace to see teams meeting together discussing project details, visiting departments as they do their research, and to have communication boards showing project plans and progress. It will have become part of 'the way we do things here', part of company culture. Department managers will be aware that their people will from time to time be engaged in cross-department projects, and are more than willing to see their people take part, knowing that it will be good for their development, and good for their own department. That is the kind of support and understanding that is necessary to help projects flourish.

'Benchmarking *visitors* show company among the "best in class"'

One way of telling if you are getting to be best in your class is the incidence of other companies who want to visit you. However, world class standard is perpetually shifting, so staying world class requires continuous improvement. When some companies see the description of Level 5 they often give us the impression that they think it is impossible to get there. It isn't. With continuous improvement companies have found themselves getting to places they never imagined were possible when they started. So will you.

IDEAS AND TECHNIQUES YOU CAN USE

Writing Best Operating Practices

Mr Taiichi Ohno, successively managing director and executive vice-president of Toyota Motors over some 25 years, is widely acknowledged to be the architect of just-in-time and lean manufacturing, processes which are today copied throughout the world. In his book *The Toyota Production System*, Ohno emphasizes the value and importance of 'standard work sheets' to the Toyota production system. Today these instructions are called 'Standard Operating Procedures' (SOPs), or in our case 'Best Operating Practices'.
Here's what Ohno had to say about them:

> Standard work sheets and the information contained in them are important elements of the Toyota production system . . . We have eliminated waste by examining available resources, re-arranging machines, improving machining processes, installing autonomous systems, improving tools, analysing transportation methods, and optimising the amount of materials at hand for machining. High production efficiency has also been maintained by preventing the recurrence of defective products, operational mistakes, and accidents, and by incorporating workers' ideas. All of this is possible because of the inconspicuous standard work sheet . . . The standard work sheet has changed little since I was first asked to prepare one 40 years ago . . . However, it is based thoroughly on principles and plays an important role in Toyota's visual control system.

The methodology

Best Operating Practices (BOPs) are designed to achieve the following:

- a description of 'the best way we know how' of performing a particular task;
- removal of 'waste' from the process;
- ensuring no-fail quality is built into the process;
- providing a safety-assured method;
- encouraging continuous improvement.

A useful place to start is always to conduct a Process Mapping exercise (see Ladder 6, Eliminating Waste). That presses you into examining every step of the current process and questioning its value. We strongly recommend you involve those doing the job in the exercise. The task is then to remove as many non-value-adding steps as possible, to make the job easy and safe to do, and to ensure a quality-assured job can be done every time.

Generally employees will consult the BOP when they are new to the job, when they haven't done that particular job for some time, or when they want to check a point that may have begun to slip over time. Pictures, drawings and illustrations are most desirable, but real model examples close to the work are best. One UK manufacturer of baths and basins has to deal with a great variety of water-managing systems, plungers and cisterns. In the cistern manufacturing section, some 30 varieties of mechanisms are mounted on boards and hung on the walls. Each time an operator has a batch to produce, he takes the appropriate board from the wall, places it in front of himself on the work-bench, and starts to work with the model product and parts right in front of him. That's good BOP practice.

In office-based situations, BOPs may take the form of a manual of ideally-completed forms. In laboratory situations, it would be the step-by-step safe sequence for executing processes. In a hospital, it is even more important to do the work 'the best way we know how'. One geriatric hospital group encourages their staff to write up their processes as a standard for the whole group this way: when the process has been examined and approved, it is entered in The Beautiful Book. Their employees love to have their name recorded in The Beautiful Book.

It is pretty common for people to complete forms inadequately. Sales people will often omit important information from their sales order forms, or job applicants will struggle filling recruitment forms when they are not quite sure what is required. The same often happens with employee appraisal forms that are only cursorily filled out. BOPs don't have to be rigid or elaborate. They just have to encourage best practice.

Example 1 shows the staff appraisal form of one company, where simple instructions in each of the boxes explain in simple language what is required. Add a model completed form to that and you have a BOP (see Figure 7.1).

Example 2 shows a model stock management system database (see Figures 7.2 to 7.4).

Example 3 illustrates a test to examine how well staff involved have absorbed the BOP for the raw materials management system used in a South African brewery (see Figure 7.5).

Example 1   Performance review and personal learning plan

1. OBJECTIVES AND ANALYSIS	
Major objectives and their measures *(to be completed by manager and associate)*	**Analysis of achievement** *(to be completed by associate)*
Use the performance guidelines to identify objectives relating to your key outputs. *You will probably identify half a dozen or so but need to agree those that will be the Key Focus for A.R.B.*	*During the year you should make notes of achievement of agreed objectives in this space.*

* Denotes ARB focus

Figure 7.1 Performance review and personal learning plan

Note: In this single status company, all employees are called 'associates'. 'ARB' stands for 'annually renewable bonus', a lump sum gained by delivering on the two or three priority objectives agreed with their manager at the beginning of the year.

2. OTHER ACHIEVEMENTS AND STRENGTHS DEMONSTRATED
(to be completed by associate)

During the year you may be involved in additional tasks not included in your original objectives.
Use the space to record what you consider noteworthy.

3. SIGNIFICANT LEARNING POINTS DURING THE YEAR
(to be completed by associate)

Make brief 'one liner' notes when you recognize a learning situation.

Figure 7.2

5. PERFORMANCE REVIEW

Performance Review Summary *(to be completed by manager)*

Your manager will discuss your performance, stressing the key elements of your role and will be looking at your total contribution, not just the agreed objectives from page 1.

When the appraisal is completed you will be required to sign to say you accept it as a reflection of your discussions.

OVERALL PERFORMANCE RATING

ACCEPTABLE/UNACCEPTABLE

SIGNATURES

1 Associate _____   3 Super Scalar _____

2 Scalar _____   4 Personnel _____

BONUS ADMINISTRATION   Pay ARB [   ]   Withhold ARB [   ]

Signed _____

Figure 7.3

The process is specifically designed to encourage a constructive discussion between associate and manager on how the associate can develop and 'continuously improve'.

---

6. THINGS I INTEND TO LEARN NEXT YEAR *(to be completed by associate)*

You should use this space to note areas of learning you would like to develop as and when you become aware of them, ie don't wait for the year end!

---

7. AGREED PERSONAL LEARNING PLAN *(to be completed by manager and associate)*

This will be a contract for development your manager and you commit yourselves to for the next year.

Figure 7.4

'Scalar' is the company's name for manager or boss. The company also wanted the boss's manager ('Super Scalar') to keep in touch with how associates in their Division were developing. Hence the requirement for that signature also.

The intention here was that every associate should take responsibility for his own development, and discuss his proposals with his manager. The manager then became a support in helping the associate realize his intentions.

Example 2 Stock management system database

1. INTRODUCTION
1.1 Data input is required to calculate the stock for manufacturing and suppliers in the short and medium term. This information assists in the planning of volumes to ensure that the manufacturing process runs smoothly. Forecasts are also made using this information.

2. SAFETY
All safety requirements relevant to the location of the Data input station must be adhered to. Electrical equipment must be registered with the Electrical Department and numbered in the prescribed manner.

3. TASK DESCRIPTION

3.1 Switch the computer on.

3.2 Type in your USER ID and PASSWORD. Press ENTER.

3.3 Select STOCK MANAGEMENT SYSTEM from the MENU.

3.4 Double click on STOCK MANAGEMENT

3.5 Enter your password.

3.6 Click on CONNECT.

ETC.

Example 3 Competency check-list.

PERFORMANCE CRITERIA	ACHIEVED	
	YES	**NO**

1.   PROCESS

AT CELLARS

1.1   Do BBT preparation at Start-up (see BBT/Brand Change)

1.2   Prepare raw material as per Brand Change

AT FILLER

1.3   Flush out/rinse the Filler

1.4   Drain the Filler

1.5   Ensure that the pump is switched off

1.6   Start infeed and discharge conveyors

1.7   Pressurize the Filler

1.8   Switch on the pump and fill bowl

1.9   Inspect crown hopper for correct brand

1.10 Switch on the crown sorter and supply

1.11 Switch on the jetter and vacuum pump

1.12 Ensure level on the gauge is the same as the set point

1.13 Visually check that the sight glasses on the Filler bowl show the correct levels

1.14 Set the Filler ready for bottle feed

1.15 Set checkmat for foaming, uncrowned and underfilling

1.16 Ensure correct jetter pressure

1.17 Start the filling process on slow speed, jetting and rejection until full 40,000b/h speed

1.18 Record on Downtime and BBT monitoring sheets

2.   PRODUCT

2.1   The Filler is running at 40,000b/h

2.2   Fobbing is shown below (immediately after crowning

CORRECT FOBBING   **TOO MUCH FOBBING**
Foam is just reaching
the top of the bottle
when crowned

2.3   There is no continuous rejection

2.4   The Downtime and BBT monitoring sheets are recorded

2.5   Start-up time is not later than planned

3.   KNOWLEDGE

3.1   Why must the filling process start-up be done correctly
       and accurately?

3.2   What is programme 19 used for and when is its cycle
       complete?

3.3   What programme is used to fill the bowl with beer?

3.4   What is programme 2 used for?

3.5   What are the set points of counter pressure and bowl
       level respectively?

3.6   Why must the crown hopper be visually inspected?

3.7   Why must the first round of bottles be rejected?

3.8   Who is responsible for recording all start-up information?

3.9   What protective clothing must the Filler Operator wear?

RESULT: COMPETENT   ☐

                NOT YET
                COMPETENT   ☐

FIRST ATTEMPT   ☐

SECOND ATTEMPT   ☐

THIS ATTEMPT   ☐

ASSESSOR'S COMMENTS

_____

_____

_____

_____

FOLLOW-UP DATES: _____

ASSESSOR 1: _____ CANDIDATE: _____

ASSESSOR 2: _____

Figure 7.5 Competency check-list

E i g h t

Teamwork

LEVELS	MEASURES
Level 1	People think of themselves as just doing a job, not in a team. Co-operation between work-groups is patchy; there is rivalry and point-scoring between teams. Workers don't act as a team with management – it's difficult to make changes without suspicion or opposition.
Level 2	Staff generally co-operate with changes the company wants to make. Work-groups have specific measurable *team* objectives. Staff know who their customers are, external and internal. They look like a team and help each other to get the job done.
Level 3	Work groups meet as a team daily, or at least monthly. Team members and team leaders all have clear roles. They make specific performance contracts with customers. They display performance data publicly in their team area. Staff are multi-skilled and can cover a variety of jobs.
Level 4	Teams are organized around processes or products. Cross-disciplined project teams used to tackle big issues. Teams set their own objectives, manage their own budgets, resolve problems and make innovations.
Level 5	Teams exist everywhere, and have become a way of life. Self-directed teams are set up and working effectively. The versatility in teams means they cope with change well. Teams celebrate achievements and expect success.

LEVEL 1

'People think of themselves as just doing a job, not in a team'

This is normally the case where staff are simply employed as 'pairs of hands' to do a specific job. They are expected simply to conform to the rules and follow instructions given by the front-line manager or supervisor. Employees usually see the work as 'just a job' and a way of earning money. They put in the hours required, and leave as soon as the work period ends. If pay is on a piece-work or hours worked basis, then that can reinforce the attitude that everyone has to look out for themselves first. Often the attitude is: 'I just look after myself and everyone else should do the same.'

'Co-operation between work-groups is patchy; there is rivalry and points-scoring between teams'

This is a common situation in many companies. A typical example is staff in the finance department feeling aggrieved that sales people get big bonuses while they are on a straight (often smaller) rate of pay. By way of demonstrating their importance, they may regularly reject forms filled out by sales people for technical reasons to help 'even the score'. Or, maintenance and production staff may counterblast each other. 'If you maintenance people did your job right,' say Production, 'this equipment wouldn't break down half so often,' while Maintenance retort: 'If you production people didn't abuse the equipment so much, we would have a lot less maintenance to do.' Production managers may find themselves at loggerheads too with the Quality department, with Production accusing Quality of being both variable or too tight in the standards they apply, and Quality feeling Production are always trying to pass off product that is obviously sub-standard.

Rivalries and points-scoring are a disaster for companies intent on serving customers well and embarking on the journey to world class performance. If managers and staff spend time arguing about whose fault a problem is, they are dissipating the very energy that should be applied to making improvements, delivering to the customer on time, achieving 'right-first-time' quality, and doing it all better than the competition.

'Workers don't act as a team with management – it's difficult to make changes without suspicion or opposition'

In many Western companies, it has become an accepted practice to declare staff redundant when sales suffer or hard times are experienced. The shipbuilding industry in the United Kingdom was a typical example of this 'feast and famine' syndrome. In these circumstances workers banded together into unions to counter the strength of employers and give themselves greater apparent security. Many companies also try to pay only as much as necessary to keep prices and costs down, and negotiate this way with employee representatives. The negotiation process generally results in both parties starting from widely different positions, the employer making a less-than-acceptable offer and the union making unrealistic initial demands. However, when representatives relay back to their members their company's initial offer, employees are inclined to feel they have to fight the company for everything they get.

That creates an unfortunate habit. Employees initially oppose every proposed change knowing that if they do, they are likely to end up with a better deal. In other words, their experience is that conflict pays better than cooperation. Any time the company wants to introduce any changes, the response they get is: 'What's in it for us?' As a result, management will often shelve perfectly sensible changes, feeling that the disruption and aggravation that are likely to result are just not worth the trouble.

Many companies continue to survive in just such situations, but we have to state categorically: no company who stays there is ever going to become world class. You cannot have management and employees playing on separate teams with different goals and agendas. Their goals have to be the same, ie where both groups feel that playing together will bring greater benefits for both parties.

LEVEL 2

'Staff generally co-operate with changes the company wants to make'

Realize that there is a big jump from Level 1 to Level 2! When staff are co-operative it is indicative of a change in expectations. Staff now expect that management in general will want to do the right thing for both the company and the people who work in it. It is possible to engender a spirit of trust by, for example, giving employees the guarantee that although changes are envisaged, nobody will be made redundant because of any changes introduced by management. That may sound risky to many, but it is exactly what a company called Pedigree Petfoods did in the United Kingdom. They intended to introduce new automated canning lines and computer-controlled raw materials storage. Many jobs would have to change in character and scope. They told their employees they would have to change to stay competitive and offer their customers continuously better value for money. 'You may not have the same job here,' they said, 'but you will have a job as long as you want and can stay part of the team.'

Two years later, there were 20 per cent fewer jobs, but no one had gone except volunteers on special financial separation packages. Some jobs had changed radically: some employees who had originally joined to handle meat and shovel fish were now sitting in front of computer screens manoeuvring materials in automated production lines. The company was now three times as productive as its nearest rival, and in employee opinion surveys 80 per cent of staff still felt 'secure in their job'.

Employees will only start working on the same team as management when they have confidence that management will keep their interests just as much at heart as those of the company. And when the chains of opposition fall away, the company can rise to quite new levels of performance.

'Work-groups have specific measurable team objectives'

People who work together are only a work-group. They become a team only when they have common objectives. Like the clear objective you see in a soccer team when they take the field. The first thing you notice when they are all dressed the same is that they look like a team. They have no time for in-team rivalry – they're too busy trying to beat the opposition. They play to team members' strengths (they don't play the goalkeeper at centre-forward). If the centre-forward scores, their goalkeeper jumps up and down as well. They all celebrate. That's because there's only one goal, and it's the same for everybody: to get the ball in the other team's net. And the measure of success is clear: if the ball goes wholly over the line, it's a goal. Finally, the competition is right in their face, and that's motivating (do not minimize the power of talking frequently about your competition to help motivate your employees).

There are real lessons to be learnt from sport for work-teams. Clear measurable goals are crucial. We also believe good teamwork brings particular added-value benefits in the work situation that are difficult to replicate any other way. Here's what we think they are:

- *Teamwork is necessary in complex organizations.* It's very seldom in large organizations that one person will be able to serve all the needs of the customer personally. A whole series of people get involved, and they need to work as one team to ensure the whole process works seamlessly together.
- *You get a variety of strengths and experience.* The variety of skills and experience you can apply in a team on any issue is unlikely to be matched by any one individual. And people learn more from each other in team situations.
- *Multi-disciplined problem-solving.* You are likely to see the problem from a variety of angles when you attempt to solve it as a team. That is likely to result in more balanced, more long-term solutions.
- *Better ideas generation.* Because one idea sparks other ideas in different heads, you are always likely to get more ideas from a team than an individual. This is not to say that individuals don't sometimes come up with brilliant ideas by themselves, but teams will consistently produce more ideas, and they tend to implement well too.
- *You get better continuity and coverage.* One of the obvious benefits of teams is that when someone is absent, another member of the team is likely to know enough to be able to deal with points immediately for the customer, rather than having to wait for the return of the specific individual. In addition, with multi-skilled team members, even with absentees, the production process can always carry on.
- *Mutual support.* We all go through difficult times, and that's when support from other team members can be invaluable. And even in success, somehow celebrations seem even better as a team.
- *More fun!* Going to work is a pleasure when you're doing things you enjoy.

But the daily banter you often get in work-teams can produce fun and humour that lights up the day.

We are convinced of the added value of good teamwork. But you also need good processes to help management teams work together and agree on their common objectives. That's where we use the TOM (Team Objectives Meeting) process described in Ladder 1. This is only conducted with 'natural teams', ie people who work together and who answer to one boss. The agenda for the classic TOM looks like this:

- Managing your time.
- Past team effectiveness.
- Behaviour change requests.

- Team objectives.
- Systems and organization.
- Obstacles to achievement.
- Staying on track.
- Super-boss visit.

The first half of the TOM is designed to examine the past year's events to see what lessons can be learned, and how these lessons can be actively applied to next year. As an example, here is the section on Past Team Effectiveness.

Past Team Effectiveness

On its performance over the last 6 to 12 months or so, rate your TEAM (ie the one taking part in this TOM) on a 10-point scale under each of the following:

- *Objectives* – the extent to which clear objectives were agreed for individuals and the team as a whole.
- *Planning* – the extent to which priorities were set, and detailed planning undertaken to achieve them.
- *Achievement* – the extent to which high productivity and achievement resulted from the efforts of the team.
- *Information* – the extent to which management information was adequate over the period for the team to do its job well.
- *Innovation* – the extent to which new ideas were generated, and resulted in significant innovation.
- *Support* – the extent to which supportive relationships and co-operation were demonstrated among your team.
- *Communications* – the extent to which inter-colleague, within-team communications were good and sufficient over the period.
- *Interface relations* – the extent to which working relationships with other key departments in the organization were constructive in helping the team to do its job.
- *Meetings* – the extent to which meetings are called at appropriate times, with known agendas, and make effective use of the time spent.

- *Procedures and organization* – the extent to which the procedures and systems used have been helpful in getting the job done.

Base your ratings on actual examples and illustrations of past events. Make simple notes as reminders either on these pages or separately as you go along. If questioned at the TOM it will be useful to show that your ratings are based on real evidence.

If the score on any item is relatively low, we ask the simple question: 'What would have to be happening for you to get a score of eight on that?' What the team says is then turned into positive actions with Prime Contractors and dates attached.

The TOM process also helps ensure each team generates common goals that everybody understands and is committed to. Having the goals simply written down and distributed to every member of the group is not the point of the exercise. The goals have to be discussed and agreed with the team so that they are committed to achieving them. In other words, they are realistic and achievable. When the goals meet these criteria, the team members do not mind publishing them for the benefit of the departments that they interface with. When the goals are made public, the team is even more committed to ensure that they are achieved!

At any point in time, each team member should be able to tell you what the team's objectives are, how they are going to measure them and where they are in terms of reaching the targets. A good measure for determining if a work group is a team or not, is to ask the members what the goals or objectives of the team actually are. If they say 'what goals?' you know there is some work to do!

'Staff know who their customers are, external and internal'

Each member of any work team has to understand that they serve a customer, whether that customer be the next person in the production line (an internal customer), or the person getting the end product or service (an external customer). We have found that when individual team members make face-to-face visits to their internal customers – not to talk about a particular problem, but just to ask them how they might improve their service to them – barriers start to come down. Furthermore, staff are much more motivated to do the job right when they know the person who is getting the result of their work, and what they in turn need to do a good job. That makes for good cross-departmental teamwork. See Ladder 2 (Customer Focus) for a full discussion on internal and external customers.

'They look like a team and help each other to get the job done'

A good working team shows the following characteristics:

1. *They know where they are going; they know what they have to do.* They know

what their goals are, because they have thought them through. You hear the same story from every member of the team. No doubts, differences or denials are expressed outside the team that they haven't expressed inside the team.

2. *They measure how they are doing.* They don't rely on hearsay or opinion. They work on facts. They measure because they want to keep their eye on the ball and make sure they deliver on their commitments.

3. *They support each other inside the team, and outside the team.* They are open and straight enough with each other to 'tell it like it is' in a constructive and supportive fashion. They don't bad-mouth their colleagues to others, ie they speak in support of their team colleagues when they are not there.

4. *They expect success.* They act confident because they are used to succeeding, ie because although they are used to setting themselves challenging goals, they don't set unrealistic or impossible ones. If they do slip up from time to time, they don't then think they are a failure as a team, just that they failed on that one.

5. *They are ready to co-operate.* They realize the work they do is to satisfy real customers. They put themselves out to meet their customers' needs and wants. Customers find them a pleasure to deal with, because basically they are a 'can-do' outfit.

6. *They enjoy their work; they have fun!* It's a pleasure to work with that kind of team. It's a pleasure to be a member of it too.

LEVEL 3

'Work groups meet as a team daily, or at least monthly'

For front-line staff we recommend the use of 10-minute 'start-of-day' meetings. They have the following advantages:

- *It serves as a roll call.* You know immediately if everyone is there and how to allocate staff.
- *Critical items affecting the job can be discussed.* For example, if a machine has broken down, or if something has come up that is urgent, it can be discussed and action taken there and then.
- *The team leader is seen to be organized.* The team leader actually has to make sure that he comes in at least 5 to 10 minutes before the work day or shift starts to get himself organized.
- *It makes better use of management time.* The manager/supervisor/team leader does not have to run around for the first half hour of the day trying to fill everyone in. And if he does, he never tells it the same way to everyone.
- *It leads to early problem resolution.* If problems arise the people on the floor bring them up at the start-of-the-day meeting, ie how something that happened yesterday may affect them today. They immediately talk it through and get it fixed.
- *Useful feedback is obtained from the team.* For instance, the team leader will get

information early on where grievances etc, may occur, and deal with them promptly before they develop.

- *It helps with team building and identification.* If team members get together for five minutes every morning, five days a week, that makes 20 days a month, or more than 200 days a year. Meeting together that number of times, the group is going to feel and act like a team even if the word 'teamwork' is never mentioned. Closeness and regular communications are foundations of good teamwork.

'Team members and team leaders all have clear roles'

In traditional manufacturing companies, where the front-line manager is called 'Supervisor' and front-line staff 'Operators', it is not untypical to have duties allocated in this way:

Supervisor	Operator
Output	Attendance
Quality	Good timekeeping
Costs	Meeting performance targets
Admin./records	Flexibility
Good housekeeping	
Scrap/re-work	
Safe	
Employee relations	
Training	

Front-line employees are expected to turn up for work, on time, to meet their production targets, and to show some flexibility in the work they do and in getting round everyday problems. Supervisors are charged with responsibility for everything else.

However, we always ask the key question: 'Where do the faults first occur?' If the systems and equipment in place allow a good quality job to be done, and the supervisor does not physically get his hands on the product, who is *really* in control of quality? The operator, of course. Using the same criteria, it becomes obvious that the *operator* is actually the person in charge of output, of keeping the place tidy (good housekeeping), scrap, rework, etc. So the first step we take in establishing team roles is *to give full responsibility where the control really rests.*

Team leaders and team members each have *unique contributions* to make to the production process, ie non-overlapping contributions that build on each other and as a team add up to more than just the sum of the parts. Rewritten in the form of Unique Contributions (see Ladder 9, Staff Empowerment and Involvement, on this), the team roles would now look like this:

Team Leader	Team Member
Overall productivity	Output
Systems improvement	Quality
Costs	Scrap/re-work
Admin./records	Data collection
Safe working arrangements	Safe working habits
Team development	Skills
Housekeeping standards	Good housekeeping
Work scheduling	

In effect, we give responsibility to the operators for the things we know they're already in charge of. If, with training, they know how to do a good job, we expect them to do that job effectively without supervision.

The job of the team leader is then to add extra value. For example, to ensure his team has the right equipment and tools to do a good job, to make sure they have all the materials in the quantities and form that they need, and to remove any obstacles preventing high productivity. He is in charge of creating safe working arrangements for his people, but they have to adopt safe working habits on a daily basis. He is in charge of agreeing housekeeping standards with his team but, once set, they undertake to keep their workplace like a clean kitchen rather than a dirty garage. So team leader and team members each have distinct and separate roles, their own unique contribution to getting the job done to world class standards.

As teams develop, and become accustomed to their more responsible roles, so we refine and strengthen their unique contributions. Generically, this is how we would see the role of the team member:

1. Meeting customer requirements.
2. Productivity.
3. Product or service quality.
4. Data recording.
5. Good housekeeping.
6. Skills and versatility.
7. Improvement contributions.
8. Safe working practices.
9. Within-team co-operation.
10. Training others.
11. Self-development.

At this stage, we see team members as largely self-managing. They are well trained, they know how to deliver what the customer wants and do it without supervision. They run the job and systems *as they are now*. The primary focus of the team leader's job is to *improve* what we have now, and to spend 40–50 per cent of his time doing just that. He is always there as adviser, helper and supporter, but largely lets his team get on with the job.

This is generically how we see the unique contributions of the team leader:

1   Taking the lead.
2. Producing whatever is needed to do a good job.
3. Reducing waste.
4. Removing obstacles.
5. Devising improvements.
6. Supplier contracts.
7. Customer contracts.
8. Safe working arrangements.
9. Team communications.
10. Team motivation.
11. Team member development.
12. Self-development

At this stage, teams display versatility and 'can-do' attitudes. Their team spirit makes it a pleasure to come to work.

'They make specific performance contracts with customers'

'They display performance data publicly in their team area'

At Level 3, team members not only know who their customers are (Level 2), they have made arrangements with customers about delivery, quality, etc, which they regularly fulfil. Normally the team leader would make the contact and have discussions with the customers they supply with material, products or information. We use the word 'contract' to indicate how seriously these commitments should be taken (see Ladder 2, Customer Focus).

And whatever teams commit to their customers, that is what they should measure and display publicly in their work area. In other words, every day they should have a reminder: Are we doing what we said we would do? (See Ladder 4, Visible Measurement Systems, for more on this.)

'Staff are multi-skilled and can cover a variety of jobs'

We prefer people in teams to be multi-skilled, partly because it makes the job more interesting for the individuals, and partly because it ensures that processes can continue even when someone is absent. It also protects the company against unnecessary overtime, ie having some individuals idle while others have to work overtime to complete their jobs. Being multi-skilled should be part of the job for everyone. This can also be connected to pay systems (see Ladder 10 on Rewards and Recognition and Ladder 12 on Continuous Learning for discussion of these issues).

When a new culture of continuous learning and multi-skilling has been established and employees actually enjoy learning new skills, it is important that management continue to show enthusiasm and support the maintenance of the culture. In this respect, it should not only be front-line employees who are continually upgrading their skills: management (and even the MD) should not be beyond learning.

LEVEL 4

'Teams are organized around processes or products'

Teamwork doesn't just happen by turning the supervisor's hat round and printing Team Leader on it, or by telling everyone they are now a team. You have to change the organization to help teams flourish, change the roles of individuals, and train them in the execution of these roles. We have described above how we distinguish the Unique Contributions of team member and team leader – they make clear the role of each so that they fit with and complement each other. You also need a set of established guidelines to structure your own form of teamwork. Here are the 18 rules we ourselves use when implementing teamworking processes:

1. *Skills exist within the team to do the complete job.* By this we mean that, for example, in a manufacturing environment the team may have engineers, electricians or maintenance staff, etc, within the team to enable them to do a complete job. In other words, they don't have to depend on hope and pleading with other departments to get their job done when they need it. All the skills are right there within the team. The technicians may seek advice from other departments on specialist technical matters, but day-to-day they all answer to one boss, ie the front-line team leader.
2. *The team deals with the complete product, process or service.* Ideally, the team will manufacture a product, or provide a service, which is directly for the external (paying) customer. Where this is not feasible, then we would want them to deal with a specific, measurable part of the process or service. This may mean actual physical re-arrangement of the factory or office layout and equipment so that the team can do the whole job.

   Let's take several examples. In an ink-making process, delays were often caused by waiting for the testing of samples by technicians in their upstairs lab (they worked for a different department). After discussion and much heart-searching, it was agreed to move the testing equipment down to the shop floor, and to train the operators how to use it. (Departments often jealously guard their equipment and protest that 'only our people can do it'.) In this case, after the move, operators learnt a lot more about the chemical properties of ink, they produced more consistent quality as a result, and experienced many fewer delays.

   In a shoe-making factory, slippers went through six different processes and departments in their manufacture. The total time taken was generally around three weeks, with part-finished product stored at every process. By bringing together the skills required into one team (six operators), and arranging the machinery involved in a close U-shaped formation where the part-finished product was passed from hand to hand, the time required to produce a pair of finished slippers dropped to under one minute, with intermediate storage of part-finished product falling to zero! This is the value of thinking in terms of complete processes and not in terms of functional departments.

IBM Credit Corporation (CC) helps its customers finance its computer purchases from the main company. For a long time CC ran applications through a five-stage process taking between five and seven days to approve such loans. Two senior managers decided to run a typical financing request through all the processes involved, and found the actual work involved amounted to no more than 90 minutes! The rest was all down to handovers and delays between departments. Rather than keep 'specialists' in different departments, the company decided to train 'generalists' who could handle the whole process. The turnaround time to get applications approved dropped to four hours! The number of deals the company is now able to handle with the same staff numbers has jumped 100-fold. No, not 100 per cent, 100 times!

3. *There is visual unbroken contact between team members.* Walls and geographic separation make teamwork difficult. Remove the barriers (whether it is walls, machinery or equipment) that prevent team members seeing each other. The international Mars company are keen believers in open-plan offices for just this reason. Not only can team members in departments see and communicate easily with each other, each department can see every other department. Indeed, the directors sit in a cart-wheel arrangement in the middle of the office, with their departments radiating out from there. No one has an office. There are well-equipped rooms all round the periphery that can be used for meetings of any kind. Mars uses the same format for their offices all round the world.

4. *They know who their customers are.* Not only can team members name their customers, they know exactly what quality looks like in their eyes, and strive to deliver just that. (See more on this in Ladder 2, Customer Focus.)

5. *Visible measurement systems are used in every area.* Once team members know what their contribution to the business is, they keep their eyes on the ball by measuring regularly how they are doing, and displaying this visibly in their work area. (For more detail, see Ladder 4.)

6. *Multi-skills and flexibility are the rule.* Multi-skilling brings two distinct advantages: doing different jobs makes the daily job more interesting; the complete job can still be done even when particular team members are absent. Of course, if you also award extra pay for the learning of bunches of skills (see Ladder 10, Rewards and Recognition), then you more effectively retain those with the extra skills you particularly need.

7. *Job rotation is standard.* Clearly, moving people across jobs on a regular basis prevents boredom in repetitive jobs, and keeps team members' various learnt skills up to scratch.

8. *Best Operating Practices are captured and used.* This involves the 'building in' of practices that maintain the best standards of which the team is capable and, where improvement breakthroughs occur, capturing these and making them available to everyone. (See Ladder 7 for more.)

9. *There is a daily team communications process.* For the reasons listed earlier in

this chapter, we believe the daily communications process is a valuable team-building tool.

10. *Continuous improvement and continuous learning is part of everyone's job.* Continuous improvement won't happen in any company unless the people themselves are continuously improving their skills and capability. To make sure the habit is encouraged we like to build the requirement into personal appraisal and development systems. (See Ladder 10, Rewards and Recognition, for a good example.)

11. *Team members 'muck in' to help each other.* Often, in high-speed production lines, a packaging or other machine goes wrong and starts covering the floor with great piles of rejected product. Team members don't just shout 'Tough luck!' and leave the poor operator struggling. They get in there and help. They work as a team – especially when there are problems!

12. *The team work area is clean and visually well organized.* The comparison we like to draw is between a garage and a kitchen. We often visit garages that are untidy, with material in piles, tools scattered all over, oil and dirt on the floor, and where it's difficult to find anything you need. People have to rummage in boxes to find tools, and forget to put things back. 'Who's taken that left-handed spanner of mine?' they shout. In a kitchen, however, hygiene standards mean it's generally clean, and the sugar and flour are usually put back in the same place every time. It's much nicer and easier to work in.

   So why work in a dirty garage when you could work in a clean and tidy kitchen? Good teams all prefer the latter, but making it like that is down to the people who work there. (See Ladder 3, Cleaning and Organizing.)

13. *Team members carry out routine maintenance.* In Ladder 3 we detailed the seven functions manufacturing operators can readily undertake with the appropriate training. We think the same policy should apply in every team – whether in a school, a hospital, an office or a shop – namely that staff be given the 'ownership' of the key equipment they regularly use; and that they be taught enough about the equipment to understand how it works, and how it should be regularly maintained to keep it in good working order.

14. *Team problem-solving.* When teams put their heads together to solve problems they have all been suffering from, they often come up with ingenious and practical solutions. Furthermore, when they own the solutions, they have more incentive to make them work. They may well be poor at it to begin with – no one has asked them to do it before. But stick at it, and use some of the processes we advise in Ladder 5, Managing for Quality.

15. *No job demarcation – subject only to training.* There has been a tradition in some industries that those who did not 'serve their time' cannot forever thereafter carry out so-called 'skilled jobs' (not an uncommon situation in the docks, engineering, and printing industries, for example). We say age should be no barrier to job-holding. The only criterion should be capability. If the person with training can perform the job to the required quality and productivity standard, entry should be unrestricted.

16. *The team is responsible for setting and meeting its own targets.* As the team

grows in experience and confidence, eventually they talk directly to their customers, and know what they have to do to meet their needs. They also seek to improve their performance continuously year by year – it is now part of the culture. At that point they can be trusted to set and meet their own targets, and the ownership that results brings its own special brand of commitment.

17. *The team is given extra trust and responsibility.* As teams grow in experience and stature, you can keep their self-esteem and performance growing by giving them ever more responsibility and trust, ie trusting them with decisions previously reserved for managers only. For example, you can involve team members in the selection of new recruits. They not only set high standards, but are inclined to promote the company positively with applicants. You can also make team members part of any team to decide on what new equipment should be bought, how it should be installed, putting together the training courses involved, etc. Eventually, in any team, you won't be able to tell the team leaders from the ordinary team members.

18. *Teams are treated like mature adults, and expected to act like mature adults.* This is so fundamental, it ought to be guideline No. 1. When you treat team members like children who are expected to hang up their brain on the way in to work, you can expect to get childish behaviour. In this kind of teamwork, team members are expected to behave like grown-up people doing grown-up jobs. And the more you treat them like colleagues rather than subordinates, the more they respond and perform.

'Cross-disciplined project teams used to tackle big issues'

By 'big issues' we mean things that are supra-departmental, ie would affect people over the whole company, for example a new pay scheme or installing a new computer information system. In such instances we would strongly recommend using cross-departmental project teams. The reason we favour such teams so strongly is that they offer such a telling list of benefits:

- *Practical, workable proposals.* The most important outcome. If team members are drawn from the departments most affected by the proposed changes, they will want to make them changes they can live with and make happen. Eccentricities of any one department's ideas are soon rubbed down by the needs and demands of other departments to make the whole chain of events practical and workable.
- *Learning about the business.* Team members learn about the wider business picture. They begin to understand the work and problems of other departments first-hand and begin to act more like businessmen rather than simply accountants, buyers or production people.
- *Breaking down inter-department barriers.* Departmentalism and parochial attitudes can be the bane of effecting change in any organization. Multi-disciplined teams overtly demonstrate that better outcomes can result from cross-departmental co-operation. In addition, when the project team has finished its work, the relationships remain. It encourages inter-department

co-ordination, as team members feel more inclined to go and consult former team colleagues on other issues.

- *Getting big issues dealt with.* Issues given to one senior manager to mastermind can often founder simply because of the difficulty of getting full co-operation from all the departments involved in making the necessary changes, ie one voice against the whole company culture. Eight convinced people in a project team, who are from different departments and own their proposed solution, have a much better chance of making things happen in practice. If their proposals also have clear top man backing, so much the better.
- *Manager development.* Taking part in a successful project team can provide one of the most important formative influences for developing managers in any business.
- *Innovation and teamwork becomes a habit.* Inter-disciplinary project teams, working together to solve problems or take quantum leap initiatives, becomes just part of 'how we do things round here'. That can keep the business constantly fresh and developing. It becomes a habit to keep setting new challenges . . . and to keep meeting them.

In setting up such teams, here are some helpful guidelines developed from long experience.

Guidelines for project teams

- The brief needs to be simple, challenging, and unambiguous. Don't hedge it round with qualifications and obscurities. Wherever possible, express the objective of the project in the form of a clear, measurable goal where the team will know clearly when they have passed the winning post. (See later for some examples.)
- The members of the team should be chosen from each department that has a material influence on the outcome, and whose commitment or expertise is needed to make any agreed solution work in practice.
- Depending on the size of the project it helps to make some of the team members full-time, the others only part-time or co-opted as necessary. Simply giving managers a project to do along with their current work means they constantly have to fight the pressure of different priorities. If you want well-researched and robust proposals you need to give them the undisturbed time to do it. And use your very best people – preferably those you cannot afford to release!
- Team members must have the authority to take decisions in the team, which will be commitments on their department's behalf. If they can't do that, the team member should be a person who *can*. In practice, if it comes to a big commitment, the team member will indicate that it is something he will need to confirm, but it is no good having someone on the team who has to check everything like a messenger boy.
- Make it a rule that any recommendations or proposals made must have the 100% agreement of the team. If you don't, the dissenting departments

will simply drag their feet and effectively kill off the proposals in practice. With the 100% agreement rule, the team has to produce solutions that deal effectively with the legitimate points brought up by members from different departments. That does two things: it produces more robust solutions, and it demonstrates that departmental barriers are an irrelevance in getting things done.

- Have the project team make their recommendations direct to the top management team in the company. The project team then treat the whole issue as of the first importance. You get much more commitment when they know they have to stand up and be counted in front of the most important executives in the business.

- Give the project a realistic but definite timescale. If it is relatively long, eg three to six months, have them report on progress every month. Fix the dates firmly in everybody's diary – and don't put them off, otherwise you give the (true) impression that the subject is really of secondary importance. Insist on substantial progress every month; don't put up with excuses.

- Insist they keep their proposals simple. If they produce good but complex recommendations, send them back with the brief: 'Now see how simple you can make it.' Once they know they have your support, they can often get surprisingly ingenious at the process of simplification.

- Don't set too many teams going at once. That can cause confusion and disruption. Go for the priorities first.

Later in this chapter we give examples of challenging project team briefs set by a series of different organizations.

'Teams set their own objectives, manage their own budgets, resolve problems and make innovations'

This is a description of a mature team truly at Level 4. It will have taken a number of years to get to this stage, and to be doing it satisfactorily. This kind of team will have developed into a 'business within the business', ie they know how to serve their customers well, and to do it autonomously. They take care of problems, they manage themselves.

At this level, companies have well-established procedures to help make good team management easy. For example, they use TOMs (Team Objectives Meetings) at least once a year to agree on team objectives. During TOMs they use clear guidelines to manage their discussions and decisions. For example:

1. Start on time, finish on time (SOTFOT).
2. Tell it like it is – constructively.
3. 100% agreement on decisions.
4. Agreements are commitments – once made, we will do whatever it takes to succeed.
5. Silence is acceptance – so say it at the time!
6. One meeting, one speaker at a time.

7. Flag confidential items – we will keep confidences.
8. We will defend each other and our decisions outside the room.
9. Turn complaints into requests.
10. Phones off during the meeting.
11. No smoking in the meeting room.
12. Cheap shots cost money (that can produce some humorous moments!).

In other words, when meeting with each other, or solving problems together, managers don't flounder around using plenty of air-time but getting nowhere. They have been trained in, and use, brainstorming techniques (see Ladder 5), they know how to write measurable objectives, they know how to construct a matrix calendar when planning projects, they can map and analyse processes, they don't manage any more by the seat of their pants. In short, the processes encourage teamwork, it is built into the sinews of the organization.

LEVEL 5

'Teams exist everywhere, and have become a way of life'

Companies who have reached this stage have learnt not to set up teams for everything. For example, individuals may come up with some brilliant ideas alone, but often it takes a team to see good ideas implemented effectively. They also realize that dedicated individuals can do good research on their own, or compose excellent reports. However, companies at this level know the value of putting together all the skills necessary for key projects, and individuals are used to being members of different teams that span several disciplines. In fact teamwork has become part of the culture of the business. It is simply 'how we do things round here'.

'Self-directed teams are set up and working effectively'

Self-directed teams are those who have no nominated team leader or boss. They work on everything and decide everything as a team. They allocate responsibilities among themselves, display versatility between jobs, produce their own budgets, make contracts with their customers and suppliers, set their own objectives, measure their own performance, and make short-term changes to accommodate unforeseen problems.

Many feel any team needs a leader, or that one will emerge in practice even if they are not appointed. In practice, some 'leaderless' self-directed teams work well, and achieve productivity and delivery performance well ahead of supervised groups. Also, team members tend to act more responsibly and are much more cognizant of their fellow-workers. These teams tend also to be quick to react to short-term customer requests and to respond to challenges.

In general, however, groups need to have been operating in 'team' mode for some time before they can make the transition to 'self-directed' successfully. You also need to have the right balance of personality types, as serious tensions can develop without it. That's where an experienced 'coach' can be useful to help teams adjust in the early stages, or to help when problems arise.

Also, communications can be a problem. For example, when the company issues general communications, say, 'to all Managers', to whom should the item be sent? Anyone in the group? Does everyone then have the responsibility to pass that on to everyone else? What if an 'internal customer' manager has a problem to raise with the group, should he just talk to anyone? If an external customer wants to phone in, whom should he ask for? Will anyone do? Most companies and customers don't naturally know how to deal with groups without a nominated leader, so all these issues have to be talked through and resolved.

However, many self-directed groups do produce outstanding performance, and team members can often get a whole new lease of life as a result.

'The versatility in teams means they cope with change well'

'Teams celebrate achievements and expect success'

Like football teams used to being at the top of their league, teams at Level 5 have come to expect success. They can see themselves winning before they start. They don't begin to doubt themselves at the first sign of failure, they are confident about their ability to keep getting good results. And it always pays to encourage teams to celebrate when they win. There are always times when it's hard work, hard going. So enhance the winning feeling when success comes along. That's a feeling worth coming to work for.

IDEAS AND TECHNIQUES YOU CAN USE

In this section we deal with the following:

- requirements for the implementation of front-line teamwork;
- examples of Project Team Briefs.

Implementing front-line teamwork

As you will realize, it takes more than simply telling existing working groups 'All right, you're now a team' to make teamworking effective. Roles, attitudes, and working practices all have to change. Here is the model we ourselves use when implementing front-line teamwork.

Front-line teamwork: GPM model

1. Employees will be treated like mature adults and expected to behave like mature adults. In practice this will mean front-line employees will be:

   - given more responsibility;

- trusted more;
- allowed to make more decisions;
- trained.

Supervisors will stop 'super-vising', ie looking over people's shoulder to make sure they don't do the wrong thing. That will not be a job any more. Employees will be expected to do the right thing without being policed into it.
2. Job roles have to change, ie:
   - what the manager does;
   - what the supervisor does;
   - what the front-line employee does.

Every job, and that also means every level of job, must add some unique value to the organization. Every job can be expressed in its measurable outputs which are unique to that position, and which will enable the job-holder to know, without having to ask his boss, when he is succeeding.
3. Supervisors will change their role to that of becoming team leader. Teams will be expected to take decisions and get the right things done for their customers on their own. The team leader's role will involve:

- *Taking the lead.* That is, leading the team to places, to levels of performance, where they have never been before. That means he needs to have a good idea (a vision, if you like) of where he wants the team to go, and taking initiatives to help get them there.
- *Adding value.* Supervising will not be a job any more – that only adds cost. The team leader's activities must actually *add value* to what the team already does, ie do something different and additional which contributes to the team's performance. He must avoid duplicating what others already do, ie supervising, checking, second guessing, and the rest. That only adds cost. They must add value.
- *Making improvements.* These activities will occupy some 40–50% of his time. That means *removing obstacles*, seeking out the causes of operational problems (especially the recurrent ones) that prevent his team doing even better. It will mean actively *devising improvements* to current methods, layout, etc, that improve quality, cut waste, increase productivity and lower costs.
- *Making contracts with suppliers.* That means getting the right information, in the right form, and at the right time. It means getting good raw materials, in the right quantities, at the right time. It means having the right tools and equipment, in fact everything they need to do a good job.
- *Making contracts with customers.* Whether outside (the most important) or inside (the next process), he needs to meet face-to-face with his customers to understand their wants and needs. At the same time he has to manage customer expectations, ie agree schedules and standards with them that his team can actually meet, and meet unfailingly.

- *Helping his team act like a team.* In other words, creating and nurturing good team relationships, keeping them productive and harmonious. Encouraging team members to take initiatives, building on each other's good ideas, 'mucking in' when necessary to handle crises, etc.
- *Developing the team.* It will mean agreeing learning objectives with individual team members, so that at the end of the work year they are better and more knowledgeable than they were at the beginning. It means communicating regularly with the team, and involving them in brainstorming sessions where they tackle their difficult problems together. It means motivating the team, challenging them to ever continuous improvements. And it means developing himself year on year through a process of continuous learning.

4. One key concept that has to be embraced is the *elimination of waste* in all its forms, especially the wastes of duplication, checking, second guessing, and doing things two, three and four times. That includes the wastes also of delay, waiting, excessive transport and storage, over-stocking, over-production, run-outs, and mistakes that lead to rework and repetition. And we need every pair of eyes and every brain in the company working on that every day.

5. Continuous improvement, in every aspect of the company's operations, has to become part of the company's culture. Improvements will no longer be the exclusive territory of managers, we want everyone in the business to see it as part of their everyday job. That means creating forums where employees can contribute their ideas, where they will get listened to, and their ideas tried out in practice.

   You should be able to say to team leaders and managers in every area and at every level: 'If you or your team are doing in six months' time exactly the same as you are doing today, then that's a failure.'

6. We must accept that continuous improvement does not just mean in operations, but also in ourselves. In other words, wherever we are in the organization, *continuous learning* has to become a way of life. But it is a way of life everyone will enjoy.

   The seriousness of any company committed to continuous learning will show in the resources they put behind their efforts. For example:

- time: by building in, say, one or two days' off-the-job training every year for every employee in the company;
- money: by having a suitable training area, good equipment and appointed trainers. Also, allocating a sensible annual budget spend for the purpose. For example, how about starting modestly with, say, 1% of payroll?
- effort: in the form of managers (at every level) realizing that part of the job is passing on their knowledge by training others, ie preparing and presenting lively and practical courses.

7. We need to accept the key concept of *measurement* – only that way will we really know if we are genuinely getting any better, ie the purpose of it all.

We should cease reliance on opinion ('Well, I *feel* things are getting better', or 'I *think* things are improving'), and find out the facts – that is the acid test. And that means measurement for all, whether in administration, engineering, research, marketing, sales, production and senior management.

In general, we will want to use visible measurement systems in every area, ie with standards of performance/parameters/goals agreed with the working team, information charts kept up-to-date by the team, and publicly and understandably displayed. And part of measurement will be the constant search for continuous improvement.

8. Teamwork needs to become part of 'how we do things around here'. In practice that will mean *team objectives* being agreed within the various working teams, who conduct improvement and problem-solving sessions together, who cover for each other in cases of absence, who learn each others' jobs, who rotate functions for variety and competence and who meet together frequently to communicate, make plans and organize tasks.

Cross-departmental and multi-disciplinary teams should become the norm to tackle larger cross-company issues, to make proposals on major system changes, organization moves, purchases of new equipment, introduction of new products or services, etc. Not only does this provide better solutions and practical proposals, serving on such teams materially helps the development of the individuals involved.

9. We will want all the people in the company *to share in the benefits and the rewards.* We want it to be as interesting to be at work as to be at home. The facts show that profit-sharing participation not only gets employees feeling that 'profits are a good thing', but it helps produce consistently better results for commercial companies. Wherever possible we would want all employees to share in their company's profitability on a known and similar basis, so that we can all gain the financial benefit and work well together as a team.

Although we must always treat our business and our customers seriously, we want to enjoy work too. We will actively look for opportunities to reward people for exceptional effort, unusual customer service, and meeting tough targets. We will celebrate success, regularly. We want our company to have the sweet smell of confidence and success about it.

There is no quick fix, some magic tablet you can take to make all this happen in a short period of time. Think in terms at least of a three-year scenario. This is not simply the learning of a bunch of new techniques. This calls for the development of new attitudes, it represents a sea change, the adoption of a whole new way of life.

EXAMPLES OF PROJECT TEAM BRIEFS

Reduce the production lead times on our top three selling products by 50% within nine months. Get the agreement of all the necessary parties to the actions that have to be taken to make this happen. Plan how the changes proposed will be communicated and implemented. Keep the costs of implementation low.
(Machine tools company)

Cut company stock-holding – raw materials, work in progress and fin-ished goods – by 50% within a year, without damaging customer service or production performance. Propose practical check systems for use in each area of the company which keep stocks at these levels. Visit other companies who have successfully cut stock-holding and build in the lessons gained to your plans. Propose further steps to cut stocks by a further 50% in year two.
(Consumer durables manufacturer)

Review our entire pay and rewards system to:

- ensure they line up with our new company goals;
- reward achievement and teamwork;
- avoid inconsistency and invidious comparisons between departments.

Keep it simple. Propose how the changes can be introduced and wel-comed.
(Hotel chain)

Revise our employee communications system so that it:

- gets management meeting information down to the lowest level in the business within 48 hours maximum;
- allows any employee to speak to anyone in the business to resolve any customer problem quickly, at worst within 24 hours;
- gets, and rapidly implements, employee job improvement suggestions.
  (Insurance company)

Propose steps whereby waiting time for patients is minimized in every area of the hospital (15 minutes max). Suggest procedures within which each department will set standards and measure performance. Propose signage that will allow even older patients to find any department easily and without fail.
(Hospital)

N i n e

Staff Empowerment and Involvement

LEVELS	MEASURES
Level 1	Employees don't want any responsibility; they want managers to be responsible for everything. Managers want employees just to do as they're told. Few, if any, team involvement meetings are held.
Level 2	Employees are treated like adults, and expected to behave like adults, ie to work effectively without supervision. Employees are given full responsibility for their own work. Teams are given all the tools and information they need to do the job. Team meeting sessions are held at least monthly.
Level 3	Every team understands its own unique contributions. Individuals know the boundaries of their authority, and take initiatives to solve problems or please customers. Teams collect data on performance and use this with their manager to make continuous improvements.
Level 4	Every job-holder knows his own unique contributions. Staff handle the whole job themselves, so managers can concentrate on improving the current systems. They meet their customers' requirements even in difficult circumstances.
Level 5	Individuals agree self-set objectives and do self-appraisal. Teams set and meet their own improvement objectives. They both meet and beat their customers' expectations. Teams are involved in recruitment, equipment purchase, area layout, producing their own budgets, etc.

LEVEL 1

'Employees don't want any responsibility; they want managers to be responsible for everything'

This is a fairly typical response of employees who have not been asked to get involved in their work, to help in solving problems, to make suggestions for improvement, etc. They say things like: 'Why should we take responsibility?', 'Nobody has asked me to do this before', 'That's what managers get paid for, isn't it, taking responsibility?' There are two answers to this: that may be how things have been until now, but we would like you to get involved in making things better here, and doing things better for the customer. Or, managers are responsible for a lot of things, but employees are responsible for that which they control, such as their own productivity, the quality of the products or service they produce, keeping their workplace in good order, etc. If managers accept this first reaction, ie 'We're not paid to take responsibility', then the company will never make any progress. That may be employees' general first reaction. But it is not how things have to stay.

'Managers want employees just to do as they're told'

There are many managers who would be glad if employees simply did as they were told, which many find hard enough to achieve. However, if that is all they do, employees will not use their common sense to solve problems, and will blame everything on the manager when things do go wrong (as they should if the manager has taken on all the responsibility). There is often a negative reaction from employees when talk about empowerment and involvement starts, but it should certainly not be taken as a sign that nothing can be done. The idea that managers are powerless to do anything unless employees agree straight away needs to be rejected.

'Few, if any, team involvement meetings are held'

The very first step along the empowerment route is getting employees involved in talking about their work, ie about quality of the products they make, about removing obstacles to productivity, about how they can serve their customers better, and about generating ideas for improvement. You can't do that if you don't talk to them as a group.

It is quite common for team meetings to be held only spasmodically or not at all. The reason is that front-line supervisors often find the process difficult, meetings may as a result have become dull and boring, and as a result neither team leader nor employees are enthusiastic about attending. But team meetings are not just about passing on corporate information from senior management as a 'duty', and listening patiently to complaints from team members. They need to be about the work people do every day, about solving problems, about pooling the ideas of the whole team to keep improving continuously, about doing the job easier, better, cheaper, faster and safer.

LEVEL 2

'Employees are treated like adults, and expected to behave like adults, ie to work effectively without supervision'

This is a fundamental concept on the subject of empowerment. It does not mean, as many managers secretly fear, that they will be deprived of all their decision-making powers and have to manage solely by consensus. That could lead to chaos. But it does mean giving *employees full responsibility for those things of which they are already in control*, ie the products they make or the service they deliver to their customers. It's management's job to provide the right materials, equipment, information and training to do the job right first time. With that back-up, it's then the employee's responsibility (not the manager's) to do the job right for their customer.

In other words, we want to treat every employee like an adult, but we expect employees to act like an adult in return. We don't want any more to treat them like children, ie chasing around to make sure everyone is getting on with the job. We want them to act like they were working in their own business. We expect them to do the right thing in terms of work, quality, communication, etc, even when the supervisor is not around. And when they do, it frees up a great deal of management time. When this philosophy is fully in place, our experience shows it releases some 30 per cent of the front-line manager's time to devote to real value-adding activities.

Given how tough business and competition has become, we no longer can afford to spend time chasing and cajoling. Those who want to continue acting like children, ie needing constant supervision, making themselves scarce during the day, lining up at the exit well before normal closing time, etc, may need to think about their continued future with the business. Every company needs adults who are prepared to use their common sense and do a good job every day without having to be policed. Most employees actually prefer to be treated like adults. When you do, you can expect a significant change in employee attitudes and performance.

'Employees are given full responsibility for their own work'

Once employees have been given the tools, information and training necessary to do the job, then that should be the person in charge of the quality of the job or the service delivered, no one else. There should be a deliberate effort to get rid of second-guessing check-ups, whether from quality inspectors or in the form of authorising decisions through the management hierarchy. Full responsibility for service, quality and output should be given to the employee doing the job.

At first, employees are fearful that they won't have some 'inspector' checking up that their work is OK. They say things like: 'That means a customer could get a product that is not right if the inspector doesn't check it', hoping you will renege on your decision and let them off the hook. The answer is:

'Do you know how to make the product right? (They always admit they do.) Well, I want you to be the eyes and ears of the customer. I'm going to trust you to get it right for our customers.' It helps to introduce 'traceability' at the same time, ie to be able to trace back to the individual concerned any problems that arise, not by way of seeking out the sinner, but to ensure the individual learns from the event, and puts the problem to bed permanently. Traceability means the company is serious, and when it is introduced, employees feel the full weight of their responsibility. That responsibility (which only managers have felt up till now) is the very thing that brings on responsible, adult behaviour.

This move means that managers have to take a risk, ie trusting their staff to do things right without their supervision. In flow-line production situations like car manufacturing, the motto for years has been: whatever you do, don't stop the line. That is why it obviously took a bit of courage when management at Ford's Edison, New Jersey plant decided to give every operator a button to stop the line when necessary to correct any quality problem that surfaced. And they did stop the line, some 20 to 30 times a day. But the average stoppage was only about 10 seconds long. Interestingly, line productivity was not affected. But in the first nine months of the experiment defects dropped from 17.1 per car to 0.8 per car, and cars requiring rework at the end of the line fell by an astonishing 97 per cent! Another positive effect of giving operators more control of their environment was that the backlog of union grievances fell from approximately 200 to an average of less than 12! Even in the toughest situations, when you finally trust employees to use their common sense to do a better job, they will do just that. But the trusting comes first.

'Employees are given all the tools and information they need to do the job'

There is no way that employees can be expected to do the job without all the right materials, tools and information, but it is surprising in how many companies this is not the case. In a survey in one large UK engineering company, for instance, as many as 80 per cent of employees said they did not have all the tools required to do a good job, and some 66 per cent said they did not have all the information required. Indeed, the skilled craftsmen had to put all their tools into the store every evening before they went home (as a result of tools previously going missing) and then queue for them at the store window the following day to take them back out again! You cannot get off the ground in your journey to world class performance unless you start by instituting trust and responsibility on everybody's part.

That applies to information too. Because 'information is power', there is a tendency for managers to keep it to themselves. In companies on the way to world class, the information required to do any job is not held in the hands of a supervisor or a production controller's desk. Employees are deliberately given *all* the information they need to do the complete job. For example, at Edward Rose, a manufacturing company in the UK making parts for the automotive industry, it is typical for the customer company (in this case Ford) to fax the information on production requirements directly into the cell that produces the part. That means production requirements do not go via the office, a higher manager or even the team leader! The team handles the whole job by themselves. They keep their office up-to-date with what they are doing and what they have done. Their manager is released from running around simply maintaining the system they have now, and spending more of his time doing his real job, ie improving what they have now.

'Team meeting sessions are held at least monthly'

The front-line manager is the face of the company that employees see every day. To them he represents the company, he is the company. That person needs to be the company's best two-way communicator in the business. If the company has not taken the trouble to treat the front-line manager as such, and to train him in the art of communicating, then the grapevine will take over as the most powerful communicator in the company. The communications role of the front-line manager is described in more detail in Ladder 11 on Purposeful Communication. We recommend that team meetings are held at least once a month face-to-face, team leader to team. We would normally expect them to cover the following four areas:

1. How the company is doing. What's happening with regard to results, the market, the legislation, customers, products, services – anything that may affect team members, or how the company operates.
2. How the section is doing. How we are doing against our standards or objectives. What is happening in upstream or downstream departments that may affect the team. Welcoming new people. Laying out the work plan for the month, mentioning any special points.
3. Team member points. This gives team members a chance to raise any point that needs discussing or resolving. Team members will know that for every problem they raise, they have to suggest at least one practical solution.
4. Team improvement project. Each month, with the whole team together, at least half of the time should be given over to tackling some problem that affects the whole section, or using the ideas of team members to plan some section improvement.

The meeting should take approximately an hour in a suitable location with either an overhead projector, flipchart, white board, or the like.

We also favour holding 10-minute 'start-of-day' team meetings, to keep teams up-to-date and working effectively as a team. This is described in more detail in Ladder 8 on Teamwork.

LEVEL 3

'Every team understands its own unique contributions'

Most job descriptions are written in terms of activities, with lots of present participles like 'planning, organizing, managing and controlling'. We are much less concerned with the activities a job-holder involves himself in, and much more concerned with how effective he is in getting the *results* required. For example, a salesperson may make a number of sales calls, but these are only activities. They only add cost. The only thing that counts is actual sales. That's the output we need, that's the only thing that *adds value*. Unique contributions are a means of making clear both to teams and individuals exactly what *outputs* are required of their role, ie the results that constitute the measurable *added value* of the job. Unique contributions have five essential characteristics:

1. They express output (not activity).
2. They are unique to the department or job-holder.
3. They lead to the setting of measurable objectives and standards.
4. They are within the control or authority of the department or job-holder.
5. They can be expressed in one to five words.

When teams first try to list the outputs they are responsible for, they generally compose a table of activities, many of them difficult to measure. It takes them time to clarify just what they are uniquely accountable for, and how they should measure their performance. But the struggle is worth it. The process changes their view about what the job really is, about what they need to concentrate on to get results, and, importantly, just how they should be spending their time. Here's an example to show just what we mean. This was the managing director of an insurance business. This was his first list:

1. Co-ordinate activities of the team.
2. Oversee group achievement.
3. Agree objectives with team members.
4. Act as figurehead – internal and external
5. Consider/propose forward activities.
6. Organize and lead roadshows.
7. Lead team in overcoming obstacles.
8. Last stage in employee grievance procedure.
9. Promote company's interests in Group.

His fellow directors felt these were just a list of activities. In discussion, they arrived at a list of outputs for which he was uniquely responsible. Underneath each are measures by which the MD would know when he was succeeding.

1. Overall company plan

   - Acceptance by Holding Board.
   - Degree to which plan met.

2. Overall company performance

   - Profit meets plan.
   - Sales growth exceeds cost growth and RPI.
   - Product profitability versus plan.

3. Longer-term company objectives

   - Existence of three-year plan.
   - Acceptance by Holding Board.
   - Objectives actually fulfilled.

4. Holding company satisfaction

   - No major inquisitions.
   - Plans accepted on first submission.
   - Acceptance of recommendations for change.

5. Company morale

   - Absence of grievances.
   - Attitude survey scores meet agreed health standards.

6. Team member effectiveness

   - Appointees meet job requirements.
   - Personal development plans agreed each year.
   - No inadequate performers more than one year in the job.

See the examples of unique contributions for an engineering division and a finance department in Ideas and Techniques You Can Use section.

'Individuals know the boundaries of their authority, and take initiatives to solve problems or please customers'

Managers can sometimes get sensitive about their subordinates crossing departmental boundaries, or discussing anything with managers at a level higher than themselves. However, this can prove a real impediment to problem solving, especially solving customers' problems. Empowering employees to talk with managers at any level has the advantage of getting problems solved with the minimum of delay. Employees can then give answers rather than make excuses (eg the standard excuse 'I'll have to check and get back to you'). Managers often fear that more junior employees will make mistakes if everything they do is not checked. Our experience is that employees don't try so hard if they know their boss will make the decision anyway. They act even more responsibility when given the authority to act.

That is why our prime definition of empowerment is:

Giving employees the authority and responsibility to do it right for the customer at the time

We say to production employees: don't hesitate to put a quality fault right whenever you see it; don't pass anything on to your internal customer that doesn't allow them to do a zero defect job; and don't even think of sending to the external customer something that you know isn't perfect. That kind of advice is even more important for service employees. Good service can only be given at the point of contact with the customer. It won't wait. It has to be done at the time.

Here are a couple of examples of service companies who have taken empowerment to heart. The hotel industry is a business where so many small things can potentially go wrong for the customer. And when they do, customers want the problem put right straight away, not sometime later. Front-line employees, however, are often afraid to go too far, just in case they get a telling-off from their boss. To make the position abundantly clear, the Ritz-Carlton Hotel Group in the United States empower all their employees to spend up to $2,000 on their own initiative to solve any customer problem they may come across that needs immediate action. That's empowerment.

Legal and General Assurance were rather miffed to find in a survey they conducted among their brokers that they were judged 'no better than any other insurance company'. Customers with claims were shunted from department to department, staff who took their phone calls inevitably said they had to check with others before they could give them a decision, and generally clients were subjected to delays and hand-offs. The company decided to change all that. Now any employee who gets a telephone call from a customer takes responsibility for handling the case, and has the authority to speak to anybody else in the company (including the managing director) to deal with the customer's needs. The company has not experienced any disasters as a result. On the contrary, 'Chinese walls' between departments have fallen, and front-line staff have been found to make remarkably mature decisions.

A word of warning here. Do not just suddenly declare: 'You can now talk to anyone in the business directly to get any problem resolved and the job done.' Unless senior and middle managers are in agreement, the old barriers and departmentalism will remain. Something has to be done structurally different to make it easy for staff to use the new channels. One sure way of measuring success is to ask staff by confidential survey if they find cross-boundary communication easier and 'obstacle-free'. Then further step-by-step action can be taken until the whole process becomes slick and effective.

'Teams collect data on performance and use this with their manager to make continuous improvements'

At Level 3 Visible Measures (see Ladder 4) are displayed in the work areas recording day-to-day performance. Teams use the data to focus on priorities, and to make steady continuous improvements.

LEVEL 4

'Every job-holder knows his own unique contributions'

Whereas at Level 3 every team will have worked through its own unique contributions (UCs), at Level 4 the process has reached every *job-holder*. Each job has been spelled out in the form of unique contributions with success measures under each. By way of further examples, here are the UCs from a manufacturing company of a team operator and a team leader. UCs are not only used to write objectives every year but also for training purposes, planning organization structures, recruitment, etc.

Team Operator unique contributions

1. Product output:

    - meets or beats production targets (in training and on the job).

2. Product quality:

    - team consistently below reject target level;
    - no reject from customer due to team fault.

3. Job skills and flexibility:

    - able to perform variety of jobs;
    - undertakes routine non-specialist maintenance;
    - undertakes training or jobs to meet company needs;
    - trains colleagues when necessary.

4. Data recording:

    - data recorded is accurate and up-to-date.

5. Safe operating practices:

    - always uses approved working methods;
    - never endangers himself or others.

6. Good housekeeping:

    - maintains team work area and equipment in 'spotless' condition;

- contributes to cleanliness of other company areas;
- consistently meets or exceeds standards.

7. Attitude and contribution:

- suggestions made for continuous improvement;
- responds positively to short-notice problems;
- works well as a team member;
- demonstrates commitment to company goals.

8. Attendance:

- no absence problems.

Team Leader unique contributions

1. Meeting section production schedules:

- schedules actually met on time.

2. Team quality performance feedback:

- quality information fed back promptly to team members;
- appropriate action taken.

3. Team productivity:

- meets or exceeds productivity targets.

4. Production improvements:

- number of improvements actually introduced;
- value of benefits realized.

5. Safe working methods:

- equipment safe to operate at all times;
- team members fully trained in safety.

6. Housekeeping standards:

- standards clear to team members;
- actually met by team members.

7. Team communications:

- relevant information passed to and from team members daily;

- commitments agreed with team;
- commitments actually delivered on.

8. Team member effectiveness:

- speed in reaching quality and output standards;
- team members increase skills year by year;
- team member co-operation and resourcefulness;
- no non-performer left more than three months in the job.

Please note: the team leader does not just supervise, ie 'make sure' team members are doing their job. That is duplication, ie waste. He must add extra value, additional unique contributions. For example, he may be in charge of 'housekeeping standards', but team members are responsible for 'good housekeeping'. He may be responsible for 'safety methods', but it is team members who have to perform within 'safe operating practices'. Each level has to add something measurable, valuable and different.

'Staff handle the whole job themselves, so managers can concentrate on improving the current systems'

The key point here is that the team member's primary job is to follow the systems and Best Operating Practices that are already in place, ie to *maintain* the current system. The team leader's key job, on the other hand, is to *improve* the current system.

In his book *Kaizen*, Masaaki Imai contends that if there is one factor that explains the difference in performance between Japanese companies and their Western counterparts, it is *kaizen*. (*Kaizen* is composed of two Japanese words; *kai* – change, and *zen* – good, and has come to mean 'continuous improvement' in the West.) His view is that Western companies are often impatient and prefer quantum leap improvements even if that involves large capital cost to get it. This might involve installing a whole new automated manufacturing line, or a comprehensive computer system – what Imai names 'Innovation'. The Japanese, however, pressed by their high-value currency and need to export into a fanatical abhorrence of waste, have preferred to make the step-by-step, small, low-cost continuous improvements (*kaizen*) that have helped make Japanese companies the success they are today. He sees every level of employee concerning themselves with 'Maintenance' in Western companies, with only senior management being involved in 'Innovation'. Figures 9.1 and 9.2 show Imai's view of the difference between Western and Japanese management styles.

With the Japanese pattern, however, *kaizen* sweeps right through the whole workforce, with even supervision spending something like 40 per cent of their time on improvement activities, and using the ideas contributed by their front-line people. We think there's a lesson here.

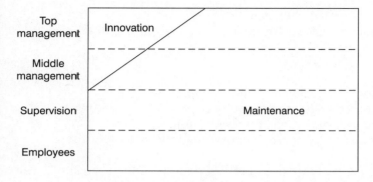

Figure 9.1 Tendency of Western management

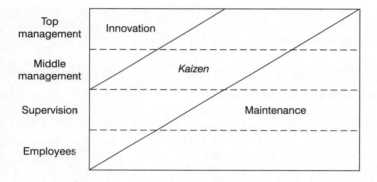

Figure 9.2 Tendency of Japanese management

'They meet their customers' requirements even in difficult circumstances'

At Level 4, team members know exactly who their customers are, both internal and external. By this stage, they have spent some time not only serving these customers but seeking out year-on-year improvements, and are therefore used to dealing with everyday problems. When more difficult problems arise, they get in contact with their customers to work out deals that ensure they can accommodate each other's needs successfully even under difficult circumstances.

LEVEL 5

'Individuals agree self-set objectives and do self-appraisal'

At this stage we expect managers and staff to take the prime responsibility for their own behaviour, performance and development. In Ladder 1, Aligning

Management Objectives, we offered rules for making objectives SMART (ie specific, measurable, agreed, realistic and time-bounded). In Ladder 10, Rewards and Recognition, we elaborate on appraisal systems designed to support employee development and motivation. At Level 5, staff should be encouraged to propose their own improvement objectives, and to assess their own performance *before* they meet with their manager to discuss how they have done, and how they can improve even further in the future.

Asking subordinates to draw up the first draft of their objectives has several advantages:

1. They have to *think* about the job. Not only must they think about their own job and what could be improved, they have to think about the objectives they propose will fit in with the company's overall goals. That is a good thinking exercise.
2. They have to get *specific*. The task of getting their ideas down on paper forces subordinates to crystallize their thoughts and make sensible proposals.
3. Subordinates tend to set themselves tougher objectives than their boss would. The boss then, instead of getting into 'argue' mode justifying the objectives he wants to hand down, can then adopt a 'help' stance to persuade the subordinate not to try and attempt too much, and to sort out the priorities.
4. Finally, the subordinate feels ownership of the objectives he himself wrote. And with ownership comes commitment.

The same is true for appraisals. If appraisees are asked to assess themselves in writing, they are generally quite realistic about their performance. In fact, more often than not they are modest in their assessment, and tend to under-claim, if anything. That gives the manager the opportunity to be supportive, positive and encouraging. However, if the appraisal consists only of the manager giving his assessment of the subordinate's performance, the appraisee tends to get defensive to justify himself. That creates conflict. The prime purpose of the appraisal is not an argument, it is to further the development of the subordinate in a constructive and positive fashion.

There are different forms of appraisal process that you can use, but with the manager firmly in his role as 'coach', this is the sequence we recommend:

1. Privately, the subordinate writes notes on his performance against his agreed objectives, the points he has learnt from the successes and failures during the year, his tentative objectives for the coming year, and his personal aims for his own further progress.
2. Privately, the manager writes notes of his assessment of his subordinate's performance, the possible learning points, some suggested objectives for the next year, and his view on further development.
3. They then meet together at a pre-arranged time, quietly, privately, for at least an hour, to conduct the appraisal. The subordinate gets to speak first, on every subject. In discussion they then come to an agreement about the key points.

4. Following the appraisal, the manager writes up the appraisal assessment, including the specific learning and development objectives agreed for the next year.
5. The subordinate initials the appraisal document to indicate he has seen and understood the assessment and learning plans.

'Teams set and meet their own improvement objectives'

At front-line level, this refers to teams agreeing what improvement objectives they think they can realistically set for the coming period. At management level it means teams conducting a Team Objectives Meeting (TOM) or the like in every department every year. (See Ladder 1 on this subject.)

'They both meet and beat their customers' expectations'

At this level teams are well educated about managing their customers' expectations. They know that just to meet their customers' expectations they have to deliver what they promised. Anything short of that will bring irritation, and maybe even loss of business. As a result, they are careful not to overclaim in the beginning, knowing that customer trust is only retained by consistent performance. They also know that they will delight their customers by beating their expectations. So they deliberately then look for opportunities to give their customers pleasant surprises.

'Teams are involved in recruitment, equipment purchase, area layout, producing their own budgets, etc'

Studies conducted during World War II showed that trainees were better able to predict who would make a successful pilot than the instructors themselves! Other studies since conducted in industry have repeated this finding, and have even shown that subordinates make better judges than supervisors. So given practical guidelines and sensible procedures, involving employees in selection procedures may actually *improve* the quality of recruits the company takes on.

Employees tend to set tough criteria for potential employees. Subconsciously, they believe themselves to be all 'good guys', and not just any person is going to be good enough to do the job they do. Therefore they are demanding. Furthermore, they don't want to tell potential employees that the company is a terrible place to work – why would they be working there if it was? So they find themselves telling candidates the good things about the place, defending its virtues. And the act of articulating the positive aspects of the company makes them appreciate it more. So the company's values and culture are advocated and perpetuated. Finally, and just as important, they are likely to choose 'people who fit', both with the company's values and with their work team. Candidates also get the chance of talking directly to the people they will be working with, and that also helps them decide whether the company is the type of organization they would like to join.

Companies at Level 5 let employees assume responsibility for training colleagues. No matter how well a person knows the job, there is nothing to teach you your own job better than having to teach someone else. It helps the individual to organize his thoughts and knowledge in a coherent manner. In addition, if the job of 'trainer' has additional status ('only the skilled and trusted are chosen to be trainers'), this can visibly increase the employee's self-esteem. The 'trainer' also starts feeling constrained into setting an example all the time for everyone. Good habits are thus reinforced. And finally, trainers find themselves speaking as advocates of the company's way of doing things – after all, they are now part of it. However, it is best to ensure that the very best person is selected to train others. Experiments conducted in the United States in the 1960s showed the value of training new recruits with the very best performers you've got. As you might expect, new recruits tend to act in the image of those who first taught them.

IDEAS AND TECHNIQUES YOU CAN USE

In this section we give several examples of processes and techniques that foster employees taking on more responsibility, that help to clarify job roles in output terms, and get employees involved in suggesting improvements. They are:

- key differences between old and new forms of employee appraisal;
- the four-step process of delegation;
- examples of unique contributions;
- an example of a suggestion form.

Table 9.1 Appraisal system differences

Old	New
Based on qualities, abilities (how do you do it)	Based on objectives/results (what you have achieved)
Concentrates on the past	Balance of past and future
Manager's view predominates	Large element of self-assessment and discussion
Assessment against others	Assessment against agreed objectives
Training recommendations focus on weaknesses	Learning objectives focus on improving strengths
Anxiety-creating	'No surprises' environment
Purpose: assessment	Purpose: motivation

Key differences between the old and new forms of employee appraisal

Most appraisees see an appraisal like an exam, and they don't often have pleasant memories of these. The appraisal systems we recommend in Ladder 10, Rewards and Recognition, are based on using the appraisal discussion between manager and subordinate as a self-development tool. These are the key differences we see between the old and new forms of appraisal system (see Figure 9.3).

The four-step process of delegation

Many managers are afraid to delegate in case their subordinate subsequently makes a mistake, and the manager then finds himself still accountable. But if the manager does not delegate responsibility, it then becomes very difficult for subordinates to grow and develop. The answer is to proceed step by step.

These are the four steps we recommend:

1. *Directing*
   Boss decides   what is to be done
                       how it is to be done
                       how it is to be measured
                       short interval report-backs
   Boss tells   how he will help
                       supervises and controls

2. *Coaching*
   Boss decides   what is to be done
                       how it is to be measured
   Boss asks   suggestions how the job is to be done, and agrees
                       longer interval report-backs
   Boss asks   what help is needed
                       supervises and coaches

3. *Supporting*
   Boss asks   subordinate to suggest what
                       he thinks needs to be done
                       how it should be done
                       how it should be measured
   Boss   discusses and agrees
                       offers help and support
                       agrees report-back intervals

4. *Delegating*
   Subordinate   takes full responsibility, and decides
                       what needs to be done
                       how
                       if and when to report back

Not everyone is ready for empowerment at the same rate. Some individuals will be ready on some aspects of their work and not on others. That's where the manager has to exercise judgement and discretion. But delegation implies trust. And trust not only enhances self-esteem, the new responsibility involved promotes development and growth.

Unique contributions

In many organizations there is a great deal of confusion between job descriptions, key result areas and unique contributions. Key result areas (sometimes accompanied by key performance indicators) focus on the results required of the job, and are essentially a performance management tool as distinct from a remuneration management tool. However, many key result areas are written in such a manner that the activity is described in detail, rather than what the results will look like when success has been achieved. Unique contributions is an improvement on the manner in which key results areas are composed.

Well-composed unique contributions have the following characteristics:

- They express output, ie what results when the job is done well.
- They are unique to the department or job holder, ie this is what the team or the individual is *uniquely* responsible for.
- They lead to the setting of measurable objectives and standards, ie if you can't measure it, you can stop doing it, as no one will notice the difference! List only outputs that are 'do-able' and measurable.
- They are within the control or authority of the department or job-holder, ie individuals or teams can only be responsible for those items where they have the *authority to act*; in other words on which they can take decisions.
- They can be expressed in one to five words.

The true test of a well-expressed unique contribution is that the job-holder will 'know, without anyone telling them, when he is doing a good job'. Normally, jobs have between 8 and 12 UCs. Each UC will have between three and six success measures.

Here are some *departmental* examples of unique contributions. We have to emphasize that handing teams a set of unique contributions is not effective. It is essential that working team itself works through the process together to 'discover' what are their real contributions to their business. That is what moves mind-sets and changes behaviour. Anything less is likely to be only cosmetic.

Engineering and Research Division: unique contributions and success measures

1. Design standards
   success measures:

   - products actually meet performance requirements in practice;
   - cost effectiveness;

- acceptance by Manufacturing for produceability;
- durability as shown in longer-term field returns.

2. System design specifications:

- specs produced within timescale;
- specs meet cost targets;
- systems actually perform to specification.

3. Material specifications:

- fitness for purpose;
- cost appropriate to purpose;
- material savings resulting from design modifications.

4. Production drawings:

- signed-off acceptance by Manufacturing;
- drawings available to Production time schedule;
- agreed modifications shown on drawings within one week.

5. Product development:

- number of new products actually launched;
- number of improvements made to existing products;
- compatibility of new products with company's older equipment.

6. Technical manuals:

- actively sought user ratings;
- no technical errors found;
- availability for product launches.

7. Technical sales proposals:

- proposals produced to promised timescale;
- acceptance by Sales and Marketing.

Finance Department: unique contributions and success measures

1. Cash control
   success measure:

- funds always available to meet company needs.

2. Financial reports:

- published within 12 working days of month end;

- easy for readers to pick out key data;
- systematic and accurate.

3. Budgets and forecasts:

- agreed budgets produced to meet Holding Board timescales.

4. Computer and telecommunications systems:

- systems meet specified requirements to agreed timescales;
- distinct, proven improvements introduced year by year.

5. Product insurances:

- insurances available as necessary at acceptable prices;
- loss ratio on underwriting account.

6. Taxation services:

- provided within budget ratio;
- underwriting loss ratios;
- client complaints and compliments;
- consultant performance meets published working standards.

7. Payroll and personnel administration:

- no failure to pay staff as a result of inaccurate or late data submitted to Holding Company;
- personnel records accurate and up-to-date.

Suggestion form example

Figure 9.4 is an example of a model suggestion form.

CONCLUSION

These are the solid benefits empowerment brings to any organization:

- helps people to grow;
- encourages them to take more interest;
- people feel more 'ownership' of what they produce;
- generates pride;
- enables managers to manage more effectively;
- fosters good teamwork;
- unleashes people's creative potential;
- produces a more effective and efficient workplace;
- encourages good people to stay;
- the customer (internal or external) gets a better deal.

They are the very benefits that help companies climb the ladder to world class performance. Wouldn't you want them in your organization?

THIS PART HAS TO BE COMPLETED BY THE SUGGESTOR
Name: . . . .   Personnel No: . . . .
Department: . . . .   Date: . . . .
Suggestions must be related to improvements with regard to: production methods, safety, housekeeping, productivity and quality
SUBJECT .... Suggestion: ....
TO BE COMPLETED BY EVALUATION COMMITTEE
Implementation date: .... Comments: .... Final result: ....
CHAIRMAN .... DATE ....

Figure 9.3 Suggestion form example

T e n

Rewards and Recognition

LEVELS	MEASURES
Level 1	The company pays only as much as it has to to get staff. Pay systems are complicated and unpublished. Overtime is frequent, often to cover *ad hoc* problems. Anomalies exist and complaints frequently arise.
Level 2	Pay systems have been simplified, are understandable and published. Employees are paid about the average for the work they do. Regular hours cover the normal work. Overtime is minimal. Additional skills acquired lead to additional pay.
Level 3	Employees are paid above the average for above average performance. Appraisal system rewards help motivate performance. Different sickness benefit and pension schemes are applied. Recognition system is in place and working.
Level 4	Surveys are conducted to ensure pay remains above average. Appraisal systems apply throughout the company. Sickness benefit and pension schemes are the same for all. Profit-sharing means staff are keen to see the company profitable.
Level 5	Staff have a 'no redundancy' undertaking. Above average pay attracts and retains the best staff. Appraisals encourage continuous improvement and continuous learning. Recognition system regularly encourages the behaviour the company wants to see.

LEVEL 1

'The company pays only as much as it has to to get staff'

Many companies do just that, on the basis of: 'Why add more costs than you have to? It all comes off the bottom line.' In theory, that sounds like common sense. In practice, however, employees may resort to tough tactics to secure a better deal. They may threaten to go slow, cut overtime, or come out on strike. Then the company is forced to negotiate. Virtually always, employees do find they end up with a better deal than they were first offered. That encourages them to oppose anything management first proposes, assuming that conflict will always pay off better than co-operation.

When staff and management are continually locked in this type of conflict situation, it leaves no chance of the company ever getting to world class. That is the fundamental problem with trying to pay as little as you can get away with.

Some companies will argue that they do it to contain their costs. But world class companies have labour costs well under 10 per cent of total product costs, many even lower than 5 per cent. So even if they added as much as 10 per cent to their labour costs, it would only add 1 per cent or less to their total product cost! World class companies concentrate on saving on major costs such as materials and overheads. That is where real savings are to be found, not in wages.

Companies basically need to structure their pay and benefits to attract and retain the quality of staff they need. Paying the lowest wages possible is not going to do that. Furthermore, if a company pays 'above average' wages, it can legitimately ask for 'above average' performance in return. That is a necessity in any company serious about becoming world class.

'Pay systems are complicated and unpublished'

This is a commonplace in many companies. What happens is management makes concessions to solve specific problems over the years until they have a tottering edifice of a pay system that has little logic left. Generally the company is scared to touch anything in case the whole structure collapses like a set of dominoes. One of the reasons the anomalies are tolerated is that elements have crept in over the years, none of which was worth protesting about by itself when it happened. In these conditions management tend not to publish pay scales in case staff find out the whole truth. That could be both problematic and embarrassing. Best to let sleeping dogs lie!

These are just some of the problems that arise:

- Different pay systems apply to different categories of staff and produce quite different rewards.
- Pay tends to drift towards the top of pay scales, seemingly independent of performance.

- Staff members falling into what can be called 'prima donna' categories are paid well above people in comparable jobs, often as a result of these individuals causing problems and having to be paid more to keep the peace.
- Some people in production areas may be allowed to go home early when they have produced their quota, while others have to stay on.
- Special payments are made for a whole variety of reasons, some remaining even when the reason for their payment has disappeared.
- Complicated piecework systems are in place that require a Work Study Department to measure work, and set pay rates. These are often then disputed, negotiated and abused.
- Departmental bonuses give widely different earning for apparently similar effort, causing invidious comparisons and inter-departmental friction.

'Overtime is frequent, often to cover ad hoc problems'

When wages for a normal work-week are low, front-line management tend to make up for that by offering overtime to boost take-home pay and keep their people happy. This has several undesirable effects:

- People create reasons for overtime even when the need does not exist.
- It is hard to rid the company of an overtime culture once it has been established.
- Every hour of overtime costs a lot more than when work is done in normal time, and that all comes off the bottom line.
- Staff get so used to having overtime boosting their wages that they adopt lifestyles to fit. They then protest if no overtime is offered, and become ingenious at finding multifarious ways of making sure it continues as before.

'Anomalies exist and complaints frequently arise'

Where pay systems are complicated, such as individual piecework systems, mistakes are often made in working out wages every week, and complaints abound. Often, only one person – the wages person – knows how it all works, and problems balloon when he is off on holiday. When you ask around among supervisors or managers what happens in this or that sort of case, generally they say 'Wages sorts all that out'. That just means they don't know how it all works.

If people are concerned about anything at work, it's their pay. If the system is full of anomalies it needs to be put right. If you do tackle such a task, our strong advice is: first get the facts. That means getting lists of pay rates for all job types, lists of earnings by pay category or even by employee name, actual overtime payments, special payments, etc. We have never done such an exercise without everyone finding out things they didn't know, and often are astonished about. Apart from giving you the essential start information you need, the data often shows you what needs to be done.

LEVEL 2

'Pay systems have been simplified, are understandable and published'

Companies traditionally have several grading structures in place, eg one for managers, one for office-based staff and yet another for shop floor staff. The latter (usually manual operators) are generally paid a 'spot rate' on an hourly basis, whereas office staff and managers are paid on a pay scale and on a monthly basis.

We believe there is no reason why everyone in a company shouldn't be paid on a single grading scale that covers all jobs from top to bottom. This has considerable advantages:

1. Everyone feels they are being treated on the same basis, ie the single pay system helps unify the company.
2. You avoid invidious comparisons, eg the 'why do they get this in their pay scheme, and we only get that?' type of complaint.
3. It makes life simpler to have only one pay system to administer.
4. When pay increases are being applied, uprating all grades by, say, 3% can be done at the press of a computer button. That also means differentials don't need to be discussed as they remain unaffected.

The structure we prefer is a single grading system with grade scales each 20 per cent long, ie the top of each scale is 20 per cent more than the bottom. This is founded on the notion that it should take no qualified job-holder (including the managing director) more than three years to become competent in the job. That would give every job-holder the chance of 5 per cent annual increments in the process of becoming fully competent. Scales longer than this simply mean paying more in successive years for effectively no greater competence in the job.

We also advocate scales that butt up to each other (kissing scales as they are sometimes called), ie the top of the scale coincides with the bottom of the next higher scale. Longer over-lapping scales give problems. If, for example, scales overlap by 50 per cent, then you find yourself:

- paying more each year simply because the scale is there, thus incurring extra costs for no measurable benefit;
- running the risk of complaints that job-holders doing jobs rated of lower value are actually earning more (at the top of their scale) than higher rated job-holders in the lower half of their scale;
- not being able to offer a raise to job-holders promoted from the top of a lower scale, even though the value of their new job is greater (not much of a motivator). Or, if you do give them a raise by way of reward, they leapfrog over others already in the higher scale.

We believe other conditions (pensions, holiday entitlements, sickness benefit, etc) should be the same or similar for all. The major difference should be pay, which should be a reflection of the value of the job to the company and of the money you have to pay to attract that type of skill or experience in the market-place. When you have a simple system like this, we normally recommend you publish it to staff complete. If you must keep senior management salaries confidential, do so, but keeping some parts of the system hidden simply causes suspicion and mistrust.

'Employees are paid about the average for the work they do'

When a company pays average salaries, it tends to get average talent, skills and commitment. If you want a company that turns in average performance, pay averagely well.

'Regular hours cover the normal work. Overtime is minimal'

As a rule, companies that do not work lots of overtime are more in control than those that do. It also means that they are not incurring negative variances on their planned labour and product costs.

'Additional skills acquired lead to additional pay'

As a rule we favour paying for the acquisition of required skills, for the following reasons:

- It encourages a process of continuous learning throughout the organization.
- Staff gain more self-esteem, become more valuable to the company and to themselves (ie in the market-place).
- An increasingly able workforce gives a company considerable flexibility as they deploy and use the skills staff have acquired.
- Virtually every asset acquired by a company starts depreciating as soon as it is bought. A continuously learning workforce, on the other hand, becomes an appreciating asset, indeed the only appreciating asset the company has.
- Competitors can buy exactly the same machinery and technology as their rivals. But they cannot have the same people. A workforce that has been continuously learning can thus become an uncopiable competitive advantage.

Some words of advice:

- Pay only for skills needed on the job.
- Bunch the skills into bundles. Give a permanent increase in pay on the acquisition of each bundle.

- Judge acquisition by using a dispassionate, objective test. This is usually based on being able to perform the task to a required speed and quality level.
- Do not create too many bundles. Staff cannot rotate around all the jobs often enough to keep their skills fresh, but you will still be paying for them.
- Make the bundles hard enough that those who haven't got them feel those who have mastered them deserve the payment.

Some Japanese and British companies have adopted a continuous learning culture and expect the learning of new skills every year as part of the job without extra payment. And it works. It is important that a company does not start paying for everything, otherwise an unhealthy 'What's in it for us?' attitude develops, and staff see every development as an opportunity to withhold co-operation and negotiate. Continuous learning ought to be part of everyone's job.

LEVEL 3

'Employees are paid above the average for above average performance'

'Appraisal system rewards help motivate performance'

When a company pays even 5 per cent above average it can attract better people and expect above average performance in return. Interestingly enough, those companies that do, tend to get higher productivity, which in turn offsets and often supersedes the extra cost.

There are three key goals of any pay system. They are to:

- attract;
- retain;
- motivate.

Better staff cannot be attracted in the first place if the company is paying ordinary money. In such cases, when the company advertises, it is forced not to publish the salary (because it is known to be a weakness) or to use a euphemism like 'competitive salary'. Potential candidates recognize this as a smokescreen. As a result, many good people do not apply. If you genuinely want better performance, you have to have good material to start with.

Companies that try to pay as little as possible find that they often cannot attract individuals with specific skills (such as computer staff or maintenance engineers). Desperate to attract the key skills they need, they may then have to secretly pay these individuals higher salaries to persuade them to join. When existing staff discover these special deals resentment sets in. That is no way to improve morale.

If you decide to improve pay in general to become a company that pays above average but expects above average performance, it is advisable not to try and do it all at once. The process should be implemented over three to five years, paying slightly more than the average earnings inflation each year. That way, staff see themselves getting a bigger percentage than their friends or other family members are getting from their companies, and this will give you several years of credit and good feelings. Make sure that staff know that the company is paying more than the going rate for a particular year, ie get full credit for the extra money being paid. But do not let expectations build up: include some motivation to co-operate and contribute by indicating that this would not be able to continue unless the company continues to progress and do well.

Good pay also helps to retain good people. But total remuneration should be built up from a number of elements where individuals have to contribute specifically to succeed. The four elements we recommend in a positive pay structure are:

1. Good base pay.
2. Payment for increased skills or responsibilities.
3. Personal performance bonus, based on appraisal.
4. Profit-sharing, whether by shares or bonus.

Let's examine each in turn in more detail.

Base pay

The 'base pay' that you would normally quote in advertisements should be the appropriate scale, which allows you to say 'in the range of £18,000–£22,000' or 'up to £22,000'. For staff or managerial jobs (ie those with higher discretion) the scale should be based on annual increases in line with the normal 'learning curve'.

The learning curve originates in the aircraft industry. There it has been long known that, roughly, the second aircraft only takes about 80 per cent of the time it took to build the first one. And that subsequently, the time taken falls to 80 per cent of that time with every doubling of production, ie:

No. 2 takes 80% of the time taken for No. 1

No. 4 takes 80% of the time taken for No. 2

No. 8 takes 80% of the time taken for No. 4, and so on.

In other words, the time taken falls quickly to start with, then reduces further over time but at an increasingly shallower rate. So it is with managers learning new jobs. Their learning rate is steep in their first three years in the job. After that, the subsequent learning rate is relatively shallow. Hence we advise the use of scales that are around 20 per cent long, ie the top of the scale pays 20 per cent more than the bottom. That way, they reward early steep learning, but contain costs thereafter.

For manual or more routine, repetitive jobs, we recommend specific payment for specific skill acquisition.

Paying for skills

Normally we prefer to build into each appraisal the naming of a specific 'learning' objective every year (or every six months for more routine jobs), ie the appraisee says, 'This is what I want to learn in the next period.' Note: this is not a training objective (that's the supervisor telling the person in 'parent' mode), but a learning objective (that's the person himself taking on responsibility for his own growth and development, ie being treated like an adult, and acting like an adult). To encourage this habit, we like to give front-line job-holders the opportunity to increase their pay by acquiring company required skills. When job-holders have acquired several skill modules and the pay to go with it, this higher pay acts as a strong retainer, ie they are better off, the company retains its most skilled people, but it would now be more difficult for them to find a similar job elsewhere that pays the same money.

Clients often ask: 'Should we pay for the skills people have learnt, or the skills they actually are called upon to exercise?' The answer is: the skills they have acquired. It just becomes too difficult in practice to record who exercised what skills, when and for how long. Also, the information has to be fed to wages, who have to make many more week-to-week calculations. And you can imagine how many disputes arise in the process. We much prefer to keep it simple.

The next question is: how much should we pay for skills? The answer is: enough to make learning, and later using, the skill attractive. A nice round number helps. For example, in the United Kingdom the average shop floor job-holder may earn around £250 per week, and £10–15 extra per week is attractive. Generally, three skill steps should cover most of what is required.

What happens when they get to the top of their skill steps, ie run out of opportunities? For some you could consider the title of 'trainer' – that might involve having been a minimum number of years in the job, being already at the top of their skill steps, and having the kind of attitude you would want to pass on to your trainees. Only give your trainees to the best people you have. For others you might consider the title 'expert'. That would mean: the person knows how to set and operate all the equipment he is responsible for, has actually made *improvements* to the installed equipment, and is regarded as the person you go to to solve any problems on that equipment. There are likely to be only a few of these high-status people.

Personal performance bonus

Team bonuses have certain associated problems. There is the argument that with team-based bonus team members apply peer pressure to get people to perform, to attend regularly, etc. That is true, but it has a darker side. People get threatened, and some team members will press management to move individuals out of the team or fire them. This often happens when job-holders are more concerned about their output than their quality. Also, dealing with the soured relations can be a problem. Team bonuses can certainly work, but they need careful structuring.

Personal performance bonuses need to be big enough to go for, but not so big that there are major disappointments and disputes when they don't materialize. At GPM we are against bonuses that amount to more than 20 per cent of base pay. There is a danger that people 'manipulate' the numbers when the bonus is greater than that, and we have seen it happen. Furthermore, there are sales people, production people, even people in the financial markets, who do excellent jobs without huge commissions or bonuses. The idea that they won't do it without big bonuses is nonsense. The only thing you have to consider is attraction and retention, ie will your total package get and keep the people you need to do the job considering what they could get for the same work elsewhere? Our advice is: don't get bounced into big bonuses for only certain categories of staff, eg salespeople. Stick to the general rule.

Sectional bonuses are also problematic, ie having different pay and bonus schemes for different sections. This can cause antagonism between sections and may also lead to compromises in quality, especially when these bonuses encourage output only. Above all, they do not encourage staff to work as one *company* team, and that is often indispensable if you are to serve your customers well.

It is much preferable to attach personal bonuses to annual or six-monthly appraisals, which includes within it team-working elements. That is what individuals can control, ie their own behaviour. And money has a part to play in motivating them to give of their best. We have found that two weeks' pay paid as a lump sum is enough to get people to respond (even directors). That, as you will readily deduce, is only 4 per cent of salary. Paid on a monthly or weekly basis it looks relatively small and may not have much effect. But it has several advantages when paid as a lump sum:

- It is easily understood and everyone can immediately work out how much it means to them in pounds or dollars.
- You can do something with a lump sum, ie buy a television, a fridge, a computer game, etc.
- It is very helpful if it is paid at useful times of the year, eg before the holidays or Christmas, etc.
- It is not added to pay permanently as a normal increase would be. So the money is not given away forever. The same money can be used to stimulate performance next year and the year after that.
- It is not added to peripheral costs, such as overtime or holiday pay. It just costs what it costs.
- You get a lot more 'bang for the bucks'.

What you are trying to do with an appraisal and personal performance bonus system is not to try and make a genius out of everyone, but to get everyone to do their *personal best*. In days gone by, work study-based consultants would argue that if they devised a good method for any job, they taught that method to the job-holders, the job-holders used the methods, and they had a money incentive, then they could increase productivity by 30 per cent. That's the kind of extra performance we want from everyone. So what needs to be done is to move everyone from wherever they are in the performance spectrum up to their personal best.

And we don't want to reserve the bonuses for the fortunate few. We want to motivate *the majority*. That is why we expect the majority to get all the money. We want the majority, not the few, to feel a success in the business. With front-line employees, we would expect, and be happy for, 80 per cent to get all the money. For, as we all know, when people feel they are succeeding they perform even better. And we like everyone to know just what they have to do to succeed.

See the section Ideas and Techniques You Can Use for examples of Personal Performance Appraisal forms.

Profit-sharing

We particularly like profit-sharing as a concept because, first, it emphasizes that we in the company are all in the same boat, ie we should all work together for our prosperity because then we can all share in it. And second, it makes it clear that money doesn't fall from the trees somewhere, we have to earn it before we can share it.

There is also strong evidence showing that those companies that do use profit-sharing experience significantly better *financial* performance than those companies that don't. A study of 400 publicly quoted UK companies in categories as widely different as building, chemicals, food, engineering, retailing, brewing, printing and textiles, compared the performance of the profit-sharers among them with the non-profit-sharers over a period of *eight years*. This is the biggest and longest study conducted on this subject that we know about. So its conclusions are hard to question. All the comparison

Table 10.1 Comparative performance of companies

Average over 1977–85 (400 companies)	Profit-sharing companies %	Non-profit-sharing companies %	Difference %
Return on sales	8.4	5.6	50.0
Return on capital	20.6	15.5	32.9
Earnings per share	16.3	12.8	27.3
Annual sales growth	15.5	13.7	13.1
Annual profit growth	13.6	9.7	40.8
Annual investor returns	24.8	18.0	37.8

factors used by the authors were financially based, and *every factor* showed a significant win for the profit-sharing companies over that period of time. The actual comparison figures are shown in Table 10.1. In other words, don't be afraid of profit-sharing. On the contrary, welcome it as a way to consistently better bottom-line results.

We should note that the profit-sharing involved differed in its form. Some companies paid out bonuses to staff during the year in the form of lump sums, and the amounts could vary considerably across grades, ie senior managers often getting considerably more than others. In some companies the profit-sharing was in the form of shares. This has the advantage of not costing the company anything in terms of cash flow, and tying the growth of the employees' capital wealth into the performance of the company they work for. That arouses their interest in how the company is doing all the time, but also makes them want to see their company good and profitable.

In addition, the authors conducted a survey among 12 of the profit-sharing companies to see what the employees thought. Not surprisingly, they liked profit-sharing as well. Table 10.2 contains a selection of their answers.

To give a concrete example of a profit-sharing pay system, we show in Figure 10.1 a representation of the system used by Pedigree Petfoods in the United Kingdom. This is how it worked.

The company was particularly focused on sales growth and profit growth, so the system was tied directly to these. There were 13 equal four-week periods in every year (shown along the bottom), and performance was measured every period. Sales were measured on a rolling annual basis, ie as you added January figures this year, so you dropped off last January's figures, so that you got a full year's sales every time. Each of the figures on the vertical axis shows growth of 5 per cent compound each time – in other words, 120.9 is 5 per cent greater than 115.1, 126.9 is 5 per cent greater than 120.9, and so on.

Table 10.2 Profit-sharing companies attitude survey

	Agree %	Disagree %	Don't know %
Profit sharing creates a better atmosphere in the firm.	65	19	16
It is good for the company and the employees	86	3	11
It strengthens people's loyalty to the firm.	47	36	17
It makes people work more effectively so as to help the firm be successful	51	34	15
It can cause disappointment or bitterness because profits can go down as well as up.	41	48	10

The profit-sharing arrangement was as follows: each time annual sales passed through a 5 per cent barrier, everyone in the company earned a lump sum of three days' pay. That is provided profit reached a minimum level. This is represented at the bottom of the chart by ROTA (Return on Total Assets). The dotted line across the graph shows the growth last year. The bold line shows they had passed through two barriers so far in the current year, resulting in two lots of three days' pay (shown as six days' pay at the top of the graph). This was paid out twice a year at useful times, namely before the summer holidays, and just before Christmas.

As you might expect, employees got very interested every period in how the company was doing (mainly because a strongly growing and profitable company was good for them personally). They asked about the competition; they asked about new products. The scheme started back in 1974 and, with minor modifications, it is still going today.

The four-part structure shown under Level 3 above is the format we recommend. Figure 10.2 is an illustration of a system based on this structure – that of Premier Exhausts, the company that won the title of 'Best Factory in Britain' in 1994. Their base pay is arrived at by conducting a pay survey in the local area (within 30 miles), and deliberately paying 5 per cent above the average. Employees can then increase their pay permanently by acquiring skills, represented by the stars shown up the vertical axis. These are called 'skill steps' as shown on the graph. Finally, employees are able to earn a Personal Performance Bonus of one week's pay every six months (shown as vertical dotted lines on the graph) based on their appraisal rating. Premier only

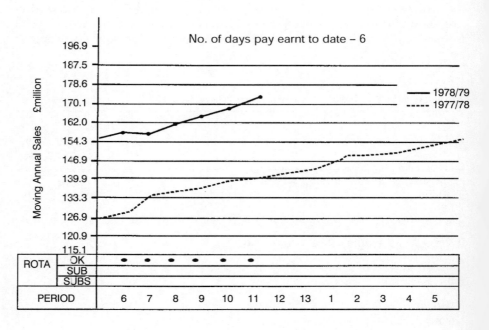

Figure 10.1 Share of prosperity, 1978–79

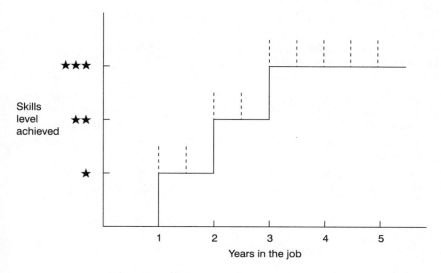

Figure 10.2 Premier Exhaust's pay structure

operate three elements of the four-part structure currently. They do not yet run a profit-sharing arrangement.

'Different sickness benefit and pension schemes are applied'

One of the features that is fairly characteristic of companies at Level 3 is that although they do operate sickness benefit arrangements and pension schemes, they tend to be different for front-line employees and management, or even between junior and senior management. We favour – even if it takes time to get there – sickness and pension schemes that are the same for all. In other words, everyone is paid when they fall sick (even if you have to set a limit to start with, eg no more than 4 per cent absence per annum, otherwise benefit is suspended). Or, everyone contributes to the same pension fund at a rate matched by the company's contribution, and so on.

'Recognition system is in place and working'

One of the best-selling books of all time is *How To Win Friends and Influence People*. The author, Dale Carnegie, says one of the most powerful ways to do that is to show 'sincere appreciation'.

Recognition is not about money: it is about appreciation. In most companies, staff find they get most attention from their manager when they do something wrong. Such companies have a 'blame culture'. Recognition is about finding people doing something right, and reinforcing that behaviour by showing you appreciate it.

Several decades ago B F Skinner, the US psychologist, in conducting a whole series of experiments investigating the process of learning, discovered that he could teach animals to perform fairly complex tasks simply by rewarding the behaviour he wanted to see. Normally he would reward performance with food titbits – what he called 'behaviour reinforcement'. It is a process widely used by animal trainers and others.

At the human level, there are all kinds of rewards and recognition that encourage and shape our behaviour. These include money, admiration of others, prizes, promotion, pleasing the boss, certificates, being trusted with more responsibility, medals, and so on. Most of us fall into the trap of complaining about the behaviour we don't want to see, but say little or nothing about the positive behaviour we do see.

Several years ago Michael LeBoeuf published a book entitled *The Greatest Management Principle in the World*. What was that principle? It's this:

> The behaviour that gets rewarded gets repeated.

It's a principle that's so important in organizations, but it's a principle unfortunately that is all too often ignored.

Regular appreciation is not going to become a habit in your company by accident. You need a system that makes it easy. This is what we see to be the overall purpose of a good recognition system:

- show appreciation for exceptional effort or commitment;
- approve (ie reinforce) the behaviours you want to encourage;
- spread good associations with work over a wide field;
- make compliments and thanks more common in the company than complaints;
- avoid de-motivation;
- get more impact for the costs involved.

Overall, recognition helps create more good feelings for more people at work. Don't leave creating good feelings at work to chance. Use a system to make giving appreciation and thanks more common than criticism and complaints. If you choose to set up a system, here are some guidelines:

- decide what behaviours you want to encourage;
- select the tools you think will do this best;
- create some fun and excitement;
- measure, monitor, and continuously improve.

That is what ICL Computers, a UK-based but Japanese-owned company, did a number of years ago. They wanted their people to focus on the twin goals of quality improvement and customer care. They decided any one of their staff could nominate for an award a colleague or team who they felt had made particular efforts in that regard. Nowadays, customers can nominate people too. Today the criteria for a recognition award are listed under eight headings. They are:

- acting as a role model;
- demonstrating we are all one ICL;
- teamwork;
- respect for society;
- professionalism and integrity;
- delighting customers;
- effective people;
- boosting margins.

You can see the detail under those headings in Figure 10.5 (page 230).

Recognition awards at ICL come in three forms: bronze, silver and gold. Bronze awards are decided upon by a Local Judging Panel, and consist of a bronze pin and a presentation of a gift chosen by the recipient from a well-produced gifts catalogue. Efforts considered particularly good are further nominated for a higher-value Silver Excellence award, decided on by the Divisional Panel and presented by the Divisional Director. Finally, each year gold awards are made to those who have shown 'exceptional achievement'. These winners can take their partners with them to a special, all-expenses-paid weekend away where they are presented with their awards, and later see their photographs in the company magazine.

ICL's efforts have been well repaid. In 1993, they won the prestigious European Quality Award. Now, you don't have to have an elaborate structure and gift catalogues to make a recognition scheme work. There are lots of things you can do to motivate staff, to encourage the behaviour you want to see, and to generate a bit of excitement and fun. Here are some of the recognition ideas other companies have used in their organizations:

- thank-you card or note;
- saying thanks face-to-face;
- badges: bronze, silver and gold;
- pens with inscription;
- plaque or a shield to display;
- signed certificates;
- personal letter from the managing director or chairman;
- photograph in company magazine;
- photograph and write-up on 'Wall of Fame';
- gifts of lasting value;
- tokens that can be accumulated and used to buy gifts of the awardee's choice;
- meals out with a guest;
- presentation events or parties;
- theatre visit;
- presenting the improvement idea directly to the Board or at an outside conference;
- time off, a day off;
- special clothing awards, eg inscribed tee-shirts or baseball caps;
- making benchmarking visits to other companies;

- use of the Chairman's Rolls-Royce for a week (yes, it really happens!).

We could go on, but you've got the idea. The key point is: use your imagination!

LEVEL 4

'Surveys are conducted to ensure pay remains above average'

At Level 4, companies will often conduct, or take part in, pay surveys in their region. If they have chosen to pay above average to attract and retain above average people, they want to check the facts that they are staying in line with the market-place. In addition, when employees know such a policy is being followed, the need for adversarial negotiation – a fundamental cause of conflict between management and workers – is reduced or even removed altogether.

'Appraisal systems apply throughout the company'

Most people don't like appraisals. They see them much like an exam at school. They hope they'll do well, of course, but they're apprehensive, scared even. Managers tend not to like them either, fearing their subordinates may not like all that they tell them, and that there might be a fight about how much their merit increase should be. So both put off the process, or do it inadequately. Appraisals should not be regarded as 'Judgement Day'. In our view, the appraisal process has two key purposes: motivation and employee development.

If your current appraisal system is not instrumental in motivating your staff to a performance level you would not get without it, you should question its continuation in its current form. We believe money has an enhancing effect on motivation, and favour the linking of personal performance bonuses with appraisal process.

We believe regular appraisals – between manager and subordinate – should apply at every level in the organization, although the process may not be in exactly the same form at different levels. For example, to avoid accusations of rewarding 'blue-eyed boys', we like to make it clear at front-line level exactly what kind of performance will get full personal performance bonus. An example of an appraisal form in use by one of our successful clients is shown as Figure 10.3 later in Ideas and Techniques You Can Use.

For staff and managers who have more discretion in how they use their time, we like an appraisal format that builds in focusing on priority objectives, deals with the soft issues of style as well as the harder measurables, gives a high value to continuous learning, and incorporates a degree of upward appraisal. The appraisal form used by another of our clients is shown in Figure 10. 4 by way of example (the box sizes shown are shorter in length compared to the original form).

'Sickness benefit and pension schemes are the same for all'

At this level, sickness benefit is likely to be paid as full pay from Day 1, but by this time there is also likely to be no abuse of the system on the part of staff. With pension schemes, standard benefits are likely to be available to everyone, with the option of contributing more from salary to purchase improved benefits under the scheme.

'Profit-sharing means staff are keen to see the company profitable'

The evidence is that profit-sharing companies do consistently better in *financial* terms than those who don't. And part of the reason is that staff are keen to help their company to win, when they know that that's how they win too.

LEVEL 5

'Staff have a "no redundancy" undertaking'

The tone of the undertaking given by the companies we have worked with tends to take the following form: 'You will not be declared redundant here as a result of changes introduced by management. If our market disappeared, then all bets would be off. Otherwise, you will always have a job here. It may not always be the *same* job, but you will have a job.'

Change is likely to be with us forever. Companies who can't get the co-operation of their workforce in making necessary changes will have difficulty surviving and competing. They are not going to get that willing co-operation if the workforce feels they are going to be the first casualties of such changes.

It's difficult to get turkeys to vote for Christmas. But what if companies need to reduce numbers, you ask? Offer voluntary packages, we say. Lump sums can often be attractive. Yes, you may lose some good people capable of getting a job elsewhere. But you need to get your costs down – that's the main thrust in these circumstances. If you nominate and point fingers, you may succeed in losing only the people you choose to lose. But you send fear and dread through the ranks of all those who stay. They say: 'Who is going to be next?' and 'It could be me!' That rekindles resistance, the barriers come up, and opposing management changes becomes the norm. You can't get to world class with such resistance in your organization.

'Above average pay attracts and retains the best staff'

'Appraisals encourage continuous improvement and continuous learning'

'Recognition system regularly encourages the behaviour the company wants to see'

At this world class level, the organization has learnt how to use rewards and recognition to keep everyone motivated to do their personal best, and year by year to make learning and continuous improvement the company's ongoing way of life.

IDEAS AND TECHNIQUES YOU CAN USE

Examples of personal performance appraisals

In the case of front-line employees, we favour a simple tick-box type of format. Figure 10.3 is an example.

Sometimes companies will make one or two of the boxes mandatory (eg Boxes 1 and 2), ie no bonus at all if these standards are not achieved. But if you get ticks in all the boxes you get all the money. Others use a standard of 8 out of 10 achieved, 80 per cent bonus, otherwise nothing. Decide the rules at the beginning, and stick with them. Most people will succeed. However, it's important that not everyone gets all the money every year. Otherwise it

	BONUS CRITERIA	YES	NO
1	Product quality meets 'Best' standard		
2	Output meets target		
3	Performs variety of jobs to the required standard		
4	Helps to train colleagues as required		
5	Suggestions made and implemented for continuous improvement		
6	Responds positively to short-notice problems		
7	Always operates within the known health and safety requirements		
8	Housekeeping above the required standard		
9	No attendance or timekeeping problems		
10	Personal learning objective achieved from previous appraisal		

Figure 10.3 Personal performance appraisal

simply becomes an entitlement and that means you lose its motivational effect. It has to be for extra performance.

When dealing with managers or staff who have considerable discretion in how they use their time, we favour an appraisal process based on contribution. This is normally expressed in the form of objectives that have been agreed between boss and subordinate at the beginning of the period concerned, and which, if achieved, would constitute for that person a stretch performance and a real contribution to the organization. In Figure 10.4, achieving the agreed Priority 1 objectives means the individual qualifies for a full personal performance bonus.

We also like to build in several other elements:

- discussion of the individual's style, and how effective that is in working in their work team, or with customers both internal and external;
- discussion of what the individual has learnt over the period (both in his everyday work dealings, or in training) that he can use and build on in the future;
- assessment of the support given by the boss, and how he might help further in the future;
- getting the individual to decide what specific learning objectives he would like to set for himself in the next period.

Box 1 lists both the original Priority 1 (must be done, no excuses) objectives agreed at the beginning of the year and actual performance in practice.

Box 2 lists any other notable achievements not listed in Box 1.

Box 3 is a subjective self-assessment by the appraisee of the softer issues of style, designed to stimulate a positive 'coaching' session between manager and appraisee.

Box 4 is designed to get the appraisee to think about what he has learnt during the year, and consolidate the learning into his habits.

Box 5 presses the appraisee into nominating what he specifically wants to learn next year to keep himself growing and improving. That keeps life interesting and makes him more valuable to the company and to himself (ie in the market-place).

Box 6 is a modest form of upward appraisal couched in positive form. In this context, we teach appraisees not just to complain, but to turn their complaints into positive requests.

Box 7 is completed by the manager after the appraisal discussion has taken place.

Boxes 8 and 9 are confirmations of the agreements made between the two parties following discussion together of the proposals made by the appraisee in Boxes 5 and 6.

Box 10. A tick in either 'good' or 'acceptable' gets all the money, in this case two weeks' pay as a lump sum. A tick in 'not acceptable' gets no personal performance bonus. Remember, the purpose of the process is to motivate. We normally expect over 80 per cent of staff to succeed, ie to get the money. We want to motivate not the minority, but the majority.

Name ....

Department ....

Job title ....

Date ....

---

1. Objectives and Achievements

Objectives/Performance Standards (Agreed between appraiser and appraisee)	Achievements (To be completed by appraisee)

---

2. Other Achievements or Initiatives Taken

3. **Self-assessment Ratings** (To be completed by appraisee)	(Put an arrow ↓ where you think you rate)

	0　　　　　　　5　　　　　　　10
Good team member	□—"—"—"—"—"—"—"—"—"—"—"—"—"—
Reliability	□—"—"—"—"—"—"—"—"—"—"—"—"—"—
Responsiveness	□—"—"—"—"—"—"—"—"—"—"—"—"—"—
Administration	□—"—"—"—"—"—"—"—"—"—"—"—"—"—
Planning	□—"—"—"—"—"—"—"—"—"—"—"—"—"—
Cross-department co-operation	□—"—"—"—"—"—"—"—"—"—"—"—"—"—

4. **Significant Points Learnt This Period**
(To be completed by appraisee)

5. **My Learning Objectives For Next Period**
(To be completed by appraisee)

6. **Support Given By My Manager This Period, and Requested For Next Period**
(To be completed by appraisee)

7. **Performance Review Summary**
(To be completed by appraiser)

8. **Agreements Reached on Manager Support For Next Period**
(To be completed by appraiser)

9. **Agreed Learning Objectives For Next Period**
(To be completed by appraiser)

10. **Overall Rating** (To be completed by appraiser)	11. **Signatures**
Good ☐	Appraisee...
Acceptable ☐	Appraiser...
Not acceptable ☐	Appraiser's Manager ....

12. **Personal Performance Bonus**

Pay ☐   Withhold ☐   Signed...

Figure 10.4 Personal performance review and development plan

Finally, in Box 11 the appraiser signs and the appraisee signs to say he has seen the finished appraisal. The appraiser's manager also signs so that he keeps well in touch with relations between the appraiser and his team and how his subordinates are developing.

Excellence awards

Figure 10.5 shows the model for an excellence award taken from ICL.

Role Model (mandatory for all nominations)

Must be recognized as role models by colleagues and/or customers by living the ICL Values.

The ICL Values

One ICL

Our shareholders enable us to serve our customers. Building the value of the ICL Group for our shareholders means we make all our decisions in the interests of the ICL Group.

Teamwork

We work energetically in teams across all boundaries to serve our customers more effectively. We share knowledge; we support each other; we build new ideas together and we respect the individual contributions that each of us makes.

Respect For Society

The information industry touches the lives of communities around the world. We all have a responsibility to ensure that the wider interests of society are considered in all our actions.

Professionalism and Integrity

We demonstrate integrity, professionalism and a continuous commitment to quality in all our relationships with colleagues, customers, division partners and other stakeholders. By doing so, we earn their trust.

Other Criteria

Delighting Customers

Winners

Put the needs of the customer first, ICL second and their division third.

Make ICL easier to do business with.

Respond quickly and accurately to customer requirements.

Always keep the customer informed.

Take personal responsibility for solving customer problems.

Effective People

Winners

Develop and support division strategy; establish structures and processes, co-ordinate resources and manage performance.

Demonstrate sound division awareness, recognizing and exploiting opportunities.

Collaborate with colleagues and suppliers across organizational boundaries to ensure the best results for the division and the customer.

Build good relationships with customers, ensuring mutual understanding and co-operation.

Introduce innovative approaches and solutions to a situation and/or problem.

Take care to ensure quality and effectiveness in implementation and delivery.

Demonstrate confidence in making decisions, taking risks and taking the initiative.

Demonstrate drive, persistence and resilience in working to achieve goals.

Influence events, activities and decisions to realize their vision and achieve a desired outcome.

Develop and maintain an effective, well-motivated team.

Boosting Margins

Winners

Prevent problems rather than simply fix them and apply true corrective action when they do occur.

Improve the quality of Systems, Projects, Products and Services.

Display a systematic way of improving processes. Reduce costs and/or increase value added.

Find new ways in which our Systems, Products and Services can improve customers' businesses.

Figure 10.5 The excellence awards criteria

E l e v e n

Purposeful Communication

LEVELS	MEASURES
Level 1	Work team meetings are patchy or non-existent. The grapevine is strong; noticeboards are poorly cared for. There are constant complaints about poor communications. People say: 'Nobody tells us anything.'
Level 2	A channel of communications from top management to front-line staff has been established. Managers are trained in, and hold, regular team meetings. Noticeboards are well sited, presented and maintained. Meeting rooms are available with good visual aids.
Level 3	Top management meets with all staff at least once a year. Managers know their messages and live them by example. Meetings are purposeful, and follow published guidelines. House journal is lively, interesting, and widely read.
Level 4	Information cascades from top management meetings to front-line staff within 48 hours. Front-line teams hold 'start-of-day' meetings, and have communication boards in their sections. Strong upward channel means front-line points are heard at senior management level.
Level 5	Company uses a variety of communication channels well, ie meetings, noticeboards, paper, computer and video. Matrix calendar of communications shows all communication channels, and who does what, when. Surveys show steadily improving communications scores.

LEVEL 1

Communication is a perennial problem in organizations. Employees, when surveyed on the quality and value of communications within their company, will generally give an average or poor rating. Some managers say that 'you can't communicate enough', the logic being that 'more communication is better'. We do not subscribe to this view. We believe that *purposeful communication* is what is required. By purposeful communication we mean first of all that every employee should have the information that he requires to do the job well; a clear understanding of the customer's requirements (whether that is the next person in the line or the external customer); an ability to understand his own job in the context of the wider requirements of the firm; and understanding how his particular job makes its contribution to the overall performance of the business.

'Work team meetings are patchy or non-existent'

At Level 1 companies may have introduced some form of downward communication via a monthly team briefing process. What often happens in practice, however, is that some front-line managers use them consistently, others only intermittently, while others hold none at all. Generally there has been a lack of training regarding the use of communication meetings, while front-line managers may not spend enough time preparing material from their own local area and simply make a recitation of what has been sent down from above. Staff may be irked that meetings are compulsory and therefore only attend under sufferance. Often they generally get bored by the proceedings, and eventually both parties are quite happy by mutual agreement not to hold the meetings at all.

It is the role of front-line managers to make their team meetings interesting, regular and lively, but they have to be given the appropriate training and backup to make them a positive force in the communications armoury.

'The grapevine is strong; noticeboards are poorly cared for'

In virtually every company opinion survey we do, when we ask from which sources employees *actually* get their information, we find 'the grapevine' comes out top of the list. The grapevine is seldom accurate or complete, of course, but the one thing you can say about it is: it is fast. That's one of the important facets of new information: people want it now, not later. If as a company you are always later than the grapevine, staff think the company is ponderous and slow-on-its-feet. Not a good image.

The problem with the grapevine is that it's generally both inaccurate and incomplete. When they hear rumours, staff may ask leading or embarrassing questions of their manager, who is then forced into a holding or a denial statement. But often the grapevine contains a grain of truth. When the full story later comes out confirming the grain of truth, staff then presume management knew all along, but denied suggestions only a few days before. Then it looks as if you can't believe what management tells you, and that's dangerous. To counter the pernicious effects of the grapevine, speed and timing are of the essence.

A casual look around any company will reveal how seriously the noticeboards are treated. At this level they are often untidy, notices out of date, graffiti appear on notices, etc. In most of the employee surveys that we conduct, the grapevine is almost always followed closely by noticeboards as their key actual information source. If your noticeboards are poorly maintained (as many are), you are effectively sending a signal every day to your staff about how seriously you regard good communication.

'People say: "Nobody tells us anything"'

This is a common complaint in many companies when we first become involved in the performance improvement process: it is obviously not always true, but the perception is very real for the employees. When one questions staff in detail one often finds they are actually quite knowledgeable, but their view tends to stem from the fact that communication is not *systematic*, but rather patchy and haphazard.

Here are a few more comments you might hear. We have heard all of these comments in our travels:

- Communicate? Do you realize how busy we are in this place?
- We communicate with everyone regularly . . . whenever we think it's necessary.
- I always communicate personally, because frankly I don't think our supervisors are up to it.
- We hold our monthly meeting . . . about four times a year.
- Noticeboards are a good thing . . . unfortunately, we don't have one.
- My people know exactly what's going on . . . I send them minutes.
- The boss should be visual. I walk the job . . . when I can.
- Ask me anything you like . . . but don't ask stupid questions!

LEVEL 2

'A channel of communications from top management to front-line staff has been established'

This would indicate top management (ie the directors or their equivalent) have a systematic means of regularly communicating the subject of their discussions and their decisions right down to front-line non-management staff. This can be through a briefing that cascades through the management chain, by specific sections in the house magazine, or via the noticeboards. It is most effective to send the message via front-line managers with a short briefing note to accompany that talk. However, despite some companies' good efforts, this is often ineffective or intermittent at best.

Exercise

One can test the effectiveness of briefings quite easily. Try this: after a few days have elapsed, ask a sample of staff from front-line jobs what they thought of some particular key subject in the last communication. A series of blank looks, or questions like 'What communication?' will tell how well (or badly) the message is getting across! One also needs to pay attention to how quickly the cascade works. If the message only gets through three to four weeks after the event, that's too long. The aim should be for the message to get down to the lowest level in the company within three days max.

'Managers are trained in, and hold, regular team meetings'

Any company keen to develop good communications has to get it right where most of the people work, and that is at front-line level. In that respect, company communications will be no better than what is delivered and achieved by their first-line managers. That is why we are strong believers that team leaders and supervisors need to be supported and trained to be the best two-way communicators in any business. And regular, well-conducted team meetings are an important way to achieve that.

The principles that the UK Industrial Society lay down for their Team Briefing system are fundamentals that should apply to any good team meeting structure. The process needs to be:

- *Face-to-face.* Noticeboards, magazines and memos are only one-way communication. Face-to-face makes it two-way. You can't ask the noticeboard questions. But if you hear directly from your boss, you can hear the information delivered in terms that you understand, and generally you can have your questions answered there and then. Face-to-face is the only way to know your audience has heard and understood.
- *In teams.* It's much easier and quicker to talk to your team all at once, rather than go around to inform them individually And that way they all hear the same story – and no one in advance of anyone else. Not everyone has the confidence to ask questions, but if someone does then the whole team gets the benefit of the answer and the clarification. And meeting as a team on a regular basis reinforces the point about acting and performing as a team.
- *By the leader.* If team leaders are ultimately accountable for the results and performance of their group, they need to be firmly in charge of the team communications meeting. If the information they give is timely, accurate and put over in an interesting way, it helps them remain the focus of

attention within the work-group. Information is power in the hands of the leader.

- *Regular.* If communications team meetings are held at haphazard intervals, it sends a strong message to everyone about how seriously their company (or their manager) treats good communication. It has to be regular to be credible. But that means it has to be useful and interesting too!
- *Relevant.* Information that is only relevant to directors and senior managers is not what front-line people want to hear. It has to be about their everyday work. That's what affects their lives and their performance. The team leader may well pass on interesting corporate information, but 70% of the time needs to be spent on locally important items, solving problems and making improvements together. The meetings need to be *active*, not passive.

The number of meetings held does not mean that the objectives are met. The content and the direction of the meeting are the determining factors, and this can be achieved by training managers in the business of running effective meetings. In some companies it will be proper to send any person who is key in the communication line on a suitable training course.

One of the key persons is the front-line manager. Part of their training will be to make their communications interesting to employees, but equally there are things that employees must understand if they are to work effectively and give of their best. That understanding should cover important questions about the job. Questions like:

- What contribution does my work make to the total job?
- Where does the work come from and go to?
- What is the end product? Who uses it? What is it for?
- What are my work targets? To what extent are they being achieved?
- To what extent can I influence costs?
- What are the safety standards we need to follow?
- What changes are being made, and why?
- What are the priorities in our work over the next month?

Then the managers need practice in making short presentations, first, in the safety of the training environment. Later, it is a good thing if those still apprehensive have a coach with them to help them over the first presentations they make on their own. The communication process is too important to throw managers into the deep end without training and hope they survive.

One of the key points to get across to managers is that communications need to be essentially a two-way process, with benefits for both the company and employees. Table 11.1 shows the benefits we see from good communications:

Table 11.1 Benefits of good communication

For the employee	For the company
Knowing exactly what is required to 'do a good job'	Getting employees to implement company aims and principles on a daily basis
Being trusted with all the information needed to do a good job	Getting employees to do a better job through full information and feedback
Feeling the company actually listens	Acting as a safety valve for good employee relations
Generating feelings of interest and ownership in the job	Tapping into the ideas and potential of employees
Feeling of belonging to a successful team	Improving teamwork and commitment among employees

Later in this chapter we offer practical advice on setting up an effective team meeting process.

If the employee feels he gets real benefit from the communication process, he will be happy to take part. Make sure it has value for both parties.

'Noticeboards are well sited, presented and maintained'

Judging again by the employee surveys we conduct, noticeboards come high on employees' list of the sources from which they get their information. It is important therefore to manage them well. These are the guidelines we would recommend to make them more effective:

1. Put communication boards in every work section. They need to focus primarily on work, namely, the targets and measures that apply to that section with indications of how it is doing on all the key measures (also see Ladder 4, Visible Measurement Systems).

    Otherwise, place the noticeboards in areas that people pass every day, ie close to the cafeteria, in the walkways where people enter or leave the building, etc. In this context, make sure the boards are placed where people can take a few moments to read them in safety, ie not where forklift trucks are moving up and down! And make sure they are well lit so that reading the material is easy.
2. It is a good idea to use different colours of paper for different types of notices. That way people can see from a distance what type of notices are on the board. For example:

Type of Notice	Paper
General company	White
Safety	Green
Sports and social	Yellow
Job vacancies	Blue
Pay and conditions	Pink

Sectioning off noticeboards tends to be less flexible, ie sometimes there's a great flood of notices on one section that then spills over into another section causing objections from the people who are looking after that particular area.

3. Make sure each notice has a 'take down' date on it. That then means that everybody has to think about how long their notices should stay on the wall, and no matter who is looking after the noticeboards, they will know exactly when specific notices are to be removed.

4. Don't allow complex notices. The language needs to be simple enough to be understood on first reading by anyone in the business.

'Meeting rooms are available with good visual aids'

In most companies there is usually a shortage of meeting rooms. Ideally, meeting rooms need to be in places that are not noisy, or untidy and unwelcoming. In addition, they should at least have a blackboard and chalk, but preferably a flipchart or whiteboard, an overhead projector and screen, a television and video player, etc. It is a good idea to have a box in which all the small items can be stored, eg felt-tip pens, masking tape, whiteboard duster, pens and pencils, etc. Such facilities should also be made available for social club or trade union representative meetings, where required. This proves to employees that the company respects the interests of its employees and demonstrates that communication is taken seriously and is not one-sided, ie it is not only important when it affects management. We still have companies where the union can only hold meetings on the factory floor with heavy machinery in operation, causing so much noise that the message cannot be properly conveyed. However, continued availability to any group should be conditional on their treating the facilities provided with care and respect.

LEVEL 3

'Top management meets with all staff at least once a year'

The reasons we commend the chief executive meets face-to-face with all the company's staff at least once a year is to inform them, 'straight from the horse's mouth' if you like, about the state of the business and the objectives the CEO has for the coming period. The act of taking the trouble to address employees directly also helps to show how much the top man respects everyone's contribution to the business, and his desire to make everyone feel part of the same *company team*. Part of the purpose is to make sure there is no dilution or distortion of the key points in any cascade down through the organization, but the key intention is to generate understanding and enthusiasm for the company's goals and future development, and to show employees they all have a valuable role to play.

'Managers know their messages and live them by example'

Messages about the company's values and beliefs need to be repeated and followed through if employees are to take them on board and live them in their everyday work. Advertisers can certainly teach us a few things when it comes to getting messages across. Generally their messages are simple, clear and consistently repeated. When Heineken tells us this week that its beer 'reaches parts other beers cannot reach', it doesn't suddenly switch to a different message the following week in case we get bored. No, they repeat the same message constantly until we know it by heart. And that is precisely what needs to be done in business if your messages are to get through to employees and actually become part of the company's culture.

The companies that use communications best are very clear about their messages. And these are no mere empty slogans. Rather, they are the principles the company actually lives by; they are statements that characterize the company's fundamental philosophy and that they carry through in their everyday operations. IBM is a good case in point. Like any good company, they have their commercial ups and downs, but they are still held in high respect by customers and competitors. Here are four of the key messages that the company's employee communications are constantly emphasizing:

- IBM knows where it is going.
- IBM is a good place to work.
- IBM makes a significant contribution to the community.
- Technology is necessary and exciting.

Indeed, if some of these message bells have not been rung for some time, the company's communications media will deliberately carry articles and items to keep them fresh in employees' minds.

But like all good messages, they have very much a two-sided effect. On the one hand, they influence employee opinion in constructive directions, but they also constantly press the company into positive actions that give substance to its messages. The company has to *show* it knows where it is going, it obviously *has to be* a good place to work, and so on. Otherwise employees see communications on these subjects as just so much hot air. Messages have next to no effect if your actions do not match them and follow through. Management actions are 10 times more powerful than their words.

And that is where the front-line manager has a crucial role to play. When we ask employees in company surveys from what source they *prefer* to get their information about the company, the front-line manager always heads the list. The following example, taken from a 2,000 employee survey, is very typical:

My immediate manager	85%
Team meetings	59%
Noticeboards	35%
Printed material sent to me	29%
My manager's manager	29%
Direct from senior management	15%
From Personnel	15%
Trade union representation	7%
Audiovisual presentations	6%
House magazine	4%
The 'grapevine'	4%

Consistently, employees vote overwhelmingly in favour of their immediate manager as the communicator they prefer. But is it any wonder? He is the person employees see every day and who understands their practical problems first-hand. When he does communicate face-to-face you can ask him questions in your own words, ie the communication is two-way and at the employee's own level. He is not impersonal like a noticeboard, a video or a magazine. He talks their language. He is the person who talks to them more than anybody else in the business. He is their natural choice.

But first-line managers cannot simply be given the prime responsibility for communications and then left to sink or swim. If the process is to be done well, they need strong and continuing support. First, in the preparation of useful and pertinent material pitched at the level of the employees' understanding and second, in the form of thorough training and on-the-job coaching until they can perform their communications role with confidence and conviction.

In fact, without this kind of support managers may well be acting to nullify the very messages their company wants to convey. Now, consider this point. Most formal company communication systems operate on a once-monthly basis. But, whether we like it or not, the front-line manager is communicating with employees every minute of the day by what he says and does. If communications team meetings take roughly half a day a month (we are being generous), and there are around 21 working days in the average month, then what the manager *does* every day has a 40 to 1 greater chance of convincing employees that that is what the company is *really* like. If what he does is in conflict with company messages, his daily actions will swamp anything the company says formally only once a month.

In the end there is really no viable alternative but to use the communications source employees clearly prefer – the front-line manager. That is also why company messages must not only be few and simple enough for the manager to carry around in his head, they need to be actionable enough for him to be *living* them in his everyday work. He is the face of the company they see every day. To most employees he is the company. If he is not speaking – and acting – in line with the company's declared philosophy every day, then they presume the mission statements and pontifications from the top are simply so many fine words and window dressing. If he does not act them out, they won't either.

'Meetings are purposeful, and follow published guidelines'

Meetings are conducted in every company, but very few have any guidelines for running effective meetings. As a result, people complain about both the number of meetings they have to attend and their quality. Training on skills to handle meetings goes a long way in addressing this problem. What also helps is to use a set of guidelines that everyone buys into. You'll be astonished at the time it saves.

Here is a set used by one of our successful clients:

1. The outcome/purpose of any meeting will be stated in advance, ie when the meeting is first requested, and at the start of the meeting itself.
2. The length of the meeting will be stated up-front, ie when first requested, and at the start of the meeting itself. Attendees may leave at any time after the stated time for the meeting has expired.
3. We will all come to meetings we have agreed to attend on time, and start promptly.
4. We will all bring to the meeting any relevant or necessary information, and our diaries.
5. The person who calls the meeting will produce the minutes.
6. The minutes will be Action Minutes, ie who is doing what, and when.
7. Minutes will be sent to attendees within 48 hours.

'House journal is lively, interesting, and widely read'

The varieties of house journals are manifold, but what is crucial is that any company newsletter or magazine should be lively, interesting and widely read. Although we don't make lengthy, detailed recommendations you may find the following ideas useful in achieving these objectives:

1. Putting in a list of 'for sale' and 'wanted' items tends to gain wide readership. In addition, employees appreciate the ability to buy and sell items at no advertising cost.
2. Competitions keep the magazine lively. Some of the items that are successful are: What name do you think we should give our new cafeteria? What should be the name of our new house magazine? etc. Also, using baby or child photographs in the magazine and getting employees to guess just who they are. That often leads to a bit of fun.

3. It is difficult to get enough material to put in the magazine if it is simply left to employees to contribute. An editor is needed who is responsible for getting material from employees and who helps meet magazine deadlines.

4. People love to see their photograph in the papers. If you have good work being done around the company, or notable achievements being produced, then it is a good idea to put photographs of the people concerned in the magazine. Not only does this please the employees (they take it home to show the family, and often keep the magazine for years afterwards), but it sets a tone of what the company values and encourages others to follow the same path.

LEVEL 4

'Information cascades from top management meetings to front-line staff within 48 hours'

To get the information cascade to work efficiently, there needs to be a well-oiled system in place. This is what we see in companies who do it well. First, there is a published calendar of Board or Senior Management Meetings. There is also an established hierarchy of Briefing Groups programmed to meet the day after the Board Meetings. A specific individual is responsible for supplying briefing notes of the Management Meeting, and where necessary overhead projection slides, to be used by the named Briefing Team Leaders. The latter will normally add the 'local information' to their Briefings that we spoke of in Level 2 above. This kind of process not only gets useful information to employees throughout the company quickly, it gives the strong impression that management is well organized and working as a team. And that's important.

'Front-line teams hold "start-of-the-day" meetings, and have communication boards in their sections'

As we indicated in Ladder 8 on Teamwork, the value of 10-minute 'start-of-the-day' meetings between front-line managers and their people are manifold:

1. It acts as a quick roll call. That helps get staff there on time (it's a bit embarrassing to be late). It also means the team leader can take early action to redeploy if members of staff are absent.

2. The team leader is seen to be organized. To run a start-of-day meeting successfully, the team leader has to come in 15 minutes or so early to find out all the circumstances affecting the job. At the meeting itself he appears then to have all the information at his fingertips, to be 'on top of the job'. That's comforting and confidence-building for team members.

3. He can immediately focus on urgent items or critical areas affecting the

job, eg whether there have been last-minute changes to the schedule of work, unexpected equipment break-downs, etc.

4. It makes better use of his managerial time. Normally if staff go immediately to their desks or operating positions, the manager then has to move around to pass on necessary information to each individual. When they meet together briefly at the start of the day, he can pass on exactly the same message to everyone in 10 minutes.

5. It makes for early problem resolution. If special circumstances have arisen late on the previous day or shift (problem equipment, shortage of materials, etc), then the manager can promptly do something about that. That way everyone is immediately aware of how the problem is to be handled.

6. And finally, *daily* team meetings build team identity and cohesion. If the team meets five times a week together briefly every day, that is five times a week, or 20 times a month, or over 200 times a year. Even if no one ever mentions the word 'teamwork' they will very soon become a team, acting together to solve problems, share ideas and make improvements.

'Strong upward channel means front-line points are heard at senior management level'

Most companies think of communication as getting messages down. And generally upward channels are vague or totally non-existent. We recommend that companies work on making the upward channel as strong as the downward. Vague generalities like 'management by walking about' and having occasional meetings between the managing director and shop floor staff are too unsystematic to be effective. Here are some examples of processes that are more systematic and more effective:

1. At Nissan, front-line managers meet with middle managers at the end of every shift, to report on the operations during that day and on any issues raised by shop floor staff that need to be resolved quickly before they become real problems. This is practical upward communication built in to the communication process on a daily basis.

2. IBM have run a system called 'Speak-up' for many years. Under the scheme anyone can send in a question to the Speak-up Controller, whose duty it is to get an answer to the questioner from the appropriate level of authority within 10 days maximum. The company publishes items of more general interest in its house magazine. Any scheme that has been going for 30 years, as theirs has, must have proven real value.

3. The John Lewis Partnership, a large retail chain in the United Kingdom, where every employee is called 'partner' and participates in profit sharing, run a scheme where questions may be asked of senior management. Their answers are published in their house magazine.

4. One Japanese company runs a scheme called Opportunity For Improvement (OFI). This allows employees to record anything that is making it difficult for them to do their job 'right first time'. This is exactly the sort of upward feedback that ought to be encouraged, ie feedback to do with the

job itself, rather than purely questions of personal interest (see Figure 11.1).

5. Several Japanese companies run a scheme called 'Scare Report'. This has to do with problems on the job or with safety hazards. Generally the Scare Report asks the reporter to say what he has done immediately to handle the problem and what else he thinks needs to be done.

OFI FORM
Opportunity for Improvement

DATE: REPORTED BY:

The following situation is making it difficult for me to do my job right the first time:

OPTIONAL:

What has already been done:

What could be done:

LOG NO ....

Figure 11.1 An OFI form

LEVEL 5

'Company uses a variety of communication channels well, ie meetings, noticeboards, paper, computer and video'

There is a great variety of media available to communicate company information and companies need to choose those that deliver their messages best. Here is a selection:

- manager/employee team meetings;
- noticeboards;
- manager information briefs;
- company magazines;
- brochures, eg on health, pensions, etc;
- trade union representatives;
- senior management presentations;
- pay packet inserts;

- campaigns;
- videos;
- posters;
- static displays;
- computerized information displays.

However, the medium is not the message. Our advice is: don't rely on only one method of communicating, eg briefing groups. Use a variety but keep your messages few and consistent. Many companies communicate far too much information, and as a result employees don't know how to interpret it all, or simply ignore most of it. You need to choose the media you're going to major on and handle well.

To do that, ask yourself the following questions:

- Who is the target audience?
- What does the company want them to know, understand and believe a year from now?
- What critical information needs to be provided to ensure that everyone in the business is able to do his or her job effectively?

Companies need to be clear about why they are communicating and what they want the results to be.

'Matrix calendar of communications shows all communication channels, and who does what, when'

A good example is shown in Figure 11.2 of the layout used by the electrical company Lucas Rists in the United Kingdom.

'Surveys show steadily improving communicating scores'

Some of the questions we ask in the opinion surveys we conduct for clients are shown in Figure 11.3 (page 246).

In a company that has worked on its employee communications, we would expect more than 50 per cent of the employees to choose one of the top two boxes on the first question and in excess of 60 per cent on the second question. This may seem easy but it's hard to do.

One of the keys to success here is to use assiduously the front-line manager, and to give them the training and support they need to manage communications well. That's when front-line managers come top of the heap in the communications source from which employees 'actually receive their information', and finally relegate the grapevine to second or third place.

It takes both knowledge and effort to keep communications healthy in any organization. David Drennan's article 'Effective Employee Communications', which follows on page 246, was written for the *Director* magazine in 1992. Its lessons are still very relevant today.

Communications Commitment

We will keep all of our employees informed about the business as a whole, and in matters of local interest to each area.

We will make sure you are receiving regular communications as detailed below, and continuously look for ways of making them better.

In addition to these formal communications, you are encouraged to raise any suggestion, question or comment with your immediate supervisor – you will be properly listened to, and given a considered, truthful and timely response.

From	To	Daily	Weekly	Monthly	6 Monthly
Management Team members	Direct reports		Cascade from Management Team meeting: • Current issues of interest • Questions and answers • Two-way communications		
Business Unit Management	Managers, Supervisors			• Feedback from monthly BU review • Key Department measures • Questions & answers • Two-way communications	
Managers	All staff		Department meeting to include where relevant: • Review of key section measures • Department measures of performance • Cascade from Management Team meeting • Process improvements • Projects • Questions & answers • Two-way communications	As weekly plus feedback from monthly BU review (or quarterly Function review)	
First line supervision	All shop floor employees (direct and indirect)	In sections with daily measures, 5-10 min to include where relevant: • Quality issues • Customer issues • Health & Safety issues • Productivity • Delivery performance • Visitors • Absenteeism	For all sections, 5-10 min to include where relevant: • Cascade from the Management Team meeting • Quality issues • Customer issues • Health & Safety issues • Productivity • Delivery performance • Visitors • Absenteeism		
Lucas Rists/SEI General Manager	All management plus TU representatives				
Business Unit Management or Corporate Management Team members	All personnel in their respective areas				• Half or full year results of Lucas Group, Lucas Rists and/or Lucas SEI • Key business issues • BU performance • Customer update

Figure 11.2 Lucas Rists' communications commitment

'How satisfied are you with the information you receive from management about what is going on in the company?'

Very satisified	☐
Satisfied	☐
Neither	☐
Dissatisfied	☐
Very dissatisfied	☐

When the company puts out information, how do you feel about it?

You can always believe it	☐
You can usually believe it	☐
You can sometimes believe it	☐
You can seldom believe it	☐
You can never believe it	☐

Figure 11.3 Opinion survey questions

IDEAS YOU CAN USE

Effective Employee Communication

Team Briefing is used by many companies as their principal method of employee communication. Yet many executives express doubts about whether the system actually adds any value to their company's operations. Often they say it does not seem to generate the positive attitudes among employees that they feel it should. But communications cannot be neatly confined to a monthly tell-it-to-the-troops slot.

The fact is, in every organization communications are taking place every day of the week, every hour of the day. It's like breathing: work cannot go on without it. And in forming their attitudes and opinions employees don't just wait to hear what the company says once a month, they watch what the company does every day. The daily actions of the company and its managers send much stronger signals about what the company is really like than the words they say once a month. If what the company does is not in line with what they say, employees just treat the company's formal communications as so much hot air. It's not really the words that count, it's the *example*. That's what tells employees what the company really values, and that's what really determines how they will behave and react.

And consider this. In most companies team briefing sessions last only an hour or so each month. But employees are at work around 21 days a month, eight hours a day, and all that time (over 150 hours) they are watching the example their own boss actually sets. If the company is pontificating about the importance of quality every month but their boss is repeatedly letting doubtful products go to keep up his productivity, then what he does will swamp whatever the company says by a factor of 150 to 1. In that case, however well intentioned, team briefing sessions will have no effect on employee behaviour at all.

If your communications are actually going to add value rather than just cost (it takes time, effort and money to prepare and deliver employee communications), then here are four pieces of fundamental advice you need to follow.

1. You have to live your own messages

It seems all too obvious to say that if you start preaching about quality you have to follow through with action. But even managing directors can soon have their convictions sorely tested. One manufacturing company, for example, anxious to improve its quality performance, coined the slogan 'Quality is number one', and launched a vigorous communications campaign in support, using meetings, posters and videos. Their stated aim was defect-free products despatched to customers. There were settling-in problems as quality inspectors tightened their standards and production managers complained of niggling rejections. However, the crunch came only two months into the programme.

It was a standing rule that all export orders had to be despatched complete (the company had painful experience of sending part orders abroad in the past). A large foreign order due for shipping at the end of the month was short of some key parts that were being specifically nursed through the plant. It was also awaiting metal casings from an outside supplier who was being heavily leant on. In the event, two of the inside parts did not clear inspection, while some of the bought-out metal casings were scratched and in one case did not fit. But the plant director decided to despatch anyway, otherwise there would have been a huge hole in his invoiced sales for the month, and he would have to face difficult questions at corporate Head Office.

The director hadn't actually said a word, but employees got the message loud and clear: 'Quality isn't really No. 1. When push comes to shove, output is still what counts. . . and meeting the boss's monthly budget. Quality is just an add-on – if you've got time.' That's the kind of cynical reaction you get when management fails to follow through on its own messages. It can destroy credibility in anything the company says through its communication process. 'If the big boss is not committed, why should we be?' say employees.

One of the things that even a committed top management does not know, however, is whether junior management is following through on the company's messages at ground floor level. . . unless they go and find out. Try this: walk around and ask a few employees what they understand is the company's position on quality, service, or whatever your company is majoring on at the time. See if the messages are actually getting through. Take action when they are not. Do this a few times and see just how quickly the quality of management–employee communications improves. Follow-up makes a lot of difference.

However, conflicting pressures can often make it difficult for junior managers to follow through on the company's messages. One company that makes complex production and packing machinery had for some time been losing market share to foreign rivals. In strategy sessions their directors concluded that to retain current customers and regain market share, they had to deliver machines on a schedule that would beat competitors both for required installation time and performance.

There ensued a great campaign to meet promised customer delivery dates come what may, and to see that machines 'worked first time out of the box' in customers' premises. Assembly complained loudly that support departments were still encroaching on their build time, and making it next-to-impossible for them to despatch on time and defect-free. An early order brought the situation to a head, when Assembly ran out of time to pack a complex machine in its special wooden case. The lorry was patiently waiting outside and had to leave that night if the load was to make the ship leaving early next morning from a port some four hours away. Rather than miss the deadline, the manager decided to wrap the machine in layers of cellophane instead. It could have been damaged by rough transport of course, but in this event when it arrived halfway round the world it was rusty. The installation crew were flabbergasted; the customer was horror-struck.

Make no mistake, whatever message you promote to your employees, there will soon come an event that tests your sincerity and your resolve. And employees will all be looking on to see if you really mean what you say. If you don't follow through, employees won't follow through either, and all your communication efforts will simply be an elaborate waste of time. So what can you do? The first rule is: don't ignore deviations and pretend it didn't happen. Instead, create a great fuss, hold an elaborate post-mortem and let everyone know you're doing it. Get together all those decision-makers whose work is key to getting that particular product out on time, defect-free.

Put two items on the group's agenda: How are we to make sure – fail-safe – that this particular problem does not occur again? What are the other vulnerabilities that might prevent on-time, defect-free despatch, and what are we going to do specifically about each one? Don't give the team a long time-scale – two weeks at the most – and let them know you are serious. Have them report formally at the highest level. That will do two things. The particular product problem will get urgent attention and resolution, and a strong signal will fly around the company that everybody else can expect the same treatment if they don't get the message.

But here's the most important point of all: employees will begin to believe what management says. You have no idea how that will improve at a stroke the effectiveness of your communications. Of course, you will have to be careful about what you do say, but you won't have to repeat yourself 64 times any more to get effective action.

2. Use the communications channel that employees prefer

Companies, like mine, who undertake employee attitude surveys, soon find out that there is a great difference in where employees *prefer* to get their information, and where they *actually* get it from. Generally the grapevine beats all the other actual sources of information. Yet it inevitably comes bottom of employees' preferred list.

There is one preferred source, however, that stands regularly head and shoulders above the others. Results consistently show that employees prefer their prime communications source to be their immediate manager. But is it any wonder? He is the person employees see every day and who understands their practical problems first-hand. He is their natural choice.

The front-line manager is in fact the most important two-way communicator in any business. He is not only the mouthpiece by which company messages are communicated downwards, but the means by which messages are communicated upwards. That crucial role can only be done with adequate training and support from the company. The best kind of training is off-the-job practice in preparing talks, delivering stand-up presentations to an audience, learning how to cope with awkward questions, seeing themselves as they really are on videotape, and having themselves critiqued by the trainer and their fellow trainees. The best kind of support is the preparation of appropriate material pitched at the level of employees' understanding, having question and answer briefs with authoritative answers to the most likely questions, and knowing where they can get answers . . . fast.

Information becomes power in managers' hands, but only under two conditions: they get the information first, and it is accurate. If the normal routine, for example, is that the Trade Union knows first, then employees naturally forget their manager.

Here's how one manufacturing company supported its managers. At the time of pay negotiations, it told its middle managers, before each meeting, the main items of their negotiation position. Middle managers passed this information on to their junior managers while the negotiation meeting was actually in progress. The company also arranged for the same middle managers to hear the outcome of the negotiations in the first hour after each meeting ended; they in turn immediately passed this on to their juniors. That way, no nasty rumours ever got started – even front-line managers seemed to know what they were talking about. As soon as negotiations were complete, front-line managers had in their hands the next day the terms of the agreement and what that meant, in figures, for all of the people they managed.

The company also circulated all noticeboard items to managers the day before they appeared on the board, with the phone number of the person from whom they could get questions answered. (Almost nothing won't wait one day, and this way managers stop getting surprised and embarrassed.) In addition, front-line managers got properly structured training and well-prepared material with question and answer briefs for their monthly communication meetings. At the end of year one, in an attitude survey that asked employees to list the sources from which they actually got their information, 'my immediate manager' beat 'the grapevine' for the first time in the company's history.

3. Talk at the level of the employee's interest

Although team-briefing meetings are supposed to be about employees' own items, they frequently consist of company-wide information sent down from senior management, and about which the front-line manager knows very little. As a result, managers often look awkward delivering the information, while employees don't quite know what the company's market share figures or acquisitions have got to do with them.

Employee communications need to concentrate on what employees understand best – their everyday work. This is something Nissan understands very well. An important part of its communications process at their Sunderland car plant in the United Kingdom is the 5 to 10-minute meetings team leaders hold *every day* with their work teams before they start work. The meetings focus on the employees' actual work, brevity forcing them to concentrate on the priorities. They talk about the day's targets, any specific problems that have arisen, and what they are going to do about them. Then they're off to work with everyone informed. The system is simple, quick and effective.

The 'interest graph' in Figure 11.4 demonstrates in a very obvious way that the interests of staff are highest when what is being communicated affects them directly and decreases in proportion to the distance the information is from their concern. However, most companies report largely on company and corporate information in their company magazine, an area where staff interest is at its lowest.

4. Listen to what your employees say

A new general manager took over the management of several manufacturing plants in a well-known UK company. He was urged by his boss to improve employee communications, and to start by visiting one plant that had 'an excellent system'. At the end of his first visit there, he was accosted by the trade union convenor who harangued him with a great list of grievances. The new general manager, anxious to make an impression, decided there and then to call all the employees into the cafeteria for an informal get-together. By the end, his ears were burning. With the factory in a built-up area, employees complained they could find nowhere to park in the morning to get into work (managers had special spaces inside the works); the lavatories were in a terrible state; doors and windows were broken; operators were being gassed. Gassed? Yes, they said, one of the main operations involved considerable fumes and operators were falling sick. Eventually the GM had a long list of points.

After the session, he held a meeting with the plant manager. Why had all these items not come up in their regular communication meetings? They had. Why had they not done anything about them? 'You mustn't react to everything they say,' said the manager, 'otherwise you would never be finished. I just use the meetings to let them have a good moan and let off steam.' This may seem like an extreme example but, believe me, employees everywhere

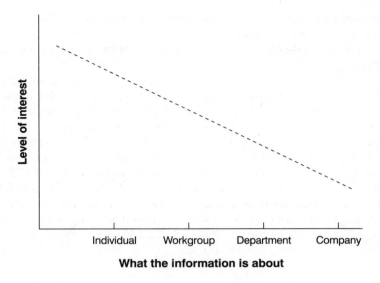

Figure 11.4 Interest graph

get very frustrated by the failure of their communication system to get things done. In fact, the failure to listen kills more company communication systems than any other factor. The answer is clear: don't engage in any management –employee communication process unless you are genuinely prepared to do something about the legitimate issues employees raise.

One company came up with a neat mechanism to help get over this problem. It invented a 'go-do' board. Any problem accepted for action by a manager in a communication meeting was recorded on the board, complete with the initials of the person responsible and an agreed date for completion. The boards were placed in a public position in every section for everyone to see. No manager ever wanted to be seen to fail or to take on nigh-impossible actions. Not only did things get done, but they were seen to be done. The large ticks that appeared as actions were completed not only helped to convince employees that their communication meetings could really achieve things, they even stimulated feelings of pride.

Communications between management and staff must not be confined to giving employees opportunities to complain. Even more important is creating specific communications avenues by which employees can contribute positively to the business – with new ideas and practical suggestions.

Japanese companies have developed this side of communications most effectively. They expect their people to do the very best they can for their company. At Pioneer, the electronic audio manufacturer, for example, every employee is asked to provide seven new ideas for improvement every month. The company doesn't expect them all to be mind-boggling ideas, of course, but it does mean that every employee in the company is thinking in a mode of constant, never-ending improvement all the time. You may think that demanding seven ideas every month is a bit much. But what about just one suggestion a month – would that really be too much to ask? No company that leaves the process of innovation and improvement exclusively to management can hope to compete with a company that has got every employee on the job every day.

Employees' ideas may not be all that marvellous to start with, but they do get better at it. Car manufacturer Toyota started asking its staff for improvement ideas way back in 1962. At first it did not get a very good response. Suggestions amounted to less than one per person in the first year, and of these the company rejected the majority (only some 34 per cent were implemented). But they kept going, and 20 years later they got an average of 32.7 suggestions per person (a 50-fold increase), making a grand total of 1,950,000 suggestions. And here's the best part: the quality had improved so much that they were able to implement 90 per cent of them. That means they are currently implementing more than 7,000 improvement suggestions every working day! That's the power of developing a communication system that deliberately taps into the goodwill and brain power of every employee in the business.

Some telling questions

So examine the nature of your own employee communications system, and ask yourself these few questions:

- Are you relying on team briefing to carry the burden of your company's employee communication system? No once-a-month system can do it all by itself.
- Are you and your managers actually living the company's messages every day? It's not the words that count, it's the example. If managers aren't doing it, employees won't either.
- Are you using – and supporting – the communicator employees clearly prefer? Front-line managers are the face of the company employees see every day. More than any other group, they have the power to change attitudes.
- Are your communications couched at the level of your employees' interest? Overwhelmingly your communications with employees need to be about their everyday work.
- Do you do something about what your employees say? Without that, your communication system may be worse than useless. However, the more you put their ideas into practice the more they'll tell you. And when the whole company is actively contributing, you will be able to compete with the best in the world.

Twelve

Continuous Learning

LEVELS	MEASURES
Level 1	Employees are not enthusiastic about learning new skills. There is minimal induction training and little off-the-job training. Experts are generally opposed to sharing their skills with others, feeling their jobs would thereby be threatened.
Level 2	Minimum of one day's off-the-job training for everyone every year. Staff are trained to handle multi-tasks in operations and office. Tradespeople are trained and operate across skill boundaries. Skill and training records maintained for every person. All inductees get initial training and are linked to a mentor.
Level 3	Learning objectives are built into all appraisals every year. Complete cross-skilling operated within work groups. Using a points-based system, the average employee has doubled his skill points. Job rotation is happening in every area of the company.
Level 4	Minimum of three days off-the-job training for everyone every year. Training facilities have become 'state-of-the-art'. Managers and directors have become trained trainers. The whole workforce becomes more skilled/valuable every year.
Level 5	The company realizes that continuous skills training turns their people into a competitive (and their only) appreciating asset. Minimum of five days off-the-job training for everyone every year. Larger companies operate an in-house university. Continuous learning has become a way of life.

LEVEL 1

'Employees are not enthusiastic about learning new skills'

This is generally the first reaction of staff who have been employed by their company for years and have never been to any training course since they started. When asked to undertake training they say things like 'Do I have to? I just want to do this job, earn my money and go home', or 'What's in it for us if we do?' This often gives management the impression that staff are unco-operative and contrary. The fact is that most of them are scared. After all, most people were ordinary at school. They never won any prizes, and generally don't have pleasant memories of the classroom or school examinations. They are scared that if they go on a training course they will be made to look stupid or dull. The best way to avoid that kind of embarrassment is just to say 'no'.

You should not be put off by these initial reactions. However, it is critically important that employees' first experience with company training should be positive, in that they experience early success. That means structuring the training into manageable pieces so that the vast majority of trainees feel they can cope, they see at the end that they have actually learnt something, and they thought learning was enjoyable too.

'There is minimal induction training and little off-the-job training'

Many companies give the briefest and most rudimentary induction training to their new employees. They are simply escorted to their department, introduced to the manager and left to find their way around by themselves. The manager may show them where the toilets are, and put them with one of their employees to 'learn the ropes'. That way, new recruits are bound to find out all the bad habits from Day One. In such companies there is usually little off-the-job training, and little evidence of training rooms with basic training equipment (ie flip charts, overhead projectors and screens). Where training facilities are available, these are often situated in the most unsuitable places, where it is cramped and noisy, and the equipment is rudimentary or poorly maintained. Managers say: 'We don't have time for all this training. We need these people on the job now to get the product out of the door.' When you hear this you know you are in a Level 1 company.

'Experts are generally opposed to sharing their skills with others, feeling that their jobs would thereby be threatened'

This happens in companies where there is little ongoing staff training, and where there is an established or even ancient tradition of apprenticeships. For example, some tradesmen will deliberately keep their specialist knowledge both from their colleagues and apprentices in order to make themselves appear more valuable or even indispensable. This is a situation no management should tolerate. Continuous improvement has become today such a standard commodity whether it is in sport, education, technology, communications, customer service, quality standards, or product value for money, that no organization can afford to stand still and survive. That means all employees have to play their part by sharing their knowledge and continuously improving themselves. This should be an essential part of every employee's job.

One company that's very clear about its policy on this subject is printing company Quad Graphics in the United States. This is what new employees are told when they join the company:

> Each employee makes a commitment to accept our values and become a student/teacher. Our first task is to learn our jobs. Our second task is to know our jobs. Our third task is to improve our jobs – since only those doing a given job can determine how to do it better. And our fourth job is to teach our jobs to each other.

> Education nurtures people. It accelerates change. It is how we find the next leading edge of technology. We create the technology to do our work at unrivalled levels of quality and unheard of speeds. Education is a way of life in Quad Graphics.

In any company keen to move out of Level 1, employees need to be disabused of the idea that their learning stopped when they left school or college, or completed their apprenticeship. On the contrary, lifelong learning is the only way that companies can stay competitive and individuals remain valuable and wanted in the jobs market-place. It's just that realization that has kept Quad repeatedly winning the title of 'Best Printer in America'.

LEVEL 2

'Minimum of one day's off-the-job training for everyone every year'

We often visit companies where employees and staff tell us they haven't been on training sessions for years. Sometimes they are wrong, but more often they are right. There are about 220 working days in the year, so allocating one day a year for training amounts to less than half a per cent of the working year! That barely scratches the surface of continuous improvement, but it's better than none at all! And making such a commitment sends a strong signal that the company is serious and emphasizes three things:

1. To stay ahead of rising customer expectations and ever-improving competition, continuous learning is not an option any more, it's a necessity.
2. No one is beyond learning, and that includes staff in the lowliest jobs up to the chairman and managing director.
3. Public announcement raises the position of learning and training on the agenda of the company's priorities. It ensures that a budget is allocated for it, and makes it less prone to whimsical budget cuts during the year.

This is almost always just the start. Most companies quickly realize that one day's training is a bare minimum and soon start increasing the number to several days per person, which in turn helps institutionalize the process of continuous learning in the company.

There are two good reasons why you should plan any training well:

- There are always costs associated with training, including the time employees spend off the job, so good planning helps get better value for money.
- If employees are only going to spend one or two days off-the-job on training, you want them to achieve something measurable and useful in the time available.

We have to say we see many vague generalities describing the objectives of training. For example: 'To gain an appreciation of . . .'; 'To have a knowledge of the law with regard to . . .'; 'To understand the principles of marketing', etc. We strongly recommend you write measurable, testable objectives for every piece of training you run. In this respect, the advice given by Robert Mager to trainers back in the 1960s on writing training objectives is still very relevant today. Here are the key points:

1. A good objective describes the intended *outcome* of the training, rather than a description of its content. It specifies what the learner will be DOING by the end, in a way that would be clear to anyone when he has succeeded.

   Consider this objective, for example: 'To develop a critical understanding of the Chiron numerically controlled machine.' It sounds very serious, but 'critical understanding' could mean many different things to different people. It's too vague. Much better would be: 'By the end of the training module, the trainee must be able to name correctly all the controls on the front of the Chiron.' That's clear to everyone. You may have to write several such objectives to cover a whole programme of course, but it is vitally important to get that kind of clarity into your training objectives right at the start.

2. You may have to describe the *conditions* under which end performance will be judged. For example, in a hospital an objective might be: 'Given a human skeleton, the learner must be able to identify by labelling 30 of the following bones' (list added). Or in a factory: 'Without reference to instructions, the learner must be able to start up the boiler equipment fault-free.' Describe the conditions so that no one could misinterpret what is required.

3. Finally, state the *criterion* by which you will judge success. One of the most obvious criteria is to describe in what time a task has to be performed; or what is the minimum number of answers that have to be right to a set of test questions. For example: 'Given a standard set of tools and product drawings, the learner must be able to repair a single malfunction in a 10 horsepower DC motor within 45 minutes.' Or: 'The learner must

achieve at least 8 out of 10 correct answers to each module test, before being allowed to proceed to the next stage.'

Notice all these objectives tend to talk about the 'learner'. Training is what you do to people. But what the learner is able to do as a result is the only way to judge the value of the process. To test the value of any proposed training, there is only one question worth asking: 'What will the learner be able to do at the end?' Don't run any training where you are not satisfied with the answer. However, the purpose is not to play the Smart Alec and avoid doing any training at all. That is not clever. The purpose is to make sure the value you get matches the effort and money you spend on it.

Another technique first developed during the 1960s – 'Criterion-referenced instruction' (CRI) – provides an excellent basic format for training. CRI is based on a number of key concepts:

1. The proposed training is broken down into a series of easily assimilated modules, perhaps as short as 20 minutes. This is to ensure the training can be digested in bite-sized pieces, and by conducting modest little 'hurdle tests' at each stage, to give trainees the opportunity to see themselves achieving early success. That encouragement is critically important in the early stages.
2. At the beginning of each module, trainees undertake a 'criterion test'. This is usually composed of approximately 10 questions. If trainees are able to answer 8 or more of the 10 questions correctly, then they do not need to undertake that module of training. Normally trainees only get one or two right.
3. At the end of the training, trainees are asked to undertake the same criterion test again. When they obtain scores of 9 or 10 out of 10 and compare that with the low score they had at the beginning of the module, they realize how much they have learnt in a short time. That success is a great spur to go further.
4. Criterion tests are also used for the following reasons:

   (a) The trainer is forced to be clear about the skills and knowledge the trainees should have when the module has been completed. Training material is therefore much more specific and to the point.
   (b) Success on the tests not only motivates the learners to carry on with further training, it also proves to the trainer whether the trainees have actually obtained the intended knowledge and skills – which is the whole point of doing the training.

5. Trainees should know beforehand that they will be tested at the end of each training module. This is not to frighten them, but experience has shown that when there is a prospective test trainees pay much more attention during the training itself. And, funnily enough, they value their achievement that much more.

'Staff are trained to handle multi-tasks in operations and office'

We encourage front-line staff to learn a variety of jobs or tasks for a number of reasons:

- Staff's multi-skills mean they can cover for absence, ie no service or manufacturing process need stop for want of some key individual.
- They increase their value to themselves and the company.
- It adds variety to their everyday work.

We would add just two words of warning: staff need to rotate round the jobs involved to keep their skills sharp; if staff have learnt too many skills they cannot rotate often enough to keep them all up-to-date. So keep multi-skilling to a manageable level.

One of the consequences of multi-tasking may be that old job titles may no longer be appropriate. For example, at Staffordshire Tableware, operators were called by their job name, eg cup makers, handle makers, emptiers (of kilns), spongers, etc. When multi-tasking was introduced their job title was changed to Team Operator. This helped to reinforce the point that people were expected both to be steadily increasing their knowledge and skills and to be versatile (depending on whichever task needs to be done), and to work together as a productive team. That change of thinking was invaluable.

'Tradespeople are trained and operate across skill boundaries'

This can be a very useful facility for companies. Demarcations leading to 'That's not my job', or 'We have to wait for the electrician before we can start this job' waste time and can be great sources of inefficiency. We would always want to be careful, of course, to keep things safe (especially where electricity is concerned). But, given safety being paramount, we believe there should be no demarcation either because of tradition, trade union rules, or exclusion of people because they did not complete the requisite apprenticeship in their youth. If the person is competent, with training, to undertake the job today, there should be no other artificial barriers.

'Skill and training records maintained for every person'

In many companies people may often go on courses but no individual training records seem to be kept. After a number of years people vaguely remember that they went on a course on a specific subject two or three years ago, but can't quite remember what they did, etc. Keeping individual training and learning records is very useful from a number of points of view:

1. If a person applies for another job or promotion, this record of what they have done can be a useful resource.
2. People forget all the things that they have learnt, and seeing a long list

makes them realize how knowledgeable they have actually become. This is particularly valuable to raise the self-esteem of front-line staff who may otherwise work in mundane jobs. They love to see the record grow longer, and it often acts as a motivator to continue their learning.
3. If grants or financial help are to be offered by outside Government bodies, such records can impress the authorities and prove how seriously the company treats training as a whole.

'All inductees get initial training and are linked to a mentor'

Some companies give new recruits as much as 12 weeks' induction training. As far as front-line employees are concerned, two days' induction training is probably a minimum, although this should preferably be broken into 'bite size' pieces. Some companies require new managers to spend time doing front-line jobs, as part of their induction training, to remind them of the work that pays their and everybody else's salary. Some Japanese manufacturing companies are particularly keen on this, insisting that both new graduates and seasoned managers in disciplines other than manufacturing spend at least four weeks working in their manufacturing plants.

Some service companies not only do their initial recruitment very carefully, but set tests during the induction training process as a means of determining whether new recruits are allowed to stay. Carphone Warehouse, a hugely successful company in the United Kingdom, adopts just such a policy. This is Charles Dunstone, their Managing Director:

> We invest a huge amount in training. It comes from the basic philosophy that if I joined the company, the very first customer I deal with should not suffer even 1 per cent because it is my first day. It is not the customer's fault. They walked in expecting a level of service, and it is up to us to deliver it. We put recruits on a three-week training course when they join the company – an induction course. They have to go through this process, some of it working in stores, but most based in the classroom learning about the networks, the tariffs, our computer system, etc. At the end we give them a two-hour written exam. If you do not score 75 per cent, that is the end of your time at Carphone Warehouse.

Do you think customers get good service at Carphone Warehouse? They love it.

It is also a good practice to attach new recruits to a mentor. By a mentor is meant someone who will take a personal interest in the new recruit, and help him or her integrate into the company successfully. They therefore act as confidant and friend during that period. However, mentors should be selected carefully. Experiments conducted by Metropolitan Life Insurance in the United States show that good sales recruits, when partnered with top sales people, do three to five times as well as the same recruits partnered with mediocre sales people. Similarly, if recruits are going to shop floor jobs, they should never simply be partnered with any employee who is available – that way they may learn all the short cuts and bad habits there are in the first three weeks. If recruits are to become model employees, put them close to people who are already model employees. Soon they'll be acting just like them.

LEVEL 3

'Learning objectives are built into all appraisals every year'

In Ladder 10 (Rewards and Recognition) examples of appraisal forms are shown that incorporate the idea of 'learning objectives'. We choose the term 'learning objective' deliberately. We want individuals to think about what they want to learn, and in which areas they want to become more knowledgeable or skilful over the following period or year. In other words, instead of the company doing it to them (training), individual employees plan their own learning (with their boss's help).

We believe the prime purpose of appraisals is motivation and development (again see Ladder 10). That is why we favour building learning objectives into the appraisal system itself, rather than be an accidental add-on. The process we advise is that both parties – manager and individual – should come to the appraisal meeting with ideas or suggestions for learning objectives for the next period, and in discussion firm up on what these are to be. That way, training officers don't have to trail round the company touting their latest training course suggestions. On the contrary, the customers (the employees) tell the training manager just what they want, and his job is then to provide a quality service.

Training courses are not the only way to foster learning, of course. In Figure 10.4, an appraisal form in Ladder 10, there is a Box entitled 'Significant Points Learned This Period' to be completed by the appraisee. This urges the individual to crystallize what they have learnt by experience, and to build that learning into their next year's actions. That learning may have come from mistakes they have made, failing to plan well enough, broken promises and disappointments as well as successes. All that is valuable learning. Don't let it trickle away between the cracks by default. Capture it and use it. That's the kind of learning that not only develops skills but wisdom too.

'Complete cross-skilling operated within work groups'

What very much helps this process is bringing together into one team all the skills required to deliver a whole service or make a whole product (advice we gave in Ladder 8 on Teamwork). For example, one large insurance company who brought together into one team all those involved in settling motor accident claims, found that not only did customers get better service, with fewer delays and mis-placing of paperwork, but individuals learnt different skills from each other, and were able to give much better continuity to customer inquiries as they occurred. Also, individuals were more anxious to take further qualifications to be able to handle better the variety of questions with which they were confronted every day.

In manufacturing situations, the greatest benefit of cross-skilling is the reduction of production delays due to the absence of particular individuals with special skills. With training, multi-skilled team members, even with absences, are always able to keep production processes running with no loss of product quality. Also, experience has shown that skilled technicians and maintenance personnel are more willing to share their specialist knowledge with their colleagues when they are part of the same team with the same shared goals.

'Using a points-based system, the average employee has doubled his skills points'

This is an idea favoured by many Japanese companies, which may be very useful in some situations. At front-line employee level, for example, tasks or skills may be grouped into useful 'bundles', which when mastered may gain the employee some reward or permanent increase in pay. That has a two-way benefit, namely the company can use the extra skills, and the employee gets the advantage of the financial reward. Naturally some tasks are more complex or difficult than others and may deserve a different points rating. This points rating is obviously useful when determining a pay value, but it can also be motivating to employees (even without any pay increases attached) to see their skill points mounting. It also acts as an overall measure for any company to see how well it is actually increasing the skills of its employees across the company.

'Job rotation is happening in every area of the company'

Job rotation is clearly a necessity if multi-skilled staff are to keep their skills alive and up-to-date. But job swaps – where individual members of staff from interfacing departments exchange jobs for a number of months – have been found by the companies who use them to be highly beneficial, not only in the additional skills and business understanding the individuals gain as a result, but also in the breaking down of the inter-departmental barriers and 'Chinese walls' that can often otherwise develop.

A number of US companies – including Proctor and Gamble, 3M and the Mars Group – are wedded to the value of developing their best management talent by making sure they get experience in different disciplines and departments. And we don't just mean the Cook's Tour training programmes some companies use for newly recruited graduates. We mean moving managers to responsible positions in different departments as their career develops. That way they believe they develop broad-based 'businesspeople' rather than just expert accountants or production managers. And there's nothing as educational as having to take tough decisions when you have real responsibility.

LEVEL 4

'Minimum of three days off-the-job training for everyone every year'

Some managers protest to us that all their people are doing on-the-job training every day. We don't denigrate on-the-job training, but clearly off-the-job training means a much more serious attitude and commitment to the process of training every year. We regard this yearly off-the-job training as a sensible form of 'people maintenance'. Yet companies will often be reluctant to allocate a sensible budget to it. You wouldn't expect your car to run well without regular maintenance, and you shouldn't expect your people to do it either. We find it commonplace for companies to allocate a budget of around 3 per cent of asset value to maintain their plant and machinery every year. We think people are every bit as important as hardware. Motorola insist all their people spend at least 40 hours a year on off-the-job training, and reckon from their quality training their return was $30 for every $ spent. So, allocate time and a budget. It will certainly pay off.

We must emphasize here that learning is not just training. People learn most by doing, and often most forcefully and permanently from their mistakes. Some years ago, Reg Revans became convinced that the most valuable learning occurred when people were actually engaged in achieving tasks and solving problems. He insisted the idea was essentially simple, and named it Action Learning. The key principles are:

1. *The task becomes the vehicle for learning.* Ideally this should be a problem that is important to the organization, but as yet had no obvious solution. Revans believed learning was at its peak when there was 'recognized ignorance', ie when the team members taking part in resolving the problem had no ready solution, but nevertheless were obliged to find one.
2. *A 'set' of people are put together for the purpose of resolving the problem.* A set would normally be composed of four to six people, who (a) could contribute to the issue in hand, and (b) had a material interest in the outcome. The key questions to ask in choosing set members are:

    - Who knows about this?
    - Who cares about it?
    - Who can do something about it?

3. *Real action takes place between set meetings.* Meetings would normally take place once a week, lasting a half to one whole day, with a trained facilitator. Time has to be taken to examine options, and develop relationships within the set, but the intervals between meetings are used to collect data, conduct research, and try out actions and possible solutions suggested by the set.

Revans was of the view that 'lectures and bookwork alone are not sufficient for developing people who have to take decisions in the real world. We all know that practice alone makes perfect'. And in that real world there are other ways of developing people effectively, including sensible combinations of the following:

- stretching objectives;
- cross-departmental projects;
- external seminars, where people can learn from not only from the speaker but from others in different businesses;
- assessment by colleagues or customers;
- bench-marking visits to other companies.

'Training facilities have become "state-of-the-art"'

By this time training has become an accepted part of the company's operations. At this level we find rooms are set aside for the specific purpose of training, and contain all the facilities that are necessary to do the training competently. By facilities are meant good seating, availability of flip charts and pens, overhead projectors and screens, television set and video, 35 millimetre slide projector, perhaps computer-controlled presentation equipment, or computers for individual training with programmes on CD.

'Managers and directors have become trained trainers'

If senior managers and directors have been promoted to their current positions through merit, then clearly they must have knowledge that ought to be shared and attitudes that should be transferred to other staff members. In other words, training need not be delegated exclusively to trainers, we ought to use the best people available. An interesting example is the case of Unipart in the United Kingdom. The company decided that every director should give at least one course at their large training facility. They could each choose what to teach but, to preserve quality, they had to present the course to their fellow directors first to get an approval rating, before they were allowed to deliver the course to other members of staff! That strikes us as a very good idea!

'The whole workforce becomes more skilled/valuable every year'

By now the company and the employees realize that the purpose of training is for individuals to become more valuable to themselves (if they ever had to find a job elsewhere) and to their company every year.

LEVEL 5

'The company realizes that continuous skills training turns their people into a competitive (and their only) appreciating asset'

It is interesting that every asset a company buys, whether it is machinery, computer software, telephone systems, vehicles or whatever, deteriorates and loses value as soon as it has been bought. However, if every member of the workforce is learning new skills every year, they become an *appreciating* asset, indeed the *only* appreciating asset the company has. An appreciating skills base may in fact be the main competitive asset of any company. Whereas other companies can buy the same technology and the same machinery, they do not have the same people. If it sets its mind to do so, any company can turn its workforce into an uncopiable competitive asset.

'Minimum of five days' off-the-job training for everyone every year'

This is the standard that has been set for many years by IBM. They make only one exception: managers must complete a minimum of 80 hours! Although we quote this standard as Level 5 there are companies who go well beyond this limit. Take, for example, the award-winning print company Quad Graphics, based in Milwaukee. Staff there work three or four days a week and then have a day of training offered every week. That equals 45 days off-the-job training every year! No wonder Quad Graphics is already at world class standard in the printing business. It is commonplace for both managers and front-line staff to take time off to prepare and deliver courses for their colleagues. Learning constantly from each other is built into the fabric of the business. This is a company that has used continuous learning both to get themselves to world class standard, and, more importantly, to keep themselves there.

'Larger companies operate an in-house university'

Obviously not every company can operate a university, but consider the idea of the Hamburger University run by McDonald's. On the face of it, it would seem you wouldn't need a university to make hamburgers. But McDonald's don't just make hamburgers, they are so committed to maintaining their product quality and service standards, they have made themselves a known and respected brand name round the world.

It was in the late 1980s that the Unipart Group in the United Kingdom started asking employees to nominate a learning objective for themselves every six months. Soon the company found it difficult to meet all the training needs employees identified, and installed computer-based training to cope with the demand. Even that wasn't enough. In 1993, Chief Executive John Neill and his Board decided to convert the whole of the ground floor of their Head Office in Oxford into a huge learning centre, which they named

Unipart University. They're proud of it, and so they should be. John Neill really believes his people are the company's greatest asset, and they intend to keep it that way.

'Continuous learning has become a way of life'

We all recognize we live in age of tremendous change. The improvements in communications, the advances in technology and the developments in science have been staggering in recent years, while customer expectations for value and service rise ever higher. Companies are not inanimate objects. They are nothing more or less than the people they contain. To stay with the changes they have to keep learning. There is just no alternative. Reg Revans, author of *Action Learning*, put it this way: fundamentally an organization's learning must be equal to, or greater than, the rate of change in its external environment. He had a formula for it: L > C. Arie de Geus, formerly Director of Planning for Shell, put it another way: 'The ability to learn faster than your competitors may be the only sustainable competitive advantage.' For every employee, learning has to be a lifelong occupation.

IDEAS AND TECHNIQUES YOU CAN USE

In this section the focus is on the following aspects of continuous learning:

- building a continuous learning culture;
- using a skill matrix;
- a human resource strategy supportive of a continuous learning culture;
- guidelines for systematic training.

Developing a continuous learning culture

Have you established a continuous learning culture in your organization? Test yourself against these 17 measures:

1. There is top team recognition that continuous learning is an essential element in the creation of a continuous improvement culture.
2. The organization invests between 2–5% of its annual payroll costs in the development of its employees' skills.
3. Every person in the business spends a minimum of 30 hours annually in off-the-job training.
4. All investment in training and development directly supports the achievement of agreed organizational goals.
5. People are made aware at the recruitment stage that they have to commit themselves to a continuous improvement and continuous learning culture.
6. All new recruits undergo a specifically tailored induction process (which includes standards to achieve), and are attached to a selected mentor.

7. Pay structures are in place that motivate all employees towards continuous learning and that reward the achievement of agreed learning objectives.
8. The personal learning needs of all employees are agreed and actioned through two-way appraisal, at least annually.
9. All directors, managers and team leaders have been trained in performance review and development skills.
10. Staff are multi-skilled in every area.
11. The company uses job rotation to develop employees at every level.
12. Every employee has a personal logbook, which contains details of the training, projects and other development activities he has been involved in, and any certificates or awards he has gained in the process.
13. Well-maintained and equipped training facilities are available in the company.
14. All in-house training is directed at the tested achievement of specific learning objectives. This is particularly focused on the mastery of BOPs in every area (see Ladder 7 on Best Operating Practices).
15. All external training is evaluated through assessment of return-to-work performance.
16. All employees who act as trainers receive appropriate training. Directors of the company conduct regular training sessions.
17. Skills matrices are displayed and kept up-to-date in every work area (see Figure 12.2 and Ladder 4).

Using a skill matrix

The Nissan car company have long been convinced of the value of multi-skilled employees. They use a five-stage process in their training, and assess front-line employees' progress on four factors; Standard Operation, Specification, Quality and Speed. Figure 12.1 shows the definitions they use.

As you see, the progressive symbols they use represent the formation of a box, but by common parlance it has become known as the ILU chart. Using these symbols, each area team leader charts his team members' current skills, and shows this publicly on his section's local communications board. This not only shows the team's current mix of skills, but encourages team members to add progressively to their skills as time goes on. Figure 12.2 is a typical visual display chart.

A human resource strategy for development and learning

A need exists for the integration of the human resource function into the total business. Personnel departments may use sophisticated selection techniques including psychometric testing, but often this is information that is not used to its full advantage. Also, selection criteria may have little in common with the strategic objectives of the organization. Company goals need to be translated into viable human resource plans that can guide the recruitment,

	I	L	⊔	▭	▣
Standard Operation	Can do with reference to standard operation sheet	Can do without reference to standard operation sheet	Completes standard operation in controlled manner to the required safety level	Can train others in the standard operation	Can improve the standard operation
Specification	Can build OK spec with reference to spec data	Can build OK spec with occasional reference to spec data	Can build OK spec without reference to spec data	Can train others in the specification	Can identify related specification errors
Quality	Understands the quality standard required	Can achieve the quality standard required	Can achieve quality standard and understands acceptable deviations	Can train others in the quality standard	Can take corrective quality actions
Speed	Can complete the standard operation in 3 x the standard time or quicker	Can complete the standard operation in 1.3 x the standard time or quicker	Can complete the standard operation in the standard time	Can train others in the standard time achievement	Can complete the operation in 0.9 of standard time or quicker

Figure 12.1 Nissan skill monitoring chart

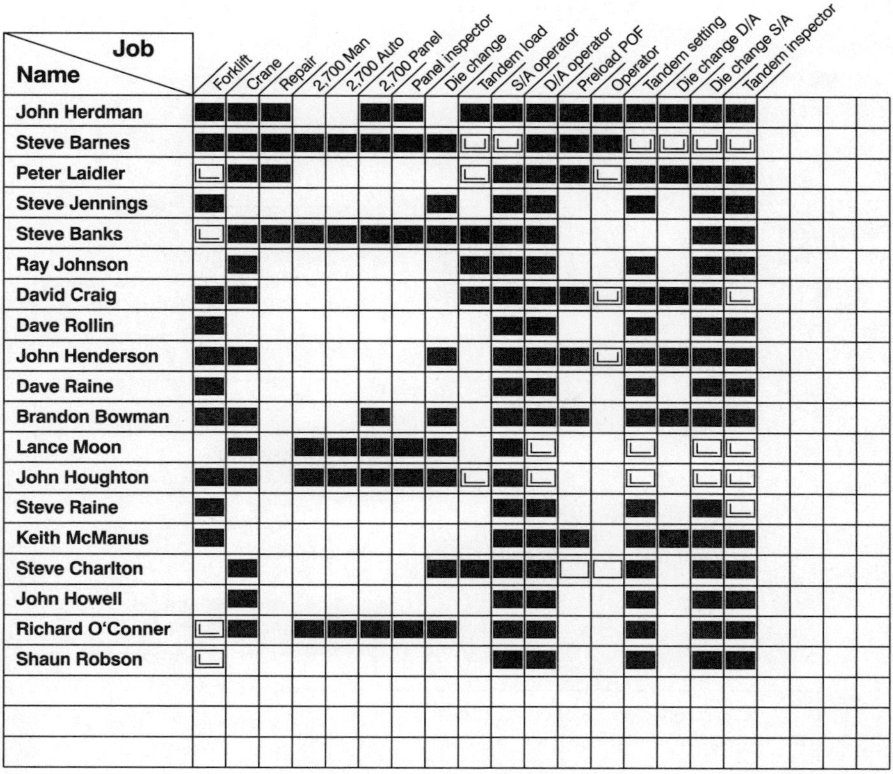

Figure 12.2 A skill matrix

placement, utilization and development of employees. A coherent HR strategy should be in place that is supported by all the role players and stakeholders; one that can be used for more than recruitment and selection of personnel and that provides *inputs* for all the above-mentioned functions.

Organizational responsibility

Development goals should be related to building capacity to perform into the future. These development goals should be centred on the following core issues:

- development of employees;
- self-development (competency standards);
- management and self-management practices;
- leadership style.

Human resource development needs to focus on three separate but co-ordinated processes (see Figure 12.3):

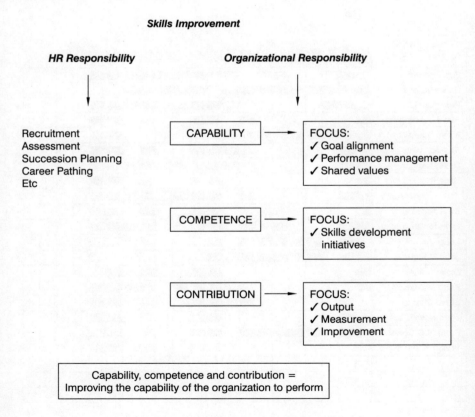

Figure 12.3 Model of skills improvement

- capability;
- competence;
- contribution.

Diagrammatically, these processes should converge as illustrated in Figure 12.4.

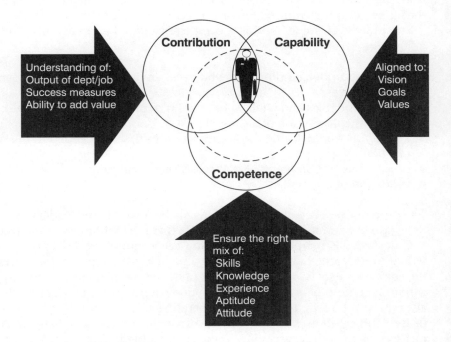

Figure 12.4 People development: the convergence model

Let us explain the key terms briefly. *Capability* refers to implementing a process within the organization that will enable staff to perform in a manner consistent with the organization's key strategic goals. Put simply, 'if every employee understands what he can do every day to help the company achieve its goals', then the organization will truly be *capable* of delivering. Ensuring capability has a number of critical elements:

- developing complete agreement on the goals of the organization;
- ensuring that every natural work team has a clear set of objectives and measures related to these goals that have been approved by the next level of management;
- regularly monitoring the performances of natural work teams against their agreed objectives and measures.

Competence is the process of implementing training and development initiatives to ensure that individuals have the skills required to do the job. Simply, agreeing what competencies are required in the job to perform at optimum level and matching these with the competencies of both the natural work team and the individual is a straightforward process of understanding the gap (job vs individual), conducting a needs analysis, implementing training and development sessions, and reviewing performance.

Organizations that implement a competency approach tend to move away from the notion of job descriptions and instead describe all jobs in respect of the agreed outputs required for each specific job or function.

The process of implementing a competency-based approach involves the following:

- gaining an understanding of the business environment and the organizational culture;
- defining the roles and challenges in the organization for specific jobs;
- development/selection of a competence model;
- identifying and defining those competencies that are needed in the organization;
- process integration (people/processes/systems/culture);
- validation of the model.

The process described above should ideally be linked to the leadership, team development and mentoring programmes that exist within the organization.

Contribution is the process of enabling each natural work team and individual to fully understand his unique area of contribution in the context of the company's goals and to understand how he can add value to the organization. It is the process of agreeing unique contributions between individuals, within the team, and between operating teams and divisions. It is the process of creating absolute clarity on contribution and being able to measure, in an agreed way, how value is best added.

Guidelines for systematic training

Senior management

Experience shows that senior managers often have likes and dislikes that can influence how well they take to the training. Based on experience, these are our observations:

- They are receptive to outsiders who have recognized authority or experience in their subject, but experts within their own company are generally treated as 'prophets without honour in their own country'.
- They welcome the opportunity to learn from the experiences of senior executives from other respected companies.
- They are very willing to visit other companies who have established reputations in the subject, eg organized visits to a series of companies with records of excellence.
- They prefer to attend training sessions with managers of the same level.

- They prefer their training sessions to be off-site, in pleasant locations where they can concentrate, undisturbed by temporary operational problems and phone calls.
- They are not keen on being trained by their subordinates.
- They hate to be treated like schoolchildren.

Training front-line managers

Front-line managers are closest to where customer services are delivered and products manufactured. As such they have a key role in any organization. This is our advice on the form of their training sessions:

- Don't try to teach too much at once. Many managers may not have been in a training or learning situation for years and can be apprehensive about it. Teach them only as much as they are going to use immediately.
- Have the managers work in small groups – of two, three or four people. That way they feel less exposed, and they learn from each other.
- Modularize the training, for example into day-long chunks. That's enough for them to absorb at any one time.
- Ensure they leave each training day committed to an action assignment that will make use of the lessons they have learnt. If they don't use the learning within three weeks of the course, they won't use it.
- Follow up on their progress. Start the next day's training module by checking up how everyone got on, discussing and resolving their problems.
- Appoint a mentor for every trainee. This can be the trainee's boss or another senior manager, and has two distinct functions. First, the mentor's role is to encourage and support the trainee in carrying out his action assignment back at the workplace. Also, it presses the boss into a support mode for the training and the company's new goals.
- Use workbooks for the training sessions in which key points are listed and in which managers can make their own pertinent notes. If the workbooks are succinct and practical enough, managers will use the material back on the job.
- Conduct 'passport' tests as you go along. Experiments in work situations show that the attention, performance and retention of trainees are clearly raised when they know they will be examined on their learning.
- It is a good idea to get the chief executive or a member of senior management to open or close the training sessions. This has a two-fold purpose. First, first-line managers hear about the seriousness of the company 'straight from the horse's mouth'. Second, they can put to him directly any resource or blockage problems that may be preventing them from delivering even better on the company's goals.

Training front-line employees in manufacturing companies

- Take the training in bite-size pieces: as a rule, no more than 20 minutes teaching talk without activity or participation.

- The training must be 'hands-on' practical stuff.
- Only train when the employees concerned are actually going to put the knowledge to use; and that within a week of the course itself.
- Don't assume knowledge. For example, most shop-floor employees will get percentages wrong, and as soon as you lose them, they switch off.
- They must experience early success with the learning. If they do, they will plague you to learn more. If they don't, they'll give up on you.
- Set little 'hurdle' tests for each half-hour or hour of the learning. Plan the training that way. Like teaching horses to jump, make the hurdles easy to start with, and congratulate them often.
- Review and extend the knowledge at spaced time intervals. Reinforcement of lessons learnt and step-by-step build-up is essential at this level.
- Give employees 'credits' when they pass through specific parts of the training. They love to feel they are getting somewhere.
- Get customers to visit your training sessions and talk directly to the trainees about your products, quality, service, etc, as they see it. Your employees will be more convinced by that than anything you say.
- Take them to visit customers on their premises and talk directly to the front-line people who are using your products. That frequently produces a quantum leap in employees' customer awareness.
- Show trainees competitors' products, literature, advertising, etc, to show them what they are competing against.

Training service employees

Unlike products that can be checked before they leave the factory, the quality of services is determined at the moment of delivery, by whoever delivers the service. In high-contact businesses, like hotels, airlines, banks and shops, the 'moments of truth' experienced by customers with front-line employees in large measure determine the reputation of the company.

Delivering the same service hour after hour, day after day, can be a pretty tedious affair. Sitting at a supermarket check-out for hours, answering telephone call after telephone call all day, or rushing around serving orders for food and drink can be pretty patience-stretching at times, to say the least. That is why service training needs to emphasize with employees the fun and satisfaction in serving the customer well if they look for the signs, and to show that customers' reactions are largely a reflection of one's own approach and attitude. Customers have different views and attitudes and, tough as it is, their satisfaction is a very personal business.

Above all, the training has to deal with everyday situations and realities, and give employees effective and practical strategies that will help them come out on top most of the time. They need specific answers to their questions of: 'What do I do if this happens . . . ?' And if the company shows it understands their problems and is putting into their hands practical ways of handling the tougher problems, employees will respond positively. So here are some pointers on service training:

- Employees need to know exactly, in detail, what excellent service looks like in the most common, standard situations in their job.
- They also need to have some idea what to do, or where to go for help, in non-standard situations.
- They need to be aware of the importance of time in service businesses in achieving customer satisfaction. Customers want their requests or complaints answered now, not later.
- The training must be strongly participative: no more than 20 minutes teaching talk without active involvement.
- Keep training groups small – no more than 20 people. The course leader can't ensure personal attention and full involvement otherwise.
- Discussing and answering 'What would you do if . . . ?' situations can be a good learning format.
- Role-playing helps make situations live and impactful.
- Taking videos of the role-plays and playing these back for comment and discussion is one of the most powerful ways to change attitudes.
- Use simple tests to reinforce the learning, to heighten attention and to strengthen commitment.
- Give 'credits' for successful course completion. Many service people live repetitive, humdrum lives and appreciate the sense of achievement and feeling more valued by their company.
- Make the learning fun.

References

Carnegie, D (1953) *How to Make Friends and Influence People*, Cedar Books, Alexandria, Virginia

Chang, R Y and Niedzwiecki, M E (1993) *Continuous Improvement Tools* (vols 1 and 2), Richard Chang & Associates, Irvine, California

Chang, R Y and Curtin, M J (1995) *Succeeding as a Self-managed Team*, Kogan Page, London

Crosby, P B (1979) *Quality Is Free*, McGraw-Hill, New York

Deming, W E (1986) *Out of the Crisis*, MIT, Cambridge, Massachusetts

Drennan, D (1992) *Transforming Company Culture*, McGraw-Hill, London

Harbour, J L (1994) *The Process Re-engineering Workbook*, Quality Resources, New York

Hirano, H (1990) *Five Pillars of the Visual Workplace: The sourcebook for 5S implementation*, Productivity Press, Portland, Oregon

Imai, M (1986) *Kaizen: The key to Japan's competitive success*, McGraw-Hill, New York

Imai, M (1996) *Gemba Kaizen*, McGraw-Hill, New York

Juran, J M (1989) *Juran on Leadership for Quality*, The Free Press, New York

Kobayashi, I (1994) *Twenty Keys to Workplace Improvement*, Productivity Press, Portland, Oregon

LeBoeuf, M (1986) *The Greatest Management Principle in the World*, Berkley Books, New York

Ohno, T (1988) *The Toyota Production System*, Productivity Press, Portland, Oregon

Peters, T and Austin, N (1986) *A Passion for Excellence*, Collins, Glasgow

Shingo, S (1986) *Zero Quality Control*, Productivity Press, Cambridge, Massachusetts

Shingo, S (1989) *A Study of the Toyota Production System*, Productivity Press, Portland, Oregon

Wallace Bell, D and Hanson, Charles G (1987) *Profit Sharing and Profitability*, Kogan Page, London

Walton, M (1986) *The Deming Management Method*, Putnam Publishing, New York

Index

World Class Audit

The exercise you are about to participate in is a 'mini audit' of where your organization is on the **12 key benchmarks of world class practice**. These benchmarks represent the Life Skills of world class practice, the elements that *everybody in the organization can do something about every day*.

STEP ONE

Read through each of the 12 Ladders contained in the following pages. You will see that each Ladder is divided into five categories, ranging from statements at Level 1 representing ordinary performance up to Level 5 representing 'world class'.

As you read through them, indicate with a ✔ in the 'My Rating' section of the scoring table at what level you think your organization is currently on the particular Ladder concerned. If you are undecided between one level and the next, eg between Level 1 and Level 2, choose the one that applies most.

STEP TWO

When you have marked where you think your organization is on each of the 12 Ladders, we would like you to prioritize the Ladders regarding their *importance* for your organization at the present time. Allocate the Ladders to one of the three categories below, putting only *four* into each category.

- Category 1: Must do, requires urgent attention in the short to medium term.
  (Remember you can only choose 4 ladders in Category 1.)
- Category 2: Should do, requires attention in the medium to long term.
  (Remember you can only choose 4 ladders in Category 2.)
- Category 3: Can wait, requires attention once we have dealt with Category 1 and Category 2 Ladders.

STEP THREE

Take action. Now that you know where your priorities lie, start taking action to get your company or your team on to the next step of the Ladders of Performance that are most important to you. And don't think that those companies already at world class level are somehow uniquely filled with exceptional people. They aren't. They simply used the best operating practices they could find, put them into use, and launched themselves on an ongoing programme of continuous improvement. Start now on your journey to world class.

Table A.1 Ladders audit scoring table

Where We are Now					THE LADDERS TO WORLD CLASS PERFORMANCE	Importance		
1	2	3	4	5		1	2	3
					Aligning Management Objectives			
					Customer Focus			
					Organizing the Workplace			
					Visible Measurement Systems			
					Managing for Quality			
					Eliminating Waste			
					Best Operating Practices and Continuous Improvement			
					Teamwork			
					Staff Empowerment and Involvement			
					Rewards and Recognition			
					Purposeful Communication			
					Continuous Learning			

Customer Focus

The extent to which everybody in the organization understands how service is measured, to recognize the needs of both internal and external customers. The degree to which the organization is truly customer-focused.

My Rating	MEASURES
1	Only general company-wide measures used. Departments tend to keep performance measures to themselves. Lack of hard data means much has to be done on 'gut feel'. Some departments think their work is not measurable.
2	Key performance measures decided on and publicly displayed. Measures show performance meeting the standards set. Budgets agreed by department and monthly data fed back. Plenty of data but often in different formats and places.
3	Performance measures publicly displayed in every department, and simple enough to be understood by all. Data shows performance continuously improving. Standards clear for every machine and every job holder.
4	Team members themselves produce the charts and graphs and update the displayed data. Visible management systems instantly make clear deviations from normal performance in production areas. One-page management in operation, ie data on key measures fed back monthly/weekly to each individual manager.
5	Company realizes that measurement is the only way to sustain continuous improvement. Senior management or visitors are able to tell from displayed data how any department is performing at any time.

Aligning Management Objectives

The extent to which staff understand the strategic and operational goals of the organization, and, in their natural work teams, have actively participated in agreeing and committing to improvement objectives.

My Rating	MEASURES
1	Managers give orders, workers only do as much as they have to. Some people don't know who their boss is. Objectives are not written; the goalposts seem to keep moving. Managers say: We don't need objectives, we know what to do.
2	Each person's responsibilities are clearly defined. There is a well-defined organization chart. Management have defined their goals but junior management are not sure what they can do about them. Objectives are written, but not seriously followed up.
3	Top management decide on their annual objectives as a team. These are turned into more specific team objectives at each lower level of management. Regular follow-up reviews measure progress to date. At least 80% of objectives are achieved by year end.
4	The company's goals are clear and actionable by all. Employees all understand exactly how they can contribute. The company is at Level 3 on the majority of the Ladders. Management co-ordinates their efforts across departments. At least 90 % of objectives have been achieved by year end.
5	Measurable objectives are agreed annually in every department. Teamwork and co-operation are expected at every level. People work to achieve the goals even under changing conditions. 100% of objectives are achieved, or exceeded, by year end.

Organizing the Workplace

The extent to which the organization has a culture of everyday organizational discipline. Factory floors, outside areas and offices tend to look like new. Organization is apparent everywhere; in reception, data collection and storage, customer liaison, inventory management, communication, etc.

My Rating	MEASURES
1	Scrap items, litter and tools are left scattered around. Walls, windows, floors and machines are dirty. The yard, car park and outside areas are untidy. Employees are sloppily dressed, desks and workstations are untidy.
2	The floors and windows are clean. No un-needed items present in the workplace. Needed items are easy to find and easy to put back. Employees are The yard, car park and storage areas are tidy. Employees are neatly dressed. Desks and workstations are tidy : you can find whatever you want in 10 seconds.
3	Equipment is cleaned up – it looks like new. Pathways are clear and without obstruction. The workplace is bright (painted). Tools and materials in well marked, easily accessible places.
4	Daily operator inspections keep equipment clean and maintained in good condition. Storage areas and materials are so clearly labelled even new employees can find them. Employees can retrieve what they need within three seconds. Any filed item can be retrieved in one minute.
5	The workplace is *habitually* clean and well organized. Work areas and the flow of operations is easy to see. Storage sites and quantities are clearly marked. Staff know automatically when to re-order. Teams earn top scores even during surprise inspections.

Visible Measurement Systems

Whether on the factory floor or in the office, staff understand and participate in displaying (for all to see) the critical performance measures of the business. Also on display will be Best Operating Practices and Key People Measures.

My Rating	MEASURES
1	Employees think sales and marketing look after customers. Managers believe they are 'professionals' and already know what customers want. Many managers and staff don't think they have customers.
2	Everyone realizes that the paying customer is the most important person in the business. In-company, people know their customer is the next process. Customer complaints are seen as a nuisance, and something to get rid of as soon as possible. At least 80% of orders delivered to customers on time.
3	The company uses real survey data to measure performance. Internal customers make contracts across departments. Written service standards established in every department. Complaints seen as an opportunity to create improvements. At least 90% of orders delivered in full and on time.
4	Customer data discussed regularly at board meetings. Service standards met and exceeded across the company. Cycle time, order to delivery, reduced by 50%. At least 95% of orders delivered in full and on time.
5	Regular surveys and focus groups keep company 'in touch'. Visible service improvements made year on year. Cycle time, order to delivery, reduced by 80%. Complaints under 0.5% and at an all-time low. 100% of orders delivered in full and on time.

Managing for Quality

The extent to which everybody in the organization understands their personal contribution to product and service quality. In process defect prevention measures are designed into processes and quality standards exist everywhere.

My Rating	MEASURES
1	People think that production is everything. They think it is the operator's job to make products and someone else's job (the inspector's) to catch mistakes. Pay systems emphasize quantity rather than quality. The primary drive is to get stuff out of the door.
2	The company has made the key mind-shift from quality defect detection to active prevention. Staff are now responsible for inspecting their own work and know exactly the standards they have to meet. Customer service measures actively measure fulfilment of service standards.
3	Corrective action taken immediately on discovered defects. Staff use the '5 Whys' technique to solve problems. The defect rate has been reduced by at least half. Customer service measures show distinct improvements.
4	Mistake-proofing devices are being implemented. Two-point inspection is now established. The defect rate is less than 0.5%. Customer service quality is measured at an all-time high.
5	The abnormality rate is tracked, ie deviations from normal rather than the defect rate. The entire company has installed mistake-proofing devices. The abnormality rate is down to 0.1%. Customer complaints are down to zero.

Eliminating Waste

The extent to which staff understand that activities that do not add value are waste. Scrap rework unnecessary storage inspection; delay and transport are continually process-mapped as part of ongoing efforts to improve the work ratio.

My Rating	MEASURES
1	Managers think that being busy means they are being productive. Things are rushed, people turn up late at meetings, etc. When you talk to them about improving the systems they use, they say 'We're too busy working for all that!'
2	People understand that all activities that do not add value to the product or service are waste. Managers realize that operators watching machines working is not work, it's waste. Teams start to use Business Process Improvement charts to identify waste. Managers use time management techniques to improve their time utilization.
3	Process waste reduced by at least 20%, eg scrap, rework, order cycle time, process steps, transport, etc. Process Mapping used everywhere. Operators look after two or more jobs or machines. Study groups meet to discuss how to reduce waste using the SPECS procedure.
4	Process waste reduced by at least 50%. The overall actual work ratio has reached 75% or higher. Operators manage whole groups of machines. Managers plan what specific value they will add every day. Equipment breakdowns are virtually eliminated.
5	The actual work ratio is at least 85%. The whole company is purposely organized to minimize waste. Stock-holding – of raw materials, in-process work and finished goods – is the lowest in the industry. Even new employees can follow procedures easily. New processes are designed to maximize added-value activity.

Teamwork

Teamworking is different from team-building. It measures the degree to which teams are the building block of the organization, where teams have full responsibility for an entire product or service.

My Rating	MEASURES
1	People think of themselves as just doing a job, not in a team. Co-operation between work-groups is patchy; there is rivalry and points-scoring between teams. Workers don't act as a team with management – it's difficult to make changes without suspicion or opposition.
2	Staff generally co-operate with changes the company wants to make. Work-groups have specific measurable *team* objectives. Staff know who their customers are, external and internal. They look like a team, help each other to get the job done.
3	Work-groups meet as a team daily, or at least monthly. Team members and team leaders all have clear roles. They make specific performance contracts with customers. They display performance data publicly in their team area. Staff are multi-skilled and can cover a variety of jobs.
4	Teams are organized around processes or products. Teams set their own objectives, manage their own budgets, resolve problems and make innovations. Cross-disciplined project teams used to tackle big issues.
5	Teams exist everywhere, and have become a way of life. Self-directed teams are set up and working effectively. The versatility in teams means they cope with change well. Teams celebrate achievements and expect success.

Best Operating Practices and Continuous Improvement

Regardless of the nature of the activity, there is always a best way of doing it. This (best practice) is benchmarked, either internally or externally, written up and implemented as the only way 'we do things around here'

My Rating	MEASURES
1	Staff don't want to get involved in improvement activities. They say things like: 'Why should we?', 'What's in it for us?', or 'That's management's job'. Suggestion boxes are little used or ignored.
2	Company realizes there is a 'best practitioner' for any job, and that they must capture this and make it standard practice. Company starts writing Best Operating Practices (BOP's). Employees contribute at least six improvement ideas a year. At least 50% of the ideas submitted are implemented. Teams are trained in improvement techniques.
3	BOP's written for all routine jobs. Employees contribute at least one improvement idea a month. Two-thirds or more of employee ideas are implemented. Team problem-solving sessions take place regularly, and teams tackle at least two major projects a year.
4	BOP's now written for all jobs, and by job-holders. Employees contribute at least two improvement ideas a month. More than 75% of employee ideas are implemented. Teams tackle three major projects a year. Benchmarking visits used to seek out and use best practice.
5	Employees average more than four improvement ideas a month. More than 85% of employee ideas are implemented. Teams tackle more than four major projects a year. Benchmarking *visitors* show company among 'best in class'.

Best Operating Practices and Continuous Improvement

Regardless of the nature of the activity, there is always a best way of doing it. This (best practice) is benchmarked, either internally or externally, written up and implemented as the only way 'we do things around here'

My Rating	MEASURES
1	Staff don't want to get involved in improvement activities. They say things like: 'Why should we?'; 'What's in it for us?'; or 'That's management's job'. Suggestion boxes are little used or ignored.
2	Company realizes there is a 'best practitioner' for any job, and that they must capture this and make it standard practice. Company starts writing Best Operating Practices (BOP's). Employees contribute at least six improvement ideas a year. At least 50% of the ideas submitted are implemented. Teams are trained in improvement techniques.
3	BOP's written for all routine jobs. Employees contribute at least one improvement idea a month. Two-thirds or more of employee ideas are implemented. Team problem-solving sessions take place regularly, and teams tackle at least two major projects a year.
4	BOP's now written for all jobs, and by job-holders. Employees contribute at least two improvement ideas a month. More than 75% of employee ideas are implemented. Teams tackle three major projects a year. Benchmarking visits used to seek out and use best practice.
5	Employees average more than four improvement ideas a month. More than 85% of employee ideas are implemented. Teams tackle more than four major projects a year. Benchmarking *visitors* show company among 'best in class'.

Teamwork

Teamworking is different from team-building. It measures the degree to which teams are the building blocks of the organization, where teams have full responsibility for an entire product or service.

My Rating	MEASURES
1	People think of themselves as just doing a job, not in a team. Co-operation between work-groups is patchy; there is rivalry and points-scoring between teams. Workers don't act as a team with management – it's difficult to make changes without suspicion or opposition.
2	Staff generally co-operate with changes the company wants to make. Work-groups have specific measurable *team* objectives. Staff know who their customers are, external and internal. They look like a team, help each other to get the job done.
3	Work-groups meet as a team daily, or at least monthly. Team members and team leaders all have clear roles. They make specific performance contracts with customers. They display performance data publicly in their team area. Staff are multi-skilled and can cover a variety of jobs.
4	Teams are organized around processes or products. Teams set their own objectives, manage their own budgets, resolve problems and make innovations. Cross-disciplined project teams used to tackle big issues.
5	Teams exist everywhere, and have become a way of life. Self-directed teams are set up and working effectively. The versatility in teams means they cope with change well. Teams celebrate achievements and expect success.

Staff Empowerment and Involvement

The extent to which every staff member has the authority to do whatever is necessary to do it 'right at the time' for their customer (internal or external). The extent to which they are treated like adults, and work effectively without supervision.

My Rating	MEASURES
1	Employees don't want any responsibility; they want managers to be responsible for everything. Managers want employees just to do as they're told. Few, if any, team involvement meetings are held.
2	Employees are treated like adults, and expected to behave like adults, ie to work effectively without supervision. Employees are given full responsibility for their own work. Teams are given all the tools and information they need to do the job. Team meeting sessions are held at least monthly.
3	Every team understands its own Unique Contributions. Individuals know the boundaries of their authority, and take initiatives to solve problems or please customers. Teams collect data on performance and use this with their manager to make continuous improvements.
4	Every job-holder knows his own Unique Contributions. Staff handle the whole job themselves, so managers can concentrate on improving the current systems. They meet their customers' requirements even in difficult circumstances.
5	Individuals agree self-set objectives and do self-appraisal. Teams set and meet their own improvement objectives. They both meet and beat their customers' expectations. Teams are involved in recruitment, equipment purchase, area layout, producing their own budgets, etc.

Rewards and Recognition

The extent to which rewards and recognition systems are simple, open, clear, and fair. The extent to which they attract, retain and motivate managers and staff to deliver superior performance.

My Rating	MEASURES
1	The company pays only as much as it has to to get staff. Pay systems are complicated and unpublished. Overtime is frequent, often to cover ad hoc problems. Anomalies exist and complaints frequently arise.
2	Pay systems have been simplified, are understandable and published. Employees are paid about the average for the work they do. Regular hours cover the normal work. Overtime is minimal. Additional skills acquired lead to additional pay.
3	Employees are paid above the average for above average performance. Appraisal system rewards help motivate performance. Different sickness benefit and pension schemes are applied. Recognition system is in place and working.
4	Surveys are conducted to ensure pay remains above average. Appraisal systems apply throughout the company. Sickness benefit and pension schemes are the same for all. Profit-sharing means staff are keen to see the company profitable.
5	Staff have a 'no redundancy' undertaking. Above average pay attracts and retains the best staff. Appraisals encourage continuous improvement and continuous learning. Recognition system regularly encourages the behaviours the company wants to see.

Visit Kogan Page on-line

Comprehensive information on
Kogan Page titles

Features include

DISCARDED

- complete catalogue listings,
  including book reviews and
  descriptions

- special monthly promotions

- information on NEW titles and
  BESTSELLING titles

- a secure shopping basket facility
  for on-line ordering

PLUS everything you need to know
about KOGAN PAGE

http://www.kogan-page.co.uk